Just When You Think...
You'll Never Be Alone Again

SUDDENLY SINGLE

A Companion Guide
To Help You Through It

Joseph Carraro, Ph.D.

Sheridan Books
ANN ARBOR, MICHIGAN

SUDDENLY SINGLE

Cover design: Joe Carraro with Amadeus Design
Book design: Ann Bottone, Amadeus Design
Albuquerque, New Mexico

Library of Congress Cataloging-in-Publication Data,
Carraro, Joseph J.
Suddenly Single: A Companion Guide To Help You Through It

ISBN: 0-9720482-0-0

*In dedication
to my sister, Arleen,
who gave me the confidence
and reason to write this book . . .
and to my friend, Katrina,
whose invaluable advice
provided its final direction.*

Table of Contents

Acknowledgements

There were so many people involved in the making of this book that it is very difficult to single out those who offered some meaning either through encouragement, assistance, or inspiration of stories. But in fairness to those of special contribution, I will try. There is of course, my sister Arleen, to whom I dedicate this book, for her unwavering confidence, not only in my capability to complete this project, but also in my being able to deal with its subject, both personally and emotionally. My friend Bernardo Alvarez, who encouraged me to offer hope beyond the despair because that's the way I am. My former agent, Ray Lincoln, who believed in the popularity of the subject, as well as the style of writing. Those who helped with editing, proofreading and layout including Karen Disner, Jennifer Doan, and Ann Bottone. Friends who assisted in so many ways including Ray Rivera, Angel Harris, Dr. Bill Krieger, Carlos De Castro, and especially Katrina Hotrum, to whom this book is also dedicated, because her insights and assistance were invaluable. It should go without saying that all those who contributed their stories were indispensable to the writing of *Suddenly Single*, especially my jungle guide Susana, who I will never forget.

Introduction

This book isn't about the seven steps to achieving financial freedom or the one-minute it takes to be a good manager. It doesn't
explain on-line trading or how to become a millionaire through
investment schemes and strategies. The topic certainly doesn't
appeal to everyone, even everyone single, although the population it talks to and about, includes tens of millions of single people.
This book deals with the most important concerns of life for those
who find themselves *Suddenly Single*. It's about personal lives;
the who, what, where, and how of our individual existence. It's
about coping and understanding the process and accomplishment
of personal growth.

Suddenly Single portrays the feelings experienced that only you
sometimes understand and gives the empathetic expressions that
you longed to hear someone else communicate. It's a helping hand
from so many others, when you thought no one else knew what
you were going through.

To people on the outside looking in, this circumstance may seem
nothing more than a minor interruption in another's lifestyle or
even just a despairing condition remedied by time. Rather how so
very much more important and long lasting this situation is to those
living its existence. And how very desperate their lives have become. If we are careful to notice, we can even see the dwelling of
their insecurities and loneliness translating to a tremendous loss of
personal productivity and even the demise of the business careers
that provide for their daily living.

If we are allowed close enough, we can observe a progression to giving up hope to sometimes life itself, and unless we have gone through a similar experience, we can never totally understand how a person in this condition feels. We can though, if we care, sense the disruption, the hurt, the anxiety and the hopelessness that makes up each and every day of their lives. Even those who know them really well can never imagine the depth or intensity of their feelings, but they try.

So, as we read our books on life's improvements, we occasionally take for granted the basic needs of personal survival that must exist before ever hoping of achieving other and greater successes. We just need to experience the taste of loneliness to understand its precedence and the importance of its resolution.

While the world of the *Suddenly Single,* by most measures, is not a fun place to be, different people react and cope in different ways. There are those who, because of their values, sensitivity, and commitment to the person they lost, experience this as a time of despair. For the purposes of this book, these *Suddenly Single* are those good-intentioned people who once hoped, loved, and were committed to their relationships, only to find themselves alone, despairing in loneliness.

I was recently *Suddenly Single,* and can now speak with experience on our feelings; our despair and desperateness; our vulnerabilities and hopelessness; and our frustrations and needs. More than anything, those of us *Suddenly Single* need someone who understands; someone who has been there and attained success. Coping with such anxiety is somehow made more bearable when you know that you are not alone in your experience. Understanding why you feel the way you do, makes "feelings" more tolerable.

With *Suddenly Single,* I am able to take you on a journey to the road to recovery, from dealing with the stages of loss to the understanding and accepting of the levels of need, and achieving a comprehension of what your physical, and emotional health is and where it needs to go. It is an exploration inward to the depths of "who" and "why" we are, where we want to go, and how to get there, ultimately with someone worthy as the recipient of our love.

I have now completed this journey of enlightenment and have put into words my experiences and those of so many others I encountered along the way. It amazed me how many other people not only endured what I had endured, but "felt" like I had felt as well. It was equally remarkable, that when removed from stereotypical roles, how similar the perceptions, reactions, sentiments, and sensitivities were amongst both men and women. When it comes to being *Suddenly Single,* the ordeals we endure after the demise of a relationship have no gender bias. Both men and women have the same capacity for loneliness and the same inclination for hopelessness.

It is unfortunate that so many of these good-intentioned people just want to give up and succumb to being lonely without having any hope for the future. It is for the hopeless and lonely that I wrote *Suddenly Single;* encouraging them to understand they are not alone in their journey and pain, and that there is a way to succeed to a place beyond their current circumstance.

For many people, without a belief in oneself to again have a successful, committed relationship, the motivation of desire and the thrill of anticipation are lost. Their spirit seems diminished, and they become resigned to joyless loneliness. They forget that when they surrender their faith in themselves and succumb to hopelessness, they are also giving up any chance that another person will be able to find them. There are so many good people who owe it to themselves, and to other good people, to persevere and not relinquish the joy that they deserve. *Suddenly Single* was written for the person in all of us, who needs that faith in self, and a hope for the future.

1

Susana's Story

I want to begin this book where this part of my story ends . . . in the jungles of Venezuela, where I met a lovely young lady by the name of Susana. Susana is a native Venezuelan who lives and works as a guide in a magnificent rain forest and became my guide to the wondrous experiences of this region of the world with its monumental waterfalls and natural beauty. It was Susana's story that I brought back home with me, along with all the pictures and memories of this glorious trip, which marked the end of a journey in my life that lasted for one year and one day. This journey is not only my story, but the story of hundreds of people I've met along the way. Those who've shared their most intimate thoughts on failed or lost relationships, as well as what it meant for them to be *Suddenly Single.*

Susana's story was atypical but certainly with many of the same emotions and inclinations toward survival that most suddenly singles have experienced. While all had taken different paths to cope with their situations, they all seem to have felt the same at some point of their journey. For most it was a heartbreaking, confusing direction in their lives with little understanding as to the how or why of its circumstance, and providing little confidence in their capability to cope with its outcome. For Susana, given the circumstances, it tended more to the ideal of how to deal with the changes that life presents, providing positive outcomes as the result of a positive attitude.

I first met Susana when I left my plane at a small airstrip in the remote jungle village of Canaima, Venezuela. She was an attractive, very personable young woman, dressed in a jungle-worn khaki uniform. I really wondered what someone like her was doing in a rugged isolated place like this. It was pouring rain, as it often does in the rain forest, and as we made our way through the mud to her jungle truck, I could tell that she wasn't impressed with me. I was wearing a golf shirt, slacks and preppie boat loafers. So when she asked whether I wanted to take the long easy way to camp or the much more rugged scenic route, I had to choose the back-breaking drive in order to dispel any negative first impressions. I had to prove that I wasn't one of those wimpy American "turistas" who wanted to experience her jungle through the window of the backseat of a chauffeured limousine.

Susana admitted that she spoke very little English, but did speak fluent German, some Italian, and of course Spanish. Although all my friends in Venezuela speak fluent English, I viewed even "a little English" as excellent in the jungle. She even suggested that she speak only English to me and that I speak only Spanish to her, to help us learn each other's language. Sometimes, however, I'd get a few words mixed up, changing the meaning of what I was trying to say—sometimes funny, sometimes embarrassing. After a few hours it was evident that I should just speak English and that she would try to understand what I was saying. Clearly, she was more linguistically talented than I.

The Change

Soon after we arrived at camp, Susana took me to a huge thunderous waterfall in which we proceeded to, very precariously walk behind. It was such a rush because of the noise, the danger of slipping, and the power of nature that when we arrived, soaking wet on the other side, I felt so relaxed and unburdened. A sort of chill and related "goose bumps" covered my body, but strangely seeming not to be caused by the tepid waters of the falls. Susana asked me if I felt any different, and I told her that I felt at peace, and somehow changed. I mentioned that I felt lighter. She said that those falls were one of her favorite places to go, and one of the reasons she was there, doing the work she was doing. She believed that when a person was immersed in a shower from the water of those falls, the negative parts of their aura was washed away.

I certainly felt somehow cleansed and different, whether it was from some negative part of my aura being removed, or from the realization and thrill of a new experience; the creation of a new memory. I felt that I had escaped from something, and maybe had even completed the journey through my loneliness. It seemed that I was now being allowed to experience, alone, the most beautiful place I had ever been. All of a sudden I felt so free, so joyful, for what felt like the first time in my life without being compelled to share it with someone I loved. It was as if I finally crossed a line of understanding the difference between loneliness and being alone. When I expressed that feeling to Susana, she told me that she had the same experience the first time she visited the falls. That first time, she felt the "change". Now each visit the waters provide her with a sense of peace.

For me however, my sense of reaching **the other side** of the falls went far beyond the feeling of peace. As I was able to contemplate what we had just accomplished, it seemed to be analogous to so many of those trials and tribulations I had just previously experienced. The daring it took to get started; the unknowns of what lied ahead; the responsibility for my care resting totally within myself; the cautious awareness of the slippery slopes; the tediousness and importance of analyzing each step; the exhilaration of seeing the light at the end of that watery tunnel; and finally the reward of the accomplishment of completing the

3

journey, all contributed to the connection between the falls and my experience being *Suddenly Single*. I had reached **the other side.**

I thought of how, with both experiences, I could have chosen not to embark on their journeys and what I would have missed by that decision. The opportunity of feeling the way I did, now of course, seemed worth every step. However, without question, they were both challenges that required the courage to seek change, the spirit to encounter adventure, and the resolve to see it through to its achievement. While the anticipation of my passage offered little clue as to what I would feel like at that point of arrival, both occasions surprised me with feelings I never expected.

That night at our jungle camp, Susana began telling me about the next day's journey to *Salto Angel*—Angel Falls. We would arise at 5 a.m., and leave by motorized dugout up the Carrao (interesting name) River for a four-hour trip; winding through dense tropical rain forest and then hiking up a steep mountain for two hours, to the base of the falls. We would have to circumvent rapids by carrying our supplies over land. It would be a hot, exhausting experience for anyone not prepared for its physical demands.

Because of all the other sights in the jungle I wanted to encounter, I allocated only one day for this excursion to Angel Falls. Susana mentioned that it was going to be a pretty rough trip to complete in such a short time, and that maybe I would want to wait until I came back again, so that I would have more time to rest and relax before trying to accomplish that sort of journey. This time, my decision was not based on the portrayal of a macho image, although I needed to prove to myself that all the working out I was doing lately had some benefit. I wanted to go because I was excited about experiencing all of these new adventures in life. It made me think of all the time I wasted, all the memories that I hadn't created because I was lonely, even when I wasn't alone. Now my being alone was filled with new adventures and new friends. The trip had just begun, but already I understood that to be able to share the joys of life with someone else, I first would have to learn how to enjoy them by myself.

At this point in my life, primarily because of my journey being *Suddenly Single*, I knew that I didn't need anyone else to experience achievement. I could become acquainted with beauty by myself, just by opening my eyes to its existence no matter where I was. I had the capability to meet the challenges of life, devoid of the necessity to lean on a warm body for support. I was able to search out those pleasures that made my life enjoyable without depending on the direction of someone else. I contemplated the future without considering its effect on a partner to its accomplishments. Although I missed the companionship, in reality, it was all I missed, because I had gained so much in getting to know myself.

So many times we become so intertwined in our partners lives, that we end up compromising who we are, and in order to accommodate the relationship, we lose our identity. For me it was this recent forced journey inward that allowed me to determine my identity apart from the responsibilities and demands of a relationship and the priorities of a partner. I was now contemplating this experience by myself, knowing myself, and enjoying myself. While finding my identity allowed me to view my life as so much more worthwhile, it also provided me with the outlook that I now have so much more to share with someone else.

That night, under a star-filled sky with some beautifully seductive Venezuelan music playing, Susana taught me how to dance the merengue. Although our relationship was platonic, the evening was wonderfully romantic. We both knew that we came to this place for a reason, and were now able to find someone with whom we could honestly share our feelings, who would somehow understand.

Beyond the Falls

It was the next morning, on our way to Angel Falls, when Susana told me how she came to this wonderful place at this particular time in her life. Of how she grew up and lived on a resort island north of the Venezuelan coast, with her very "close" and loving family. How she met a man from Europe working in Venezuela, and eventually fell in love and married him. She thought their marriage was perfect and she thought that they were perfect for each other. There were, of course, the minor problems that it seems every marriage endures, but she thought that her marriage would last forever.

Susana said she gave up a lot of her desires and ambitions in life to be a good wife and to be committed to her marriage, but felt her love was so strong, that she didn't remember having thoughts of what she was missing. She had studied to become an interior decorator and had hopes of someday starting a business, designing furniture. She also loved to be involved with nature, not just viewing it, but also living it. Changing the direction and even the circumstances of her life to experience "love" was worth any such sacrifice.

Susana even left her country and her family, to move to Europe with her husband when he received a job transfer. She felt their relationship was getting better, her love was getting stronger, and her commitment was being rewarded. Circumstances looked even brighter when he was transferred again and they moved back to Venezuela, to her island home, so that she could be closer to her family.

Everything seemed great, and then one day she went to the beach with her family, as they usually did on weekends. Her husband, who was feeling sick, didn't want to go that day, but wished her well. After a couple of hours at the beach, there was a downpour, which only lasted for a short time, but, Susana decided to leave her family and go home to be with her sick husband. When she arrived at home, earlier than expected, she discovered her husband in bed with, as Susana put it, a woman whom she recognized, but did not know.

Coffee Anyone?

That part of Susana's story was sad, and unfortunately not that unusual. Many good-intentioned souls like Susana whom I've encountered, saw their marriages disappear because they were with someone who could not be trusted, who lacked the honor and integrity to maintain the promise and commitment of their vows. The part of Susana's story that I found not only unusual, but amazing, was how she decided to deal with it; how she determined what, at this point, was really valuable in her life.

When Susana discovered her husband in their bed with another woman, in their house, she calmly went into the kitchen and made coffee. She then invited these two surprised and shocked lovers into the living room for coffee and "talk". The three of them sat down and calmly and briefly discussed how this had happened and what should happen next.

Susana said that she was able to deal with this violation of her marriage in such a way, because she knew at that moment, it was over. There was nothing that could be done or said that could erase what had happened. She felt hurt, sad, disappointed, betrayed, angry, and for the first time, alone. She knew, at that very moment, that her life was going to change forever, and decided not to fight that change. She, even surprising to herself, was able to accept what had happened and move on.

When I told Susana what I would have done, she laughed and said that there was "no pistola handy." At no point did Susana ever say she felt desperate or hopeless or use words with similar meaning that would describe her feelings or actions at that moment of discovery or since then. There was no denial for Susana, as there usually is for those of us who hang on too long. It seemed her intellect had overcome her emotion. The moral boundaries of her marriage were always very clear to her, and once they were violated, she could no longer exist in this kind of relationship. Her choice was to either hang on with time, effort, and all the exposed feelings, knowing that her marriage would never have the same meaning, or to accept the changes and move on.

You Do What You Have To Do

Susana viewed life as full of changes, and felt that the more we fought them, the more valuable time we wasted, and the harder life became. She felt that anyone who could treat her in such a way and bring mistrust into her marriage wasn't worth the time— her time. She decided she should rather spend her time discovering what was going to make her happy and cause her to forget, as best she could, what had transpired in her marriage. To Susana, time was very valuable, and although she didn't view the time she had spent with her husband as a waste, for her to stay with him or to fret over the circumstances, would be.

Susana was able to leave her marriage without the bitterness or hard feelings that usually accompany such a breakup. She was thankful for the experience, saddened by its outcome, and determined to make the best from this change her life had presented her. The strength of her personal commitment never changed, just its focus; from now on, **her commitment was to herself.**

She escaped to the beauty of nature, to ride the rivers and hike the trails. She was cleansed by waterfalls and tanned by the sun. She worked hard and was excellent at her job, and her joy came from knowing that to her, it was not really a job, but rather another beautiful experience in life. She told me that she feels blessed meeting people like me with whom she is able to share her adventures. When I left Susana, she was planning on going into business with another guide whom she met at the camp, designing and manufacturing furniture.

Susana has made it to **the other side** in a short period of time, because she didn't waste time feeling sorry for herself. She never felt that she had anything to prove to anyone else. She didn't spend time in denial, or punishing herself, or getting even, or wondering how she was going to survive alone or what her future was going to be.

Susana has moved on from her past and is creating her future. There is quite a difference between Susana's story and just about every other story I've heard, including my own. Those who wallow in despair and anger, and who react out of desperation and frustration, are just postponing the inevitable—dealing with it. The longer one waits facing the inevitable, the more opportunity is lost, fewer adventures are experienced, and the hope of the future is delayed.

To be cleansed by the waterfall, you have to face its uncertainty and relish its adventure, and "move on" right through its unburdening shower to begin creating new memories and a new life on **the other side**. It took me a lot longer than Susana, but its benefit was just as real. Deep inside, we all know that we will be unburdened at the conclusion of our ordeal; we just have to have the courage to realize it to its end.

2

Love Lost

Susana has missed a lot by choosing the path she did. She missed out on the false hope that we experience, when we are sure that the bad-intentioned deed or the decision to separate is just a temporary setback. She missed out on the daily despair of thinking about what might have been, or the constant reminders of her married life visually confronting her every day. She never experienced the extremes of loneliness and depression, or the fear of what lies ahead. Susana lost the opportunity to dissect every moment of her married life to try to figure out what went wrong, and then spend the rest of her time planning what to do about it.

Susana didn't have to deny or forget love because the definition of her love was separate from the boundaries she set allowing its expression. That's one thing we all have to do to escape the confines of a failed relationship; we must separate our love from the boundaries in which it is given. That is, the person we express it to does not define its meaning. Once we realize that the definition of true love does not lie in the characteristics of the other person, but begins when first loving ourselves,then we can realize that we are not giving up our capability to love or even denying its previous expression. We are just recognizing the integrity of its confines. That's what Susana did.

Of course, we will distinguish this love as different from the love of a father, mother, of children, family, or friends. The love we will define is the "love of our lives." It's a love that requires both a life long commitment, and continual attempts at making this person, this object of our love, happy. When you love someone in this way, you have a feeling that seemed bottled up inside, bursting forth to be shared in something that resembles a geometric progression. It grows and gains confidence every day of its development. It sometimes seems alive, with a distinct personality that just the two of you have created, like the baby that sometimes becomes its physical outgrowth. To both of you, it seems to be a different feeling that no one else could experience in quite the same way. It's a comfort; a trust. It's knowing that a major part of your life has been fulfilled, and you don't have to be or worry alone, anymore. It's the most beautiful thing you've ever experienced, and something that you know will somehow endure even through death.

Then somehow this love appears as if it's lost, gone, finished. It doesn't matter if it appeared to be happening gradually or all of a sudden; suddenly it's over. You realize that the love you had given had to be shared to seem alive. It's like your "baby" has died. The dreams and securities of your happiness have been dashed. Your feelings turn to despair, mistrust, anger, frustration, loneliness, and on and on. All of the plans with which you trusted this love have been terminated. You have a feeling that life has played a cruel joke on you. You realize that because of the mistake you made in choosing the object of your love, you've wasted time, and maybe even your life. You feel that you should have chosen a different path, one that was traveled by someone who shared the love you had.

"Until death do us part" should have given us some confidence that there would have been a reasonable finality to the sharing of our love. The "good times," and "in health" part of our vows, are pretty easy to accept, but the "bad times" and "in sickness" are what should bring about the strongest displays of love. Then, to seemingly lose our love because of a loss of attraction: whether it's a good-looking co-worker, an attractive waitperson or bartender, or the excitement of a chance encounter. Or perhaps, it was a lack of communication, escalating arguments, finances, or growing apart that seemed to indicate that the commitment given and entitled by that beautiful shared emotion and vow never really existed or to at least one, was never shared. There was a need for that wonderful love, bottled up inside, to come bursting forth to strike a target. It is now obvious that this target wasn't deserving or ready for its aim.

So many marriages end because one party feels stifled, and longs for freedom. That's why we hear so much of lost independence or of searching for oneself; of changing direction in one's life, and of seeking a different fulfillment. When the target of your love isn't committed, and believes that the grass is greener on the other side of the confines of marriage, that person becomes just another person in your life. The love of your life is so much more encompassing and permanent and is a target still out there, waiting. When the boundaries of Susana's marriage were violated, she left, taking her love with her and leaving behind all those things that were temporarily in her life before.

It's unfortunate when the sharing of love becomes a temporary condition. Even though you were the only one experiencing this commitment and trust, chances are that you once had to tear down barriers to your heart to share this now unrequited love. You needed to trust, even though you knew there may have been good reasons not to. You had to share your thoughts, even though you knew they could be used against you. You probably shared your income, possessions, family, religion, and your dreams. If you thought you were in love for life, you probably let every part of your life become involved. So where are you today? Have you learned anything from all the disappointment and heartache you have just gone through? Perhaps, you've learned that the mistake you made was not that you allowed your love to come bursting forth, but rather that it was directed toward an object that was not worthy of it, and like Susana you are able to "move on," taking your love with you.

But by now the barriers have reappeared. The fear has set in. The suppressed doubt in yourself and others has resurfaced. You mistrust your trusting nature. You protect your feelings by isolating their expression. Sharing your thoughts, become a cautious communication. Your focus becomes on protecting what little you have left, and your spirit becomes diminished by its self-imposed confinement. The meaning of love escapes your definition of its value. You become a prisoner in a cell of despair. Your confusion stifles any thought of looking ahead to the future. If this is the way the supposed love of your life has turned out, what are the odds that you'll ever have, or want to have, that same feeling? How could someone who has been through what you have just endured, ever trust, ever plan, ever share, ever depend, and ever love someone again?

It is at this point that you have to take possession of your love again. You must understand that your love has always been personal, inside of your being, just longing to be shared and expressed. It belongs to you; it always has, it always will. It's of your life, not anyone else's. It hasn't escaped your being, just because the object of your love has disappeared. Like Susana, our love stays with us. It's not something that's lost and left behind, it belongs to us and we allowed it to be shared. It's a gift from God, like all those characteristics we possess as individuals; a part of our being, that differentiates us from everyone else. Love is ours to share again and its capability can grow with experience, if we allow it to, and refuse to confine it by the barriers presented by our fear.

Love's Emotion

When we stifle love's expression we add to the confusion of our ordeal because it makes up such an important part of our being. It's as if we can't scream out in anguish when we are in pain, or are not being permitted to laugh when something extremely funny happens. It's so much more than that. It's attempting to choke the expressions of emotions of which we have no control. It becomes an unnatural undertaking.

We become confused because love is such an important part of us and yet seems worthless without its expression. Then, we have to battle within ourselves to deny its exposure to its previous pairing. We can't let it exist out there by itself, pining for recognition from someone who denies its worth, but its nature doesn't allow it to be satisfied being alone. The choices we face become the contradictions of self-protective barriers eliminating hurt or the openness of feelings exposing the defenselessness of love.

The compromise though is to recognize that love is an emotion that is ours to behold and share, thus giving the opportunity to be selective in its exposure. Being selective means that there will be barriers. However, they are not the barriers that totally deny its expression, but rather barriers that direct a focus toward a reasonable expectation that its worth will be recognized. Of course, we can all argue that we provided that direction before placing us where we are today. Obviously though, not enough care and analysis was given prior to exposing our love in the past to the realities of its environment. Too many times our wishful imaginations, which result from the compelling tendency of love to escape its confines of expression, cloud that reality.

Therefore, before you ever get to the deciphering of image versus reality with your new love interest, using the experiences of past relationships, you need to honestly evaluate your own emotions. This can be a long and involved process that will have to consider whether it is really love that is being offered or the result of a vivid imagination. Many times the emotion of love has been heightened because of that convincing need to love and be loved. It's called vulnerability. We need to first recognize and admit that possibility, the false images that it fosters, and the desperation that causes it, before we can ever have any hope of searching out true love.

Initially, to help my body work through the trauma of a failed relationship, and eventually to deal with the stresses of every day life, I would pamper myself with a massage every couple of weeks. While these deep tissue kneading sessions provided me with much needed tension relief and relaxation, they also allowed for an escape from reality for a couple of hours: At least an escape from my reality. It seems that no matter where I went or what I did I was always being presented the reality of someone else whose relationship had failed. And, getting a massage was no different. Not that I ever minded hearing about others' problems because we were all seeking relief, but it just amazed me how many people were suffering with loneliness.

The two women, who I frequented for this massage therapy, were very different, as were their massages. Mary was a single woman who had just broken up with her boyfriend of four years, while Clarissa had just gotten divorced from her husband of six years. Clarissa also had a four-year old son. When I first started going to each one we knew very little about each other and I was able to doze off while in their care. After we got to know each other, we were able to share our stories about the recent demise of our relationships and my dozing ceased. And, while their lives and

16

massage techniques were different, their stories presented many similarities, as I was to find out did almost everyone else's story.

Mary knew for sometime that her boyfriend was being unfaithful to her. Of course, when she first met him he was dating someone else. As she reflects back, it seems at that time of their meeting all of his coupled friends, including the married ones, were also dating someone else. But, he told her she was the one for him, and he was good looking and personable and it had been awhile since she had dated. She considered herself lucky.

At first, her boyfriend's cheating was continually being denied, and then later it just wasn't being discussed. It had happened to her before in a previous relationship and she was actually almost at the point of accepting that it was going to happen no matter whom she was with. Besides, there was a lot of time invested in this relationship and she thought that she was in love. She had tried to break off the relationship before, but was always drawn back because she was lonely and thought that "something was better than nothing." While this abuse of her love and devotion continued for many years and became more blatant as time went on, it was just recently that she had the courage to leave for good; at least that's what she says.

Clarissa's husband also had a wandering eye as well as other parts of his body. They had gotten married fairly young and in the beginning of their marriage would go out dancing and partying with all their friends as they did before they were married. She now thinks the reason they got married when they did, was because they didn't think they would find anyone else as suitable, and why take the chance of losing each other to someone else; at least that was her thinking at the time. And, there was always that danger with him, since other women were always flirting with him because he was so popular.

His infidelity went on for years while his wife continued to excuse it as an extension of his boyhood shenanigans. She was sure he still loved her and would grow out of his reckless behavior, until he briefly left her for another woman. It was only then that she decided to leave him and start over in life. She said she couldn't make that decision before because of her baby. She also reflects that maybe her dreams of him being a great husband and father were probably an over-extension of her view of him as a great dancer and lover.

These stories weren't unusual to me because I had heard so many with similar beginnings and similar endings. Just names and genders were substituted for each other. It seems in almost every case there were two parties with tragic flaws. There was the one party with a lack of respect that was masked or diminished by the possession of other attractive attributes. And, there was the other party with a low self-esteem who was willing to diminish their self-respect for the ability to attract someone who they either think they didn't deserve or didn't think that they could do any better.

Both these women are attractive, intelligent, personable, and give great massages. I wonder what made them think that they had to settle. Their fear of rejection or loneliness may have led them to these disrespectful relationships. And, their desperateness to share their love in a familiar union probably cause them to remain. But, for as long as each one persevered, maybe they were also lazy, subjugating their self-esteem and attaching themselves to another's identity.

It is our own vulnerability—our desperate need to love—that allows and sometimes encourages a false image to be presented. Our emotions become so strong, that we are blinded from reality. We dismiss and excuse behaviors, because we are afraid to admit that our lifelong commitment, our sharing of our hearts and souls, was just based on an image. We see our criteria for a match for our love being fulfilled in so many others ways—attractiveness, personality, intelligence, and even financial security—and forget that the result needs to be a match for our love. We are afraid of being alone; of being unwanted. We become attracted to people because other people find them attractive and we feel lucky to be considered. We want it to succeed so much, because we just know they'll be good for us and we'll be good for them. Our vulnerability strengthens our resolve to make it happen. Our benevolence, which in reality is probably our greatest strength, becomes our greatest weakness. We let our passion for love, its beauty, generosity, and kindness, lower the barriers to deceit. The hurt and the pain will eventually follow.

Is the answer to just be more careful and cautious? Should we just take our time and get to know the reality of the person we desperately want to be our love? Is the solution to somehow figure out how to hold back the explosive tendency of this emotion, and control its release? We know the result we want to accomplish, and in truth, we know the paths we must take in its achievement. With our vulnerability, it's easier said than done.

It is, to say the least, difficult to plan how, when and with whom the realization of your love will be experienced. Good human emotions do not allow for the same calculating agendas that those with bad intentions employ. Chances are that you have allowed yourself to believe, as those others in society have professed, that your good intentions are your weakness, because after all, it is your benevolence that has been preyed upon. It's easy to believe, especially when you see the inflictors of pain profiting through life while you suffer. It's easy to visualize yourself as weak if you don't understand the value of your love. You must begin to understand that love is a quality that gives you worth.

Actually, it's sad to think that there are those out there with all their agendas and lies, who will never possess the wealth of true love. It may be difficult finding the recipient of your gift, but can you imagine how empty you would feel wandering through life, not having the capability to truly share love. The problem is that those who have that capability miss sharing it, while those without the capability don't know what they are missing. Why is it that the good people always have to suffer? Well, they have something that can be fulfilled; something of great value that needs to be satisfied, and they long for and miss that satisfaction. When they do satisfy their love, theirs is a happiness and security that those without that capability can never experience.

Our capability to love is our strength; our inability to control the desperation that we have to share it is our weakness. It is this pressing urgency of emotion that needs a plan, which will not only enable us to give our love, but in a more controlled setting, to find the recipient of our love. Of course, we must understand that we have to be able to love ourselves before we can begin to be lovable to another person. It is when we are able to display this love of self that we also portray an inner strength. We allow our vulnerability to show through when we compromise our love and all those good-intentioned positive attributes that we not only possess but should demand in others as well. Our weakness becomes treating our priorities as secondary in order to achieve a less than desirable goal. It is usually a goal that only provides a short-term satisfaction. It is usually a goal, whose formula over time will provide very little hope for the future, because it just presents the failures of the past as part of its equation. To be able to have hope we must analyze and dispense of both the imagined and real errors of our past and begin to experience the realities of tomorrow.

Love's Hope

Sometimes this examination of self bothers people of good intention because, even though their intentions were "just" and they cared and loved, they somehow feel guilty. They confuse their perceived part in the failure of the relationship with the individual qualities they possess. They blame themselves for their partner's lack of interest. Then, there are the "maybes" and "what ifs" of life, that constantly resurface in these situations. Suffice it to say, nobody's perfect, and everyone we know has made mistakes in their relationships. However, we must realize that the failure to dot the "i's" and cross the "t" in relationship is not what caused us to be single. It was a lack of commitment, an unreal image of love, a failure to communicate, and because both parties didn't feel the same way about the value of the relationship.

If the commitment of a relationship is not valued, the problems inherent in any romantic partnership will become more intense and the solutions less important. If you are pledged for life, the obstacles and dilemmas will have to be resolved, unless, of course, you're foolish enough to accept misery as part of your life. Without that eternal union, **problems become a good excuse for dissolution, and solutions become an obstacle to freedom.** People without that commitment look for problems and refuse to work hard on solutions.

To dwell on the "**what ifs**," permits the negative presence of our departed lover to continue to exist in our lives in the form of **our guilt**. It's easy to say, "move on," but that's what we have to do, and it is not as difficult as we sometimes portray it. The reason many hopeless romantics cling to a lost relationship, is because they still have hope, and hope is such a wonderful feeling. It's like our mothers and fathers, when we were little children, telling us everything was going to be all right. Hope is a trust that our goodness will somehow be rewarded, that we will be protected from wrong, and that our mistakes will not be held against us. It forestalls desperation and anguish. If we learn how to focus it in a different direction.

This hope needs to be focused on the future of our love being valued by one, who we can trust to understand its importance. We have to believe that person exists, waiting for us to appear. It has to be a hope that's patient, and not just an answer to urgency. **A resolution of a desperate pressing need, usually requires throwing caution to the wind, and adjusting our criteria to meet the qualifications of the first person who comes along who's nice to us**. We've seen it happen before to others, and ourselves as well. If the most basic of needs is met, all the other criteria are thrown out the window. We are so desperate to have those basic needs met, their importance overshadows any demands of those good qualities we believed were essential to a lasting relationship. The fullment of these immediate needs is a ticket to another failed association. The need for intimacy, companionship, and security can be fulfilled by a lot of people for a short amount of time. But unless a partner who conforms with your feelings satisfies these needs, their complement is destined to be short-lived, necessitating another search for fulfillment—or worse.

So it will go on and on, until you get beyond the desperation, the urgency, and systematically plan how you are going to meet the real person for you, rather then settling for someone—anyone.

Then, you will begin to realize that there are others who share your emotions and who have a similar priority of values. You will search for someone with comparable sensitivities and a kindred spirit. When you find someone like this who "feels" as you do, then this is a person who can satisfy your needs because they can understand and empathize your feelings. These feelings might be more difficult to ascertain then other more apparent traits, but they are so much more important in the successful equation of a relationship. It's the feelings we need to hope for, because that's how we experience our love.

This Thing Called Love

My good friend Andrew, who is a bit older and a very cultured artisan has an interesting observation and definition of love. Since he is originally from Italy I would have expected his understanding of love to be a traditional one, but now that I have heard his explanations many times, I view it as one with tremendous insight and perhaps a different tradition.

In his explanation, which is laced with wonderful Italian inflection, he states that love only exists between parents and children. He believes it is somehow related to genetics and unconditional dependencies. He feels that is why it is so rare to find children and parents "divorcing" each other—splitting up and going their separate ways.

He believes that the reason there are so many divorces between husbands and wives is because real love doesn't exist in those relationships. He believes that in a relationship between a man and a woman, there is only passion; or as Andrew says it, "pash-e-own." It is this passion that grows between two people and eventually when they get older becomes even stronger than love. At least that is what Andrew has told his wife of many years when defending his thought of love.

He espouses that love doesn't diminish or grow but remains as a constant in those family relationships. It is the passion however, that has the ability to fly all over the place. By its very nature it is volatile and dynamic. He feels that is why so many people get divorced, because they lack the understanding that what they possess is passion and rather think they have a love that is guaranteed to remain constant throughout their relationship.

I believe that with regards to family, love can begin before birth (at the time of pregnancy) and endure after death (in the form of memories). In a newly formed relationship between a man and a woman, it is probably the passion that draws and binds each one to the other. It is love however, that bursts forth and collides to create this passion. If nurtured over time, this passion then binds these two loves together. That can only occur when all the barriers have been dropped and a true sharing of love can be experienced. It not only takes trust, but also presumes that every one involved has the same definition of love.

I believe love is the most valuable of all our qualities, and must be treated accordingly. It should never be easy to say. If you have it, you'll know it, you'll feel it, and you'll desperately want to share it. That's part of its character. It can enrich your life and those you share it with, beyond your dreams, because you can never imagine the beauty it beholds until you experience the power of its feeling and the dedication of its purpose.

Love is the ultimate of giving of your self and should know no bounds of containment. That is why it is so important to understand its personal nature. That is why it's so important to give this love of your life, only to someone who appreciates its value, and doesn't diminish it by demanding you continually prove it. Love should transcend human embodiment so that when you look into the love of your life's eyes, you feel like you're looking into their soul, and no proof by action, word, or gift, can ever have a more profound meaning.

Without question, love is the most powerful of positive emotions, and yet when left unrequited, evokes so many negative emotions that seem so much more intense. This is because the more we value our love, the more abused we feel when it is diminished. In reality, the intensity of our bad feelings just equals the intensity of our love. It's like when someone dies who is close to us and we miss them terribly and exhibit such intense grief. It is because they had so much value in our lives. The harder we love, the harder we fall when that love is no longer supported, and returned.

Alfred Lord Tennyson once said, "It is better to have loved and lost, than never to have loved at all." Well, it is certainly better to have the experience of love than never to have the capability to love, but to have given your love totally to someone and to have them toss it aside—no one needs or deserves that. With some of the stories I've heard from people about how their love was abused, I'm sure they would have preferred to forgo those negative experiences. But, we all need to know that we have love and its capabilities within us.

If you're reading this book, chances are it's too late to forgo your experiences. Since I'm writing this book, it means the same thing to me. We now need to understand the characteristics of this love that is inside of us waiting to burst forth toward what we hope will be a deserving target. The more we know about it, the better we will be able to channel it, and the more we will be able to appreciate it.

I'm sure we would all agree, that love grows. The first love we had, while probably emotionally exciting, most likely cannot compare in intensity or, sometimes even dedication, to our most recent love. This growth of love is a process, which involves not only our experiences with relationships, but also with our own emotions. What attracts us to the people we love are those qualities that we ourselves value as being necessary for our love to be recognized and appreciated. We search for attributes in others that, even though they are not exact duplicates of us, there are enough similarities to warrant that our loved ones "feel" as we do. Of course, in the past we were probably so desperate to share our love that we were with someone whose "feelings" were not real, but rather a product of our love-starved imagination. But through experience in relationships, we learn about human nature. We learn about our, and others', integrity, respect, willingness to sacrifice and commit to others. We learn to recognize how different we are from each other, how we prioritize our values and what makes up our individual natures. We hopefully no longer create images to suit our criteria.

Through time and experience, we have a greater capability to decipher fact from fiction. We've been there, and really don't want to do it again. We now have the insight to recognize the traits of those who have placed us in this despairing position of lost love, and can avoid such intense involvement with people like this in the future. However, we must remember, that the inclination is still there, because obviously there was something that attracted us to them and/or them to us. It could be our similar interests or physical attraction. It could be that our strength complements their weakness or vice versa. Or even less complicated, it could be that we are filled with a need to love, our cup is running over, and their type always seems to be there when we need them, providing comfort for our despair.

If ever we experienced, what we perceived to be **true love**, we experienced it with someone who had certain comforting qualities, real or imagined. Those qualities reflected our feelings, values, and caused us to trust that person with our future. We must now continue the search to find those qualities that afford us that same comfort level. We trust that our experiences have educated us to get behind the image, to discover the true being who will be the final recipient of our love. The promise of our hope is that we have learned valuable lessons from our ordeals and we need to continue to search for the person most worthy of receiving the love of our life. **An education is a terrible thing to waste.**

Climb Every Mountain

It still amazes me how we wish, hope and pray for that soul mate to enter our lives, and then somehow think they have magically arrived because we're sexually attracted, or because they have nice personalities. We need to ask ourselves, after our prayers have been "answered," if we truly believe that God is really that shallow. We need to be sexually attracted to people with nice personalities, but before we ever believe that this even could be the love of our lives, we have a whole other mountain to climb. Its slopes are slippery and its dangers are concealed; they're certainly not as apparent as a nice body or a happy smile. Climbing that mountain is a long, involved process that is time-consuming, and not meant for the impatient, basic need, "fulfillee." It is the kind of methodical struggle that is necessary to ensure that you are not victimized by the slippery slope that uncommitted unions present. **Time does heal wounds, but caution prevents**

them. And caution also takes time.

It is so much better for one's emotional health to take their time and be cautious. It's the slow, careful progressions in life that provide the emotional stability necessary in successful relationships. It's the sure-footed with a plan who can usually avoid the slippery slope and reach the plateau of love they have worked so hard to achieve. We must also be cautious enough to take the time to think that this may be a different plateau to reach than one we have been climbing for in the past. This plateau— these characteristics of a relationship—might have changed over time and experiences. This would now be a good time to evaluate its location.

This evaluation needs to provide a comparison of the place and time of past experiences with present expectations. This assessment assists in a decision-making process that will determine whether to move forward toward a goal of expected success or backwards to a goal of experienced failure. Many times it is the expectations of our past that remain with us as our potential for the future that, either continually provides the same result, or promises unreachable goals. For us to be successful, **our assessment must honestly consider what is actually good for us rather than what is desirable.** What is good is what is important; what is desirable is the fluff that dreams are made of. We can have both, but to be happy and secure in the future we need to prioritize our expectations.

> *It had been a while since I saw Mary. She is still single waiting for her white knight to come riding into her life. Apparently knights have come and gone since we last had visited. She was always attracted to the same type of man; extremely good-looking, well educated and traveled, very rich, classy, and with great personalities. I always seemed*

to get the feeling that she felt some sort of a sense of accomplishment to have others observe that she was lucky to have found someone like that. It also seemed that she felt that she didn't deserve anyone "less."

Now, Mary's no slouch. She's attractive, has a great job, dresses great, and lights up the room with her persona. The problem is, she doesn't seem satisfied with just a mirrored image of the qualities she brings to a relationship. She always has to find someone who appears a step above her characteristics and capabilities. Of course, I'm pretty sure that she never analyzed what she desired versus who was good for her.

Her situation makes me think of how many ideal matches, from the point of view of important qualities, are never considered because someone either has an inflated sense of their own image or are just too demanding as to what they think they deserve. And while, there are so many people out there with what might be considered an unattractive package today, with confidence and support from another person they can become that ideal match. But that doesn't happen to people like Mary. She's all about appearances and yet thinks that love is somehow going to be derived by the way someone acts, or what they have, or the way they look. Even to hear her tell it, all the knights in her days have been about "fluff," lacking in any substance that would equate to the giving and sharing of love. But, in a sense, while Mary's a terrific person, she is getting everything she is offering and demanding. Her priorities begin with her desires, with an anticipation that they would evolve into something that was good for her. I think even she must realize that to place such an emphasis on the "attractiveness" of a relationship can at best provide just a

> *superficial condition. Love involves a different set of priorities and direction.*

Love is not something to be treated lightly. If we feel it is not fair to treat our love with little importance, it is certainly not fair to offer it that way. And when we look for love in all the wrong places, what right have we to expect to find it. **All we can ever hope to deserve is what we are searching for.** It is when our priorities become misdirected that our search for love becomes futile.

Our search must always include what we hope to gain through its pursuit, but must also consider what it is going to take reach its goal. Like Susana's waterfall, to reach **the other side**, will involve some unknown risks, anxious moments, and the labor of the experience. Of course, the alternative is to stay right where you are wondering if your life will ever change. Just making the decision to proceed seems a difficult task, but as with many things in life, if it's worthwhile, it's worth it.

You reap what you sow, and it will be that way throughout your search for the love of your life. **The easier one makes it to find someone, the easier it will be to lose someone.** The more you diminish your standards for the expression of your love, the easier your search will be. Of course, the easiest path is to give up and not search at all, but that direction provides little, if any, chance of achieving the love for which you now long. Easy, in this case of self-motivated direction is lazy, and eventually leads to despair: settling on someone or no one. In either case, loneliness is the result. The only good answer is to tough it out, and be committed to working hard to achieve the goal your love deserves.

People work hard to buy cars and homes and provide for those things they desire. They work eight hours a day to buy things they are attracted to; things they need and want. They go into debt to their future for something so important that they need today. All that time and effort; all that money spent to be happy and to provide a sense of security. Some people even spend money and time to try to replace or forget love. Time and money well spent for what they believe to be something of value.

But, is all of this effort enough to ever equal what sharing your love is worth? Not to the people I've been talking to—not to me. We can even try to substitute for love, but we must agree that there is nothing as valuable. Yet working hard for a love that will mean more to our future than a car or home, or all those other "necessities" and luxuries, sometimes seem out of reach. It's probably because we know what things cost, and we know what it's going to take to pay for them. With an intangible like love, it is more difficult to ascertain and visualize its cost or its surety. But as with other things of our desire, we could put a price on it. That's where we must begin our search, by putting a value to the sharing of our love, concluding with what we are willing to do to pay for it and deciding whether we're willing to climb a mountain find it.

3

You Reap
What You Sow

So here we are trying to put a value on finding a recipient for our love. How much is the expression of our love worth? Or maybe the question should be: how costly will it be, for the rest of our lives, for our love to remain insulated from someone who desires its expression? I keep thinking that we only go around once in this life and shouldn't waste time. We need to think how valuable the minutes sharing our love can be, not only to ourselves, but to its recipient as well.

All the blessings and capabilities we have are related to time and experience. They've either taken time to learn and develop or time to evolve. They all have a limit of experience in time. The longer we wait to utilize our talents, to share our blessings, and to express our capabilities, the less time we have to enjoy the fruits of their existence. So no matter how much we need to be in despair, or how comforting it is to be lazy, or how secure it feels to lock ourselves behind the barriers of mistrust and self-pity; if we really want to honor all that was given to us, all that we possess, the time to act is now. The seeds—all the assets we possess—have already been sown. Now is the time to decide whether we are going to nurture these dormant possibilities of growth to become fruitful expressions of our being, or let them wither beneath the surface, never allowing others to visualize their beauty.

How do we nurture seeds? We water them, fertilize them, and pull out all the weeds around them so they not only can reach their potential, but so they can stand out on their own, appearing a lot more brilliant than if they were surrounded by non-productive clutter. The first thing we have to do is find out what and where the seeds are. No sense in nurturing things that aren't there—it just takes away from the care needed to fulfill the potential of the things really important and achievable.

We must first identify who we really are—our positives and negatives—the pros and cons of our existence up to this point. Most of this type of soul-searching can be done on our own, but a complete and final objective look, will involve family and friends who we can trust to offset our vision of ourselves. While our own-mirrored image is an indication of what others see, it may take a much more thoughtful and honest vision to accurately portray who is looking in that mirror.

People who truly care about you have a clear enough concept about who you are to be able to tell you what positives you need to accentuate, and what negatives you need to change. Sometimes we will seek out and accept their advice, and other times we won't. Sometimes they are concerned and caring enough to offer advice and observations, and other times they aren't. Regardless, their perception is important, because even though it may not be the way you really are, it is the way you appear to other people, which in reality is the way you really are to other people. Of course, you must always consider the source and their perception of your life before ever considering change.

Lo and behold, there are just some things we can't change! But once again, we usually spend so much time fretting over those few, permanent characteristics, that so many important possible changes go unnurtured, unwatered, unfertilized, with "needs" growing all around. Then, we sometimes get stuck in the despair and laziness of the acceptance that we don't have a green thumb when it comes to our personal growth.We are willing to accept that this nurturing of our positive attributes and the changing of those negative characteristics, are unattainable. The gardening involved in personal growth is not easy, but at least we can figure out what has to be done, and confront ourselves with the possibilities of change. Of course at this initial stage of analysis we will probably come to the conclusion that what has to be done is going to entail hard work, but we should also come to the realization that the benefits of a fruitful existence is always worth it.

Looking Good?

I can now honestly look back at my physical appearance at the ending of my relationship. Granted, I was dealing with an undiagnosed thyroid condition and what seemed to be overwhelming burdens in my life, including a failing relationship. But my physical appearance changed in a few short years from my being an "attractive" man in good physical shape, to one of an unrecognizable appearance. I had gained fifty pounds, my face was swollen with bulging eyes, I was losing my hair and my body's stooped posture portrayed a man 10 years older. My justified burdens now had the companionship of the depressed state brought on by my appearance. These began playing off each other, causing me to become more depressed.

And how did I deal with these emotions? I ate more and exercised less. I became well known in every all-you-can eat restaurant in town. I wasn't eating to satisfy my hunger; I was eating to deal with my feelings; stuffing emotions inward to satisfy needs. And, my feelings had an insatiable appetite. All the food I was consuming was just feeding my depressed emotional state. I, and it, just kept growing big-ger. I also started drinking alcohol to forget my burdens—not that much since I hardly ever drank at all— but enough to have the depressing effects of alcohol exaggerate my condi-tion while causing my face and body to swell up even more. While always athletic, I refused to exercise because I was al-ways tired and thought I was too far out of shape for it to be effective. I was wallowing in self-pity and the self-pity be-came addictive. When I was searching for the answers to my despairing and its related condition, I didn't know what ques-tions to ask. I was looking for easy solutions and advice and help from people who couldn't do what I had to do for myself. I became lazy in my search for the truth.

The truth was that the object of my love wasn't blind, al-though subconsciously I may have wanted my physical ap-pearance to be a test of that commitment. It was also true that I was giving a very valid perception that I didn't love myself or care what I looked like by not taking the mea-sures necessary to improve my physical appearance and condition. It seemed that I became lazy and somehow sat-isfied with my appearance, not understanding the effect it was having on others and me. It appears sometimes, that many of us don't want to know the truth, so that we can continue believing that love is blind and that our physical appearance shouldn't make a difference as to who we really are.

But, it does make a difference. It made a difference to me. Now that I have gotten back in shape, I look and feel younger. My confidence is exhibited by the way I walk and talk. I am self-assured in everything I do. I don't have to worry anymore about getting back in shape, just getting in better shape. I found that the exaggeration of my burdens, by the despair brought on by my poor physical appearance, are now reversed. By feeling good about myself, it is so much easier to deal with the rest of life.

I accomplished this reversal by being honest with myself, and realizing that there are some things in life that cannot be changed and others that can. I was no longer going to allow my satisfaction with laziness or the misguided belief that the way I looked didn't matter, not to be changed.

Sometimes the last thing a person wants to hear, especially when other negative influences are happening in their lives, is the truth about something as sensitive as the way they look. But to have family and friends now approach me and tell me how bad I looked, makes me wonder why they didn't approach me earlier. It was probably to save hurting my feelings, and they feel more comfortable now that I look so much better. But I could have felt so much better and dealt with my life so much easier had I known and been encouraged to do something about it. Although, I guess I could have accomplished all that by just being honest with myself.

The easiest part of our self-evaluation to figure out should be the visual nature of who we are. Although beauty lies in the eyes of the beholder, we should be able to come up with some sort of general concept of what we look like. We can of course stand in front of that sometimes, deceitful mirror, and examine the being before us in a manner that is devoid of personality and other reflecting characteristics which might cloud or enhance its image. What do we see, and what are we looking for? What we see is a person, not unlike people we cross paths with on a daily basis, some of whom we might be attracted to, and others who we wouldn't give a second look. At this point we might think, "How cold and shallow. If someone wants me just for my looks then I don't want them". And yet isn't it something about a person's "looks" that attracts most of us initially?

Granted, we all don't have the same tastes, and we would like to think that what a person looks like is nothing but superficial criteria in our formula for finding the successful recipient of our love. But, the first visual impression triggers a brief, ostensible image of who that person is. Remember, it's when we stop the examination at this point and create the person to fit the rest of our criteria that we run into trouble. Realistically though, their look is usually our first attraction.

So when we examine that figure in the mirror, we need to somehow look at ourselves, as others would see us, as we would visualize someone if they were standing in our place. If you were looking at this person before you for the first time, would you be attracted to them? And if not, what would you recommend that they do to catch your eye, realizing again, that everyone has different tastes.

Is the "look" reflected portraying a happy spirit, a trusting nature, a pleasing personality, and a welcoming glance? Are there flaws present that would prevent someone like you from seeking a more in-depth observation? Is the look presented, one that makes others feel comfortable?

Over time, I was able to observe in others many of my own flaws that were reflected in that mirror of self-observation. I thought back to not only that physical appearance and what had caused so many of us to reach a level of neglect, but also what decisions I had to make to change the outlook that reflected the image I portrayed both physically and emotionally.

I had obviously felt out of control, as so many of us do when we become *Suddenly Single*. Looking back at myself and others with similar circumstances, it was a perfectly natural feeling. The reasons our lives sometimes feel out of control so quickly is so many times due to the perceived suddenness of separation, even though we may have been aware of it's happening for some time. Turmoil exists because the "suddenness" doesn't allow us time to prepare for a better outlook.

This uncontrollable turmoil, caused by the effect of an unexpected loss seemed to affect every part of our lives. There was no longer anything "normal" to rely on. Of course, there was no companionship, and that even affected our identities when the relationship was split in half. The unplanned and undesired changes in the routines of our lives occurred, when just a short time before everything seemed to be taken for granted. Our lifestyles then projected not just separate identities, but different financial, household and even parental responsibilities.

Just like adding salt to the wound, emotions were allowed to enter this chaotic state bringing the feelings of rejection and the accompanying self-doubt and guilt. Every time an idle moment attempted to exist there was a bombardment of questions that began with "Why," "How," "What," and "With whom." While the answers seemed to go on forever, the cloudiness presented by all the surrounding turmoil only offered unclear and unknown conclusions.

All this confusion rains upon our minds and bodies. It plays havoc with our emotions and spirit. Our self-esteem becomes diminished to the point of giving up. Some people might then realize that their lives are not only out of control, but that they also lack self-control. They substitute their human companions with the addictive companions of alcohol, drugs, cigarettes and even food. They stuff their emotions with these comforting substances. There are so many people like myself, who ate so much food to stop the hurt. Then there even were others who sub-consciously used being over/under weight as a tool not to be attractive to the opposite sex so that they could avoid the vulnerability of being loved again.

We have to understand that we have allowed ourselves to participate in a vicious cycle. We wallow in our depression by eating more and gaining weight. We then become angry with ourselves for not being able to control these emotional urges satisfied by overeating. Then the depression follows again because our appearance, even to ourselves, becomes distasteful. The trauma left by the circumstance of our failed relationship is built upon by the trauma left by our failed appearance.

So it goes on and on with a cycle of emotional distress responding to the despair of lost love searching for comfort and finding it by embracing the food, alcohol, drugs or whatever other over-indulgent companion is available. It is then regrettable because we realize we have lost not only control, but have also lost ground, since we fall further and further behind in the journey necessary to provide a sense of stability to our lives. But then it's too late because the depression cycle begins again by our not being able to cope with the habit-forming satisfactions that now control our lives and ruin the attractiveness of our being.

It is the traumas and depressions seeking their satisfaction by feeding upon each other that cause the problems and conditions to grow. There is then even a point reached where it is difficult to ascertain what is the primary cause of the current despairing and depressed state because of all the intermingling of reasons for emotional stress; whether it's the circumstance of the failed relationship or the condition allowed by cravings for comfort. Eventually, it doesn't matter. What matters is that we change the course of our lives to exhibit that we are once again in control. While we may not be able to quiet the anxious urges that occasionally surface, we certainly can determine a more productive and less harmful way to bring about their satisfaction and break the cycle of despair.

It all seems so overwhelming and complex. After everything we have been through we certainly don't feel like we have the energy or stamina to reach the point of taking back control of our lives. Our despair and the resulting depression have taken its toll on our motivations, and the tasks of improvement seem taxing beyond our capabilities.

Somehow we have to move on to reach **the other side**, and get beyond the burdens that hold us down and inhibit our motivations. We must begin by honestly evaluating our condition from our physical appearance to the effects it has on our entire lives. It is then we will not only have the energy and stamina to continue our journey, but the self-esteem to know where we want to go.

The First Step

As we all know, from everything else we do in life, the hardest step you make on the road to physical recovery is going to be the first one. How many times have we put off something we viewed as distasteful, hoping that it will disappear? How many times have we prolonged the planning and strategy of an endeavor to where it seems like we have prepared it to death? Don't get me wrong, there's got to be a plan; there's got to be preparation. However, the nice thing about exercise is that you are allowed to think while you are performing its task. The key is to begin to exercise today and while you're at it, plan for tomorrow. Procrastination just leads to more procrastination, and in no time, all opportunity is lost.

What you need to think about is that mirrored image, and what it's going to take to improve it. Since there has to be a payoff to encourage lasting participation, imagine the achievable result. Envision the type of person to whom you would be attracted, and then allow yourself to fantasize about what you would look like as the finished product of your effort. Just remember, just about anything is possible; some people just have to work harder than others.

To have a better understanding of what has to be done to accomplish a fit and more attractive you, you need to start by going to a physician to find out what you can and can't do. That usually should prompt a physical exam, including all the necessary tests to indicate, not only your exercise capabilities, but also to ascertain if you have any illnesses. We hear, so many times, of how depression and stress affect people's physical health. It would be wise to check out the effects that your situation and lifestyle has upon your body.

I have known so many people who have had a debilitating condition that no amount of exercise would have corrected, and their bodies would have shown little improvement, no matter how hard they worked. In my case it was a thyroid condition, and at 270 pounds, even if I could do the aerobics, my body would not have responded, as it should to reach the more desirable 220 pounds that I now maintain. It was an ailment that coincidentally Susana shared, and caused her to have, as she said, " a very heavy body." We both agreed that this heaviness, also weighed upon our minds and relationships. Not knowing what was causing it, proved very frustrating. Without the diagnosis and treatment of our thyroid conditions, we would not be looking at what we each thought was a physically attractive person.

I don't know what Susana looked like before, but if she was anything like me, she probably didn't think of herself as very attractive. Now she looks very healthy and I guessed her to be eight years younger than she was. It is amazing how much being healthy and physically fit can change your appearance.

Of course, exercise alone will only tone up the body you have. To shape your body usually requires changing your diet. By that I do not mean going on a diet. I mean changing your eating habits. Typically, people who I have talked with who have gone through a sudden, negative relationship change either don't eat because of the stress and emotional turmoil their body is absorbing, or they eat everything in sight as a reflection of their anxiety and despair. Many of those that overeat, do so as an attempt to "control" a part of their lives, or as an attempt to stuff emotions inward—the emotions once expressed outward to the one they loved. Once they get past the pain, they are left with an out of control appetite and the body to match. So very quickly, they either lose or gain a lot of weight. Either way their bodies portray their psychological and emotional condition.

Eating healthy and listening to what your body craves enhances the speed of the effects of exercise. Fast foods, fatty foods, salty foods, all the foods a depressed body doesn't need but constantly gets, must be eliminated and replaced with nourishment. How hard is it to change your diet so drastically? It is only about as hard as it is to begin an exercise program. It's done one step at a time. Once again, if it's important enough for you to increase the opportunities of expressing and sharing your love again, you'll do it.

You need to be honest when you tell yourself that you shouldn't have to go through all this trouble, and that you are just fine just as you are. If you're honest, you'll say that while you may be too depressed, or stressed, or even resolved to being alone, that you really do want to improve your condition. It also may be that you don't know what to do to achieve the results you desire or don't have the confidence to think you can accomplish such lofty goals. After all you have been through, it is certainly understandable to be timid about attempting anything outside the barriers you have constructed. But, if you truly want to have your love expressed, then you really have to begin, slowly though it may have to be, to improve your chances.

Of course, there are some people who have become conditioned to being lazy, or comfortable in their current setting. It could very well be because they are tired both physically and emotionally from their last ordeal. It is so important for them to understand that becoming healthy not only makes them look better, but can make them feel better as well. Diet and exercise tones the body, relieves stress and can aid in combating mild depression by releasing endorphins—the happy hormone—and also aid in weight loss and regulate the body. All of this results in improving self-esteem. And, as goals are accomplished, they may realize that this is the first significant thing they've done alone since becoming *Suddenly Single*—further enhancing they're confidence. They soon realize that their previous comfort zone was not that comfortable.

Feeling Good

Getting in shape is the first step to feeling better about yourself. That's when you come to realize that this personal fitness stuff, while presenting an attractive package to others, really becomes all about making yourself feel better. So harboring all those guilt feelings about giving in to societal pressures, or feeling superficial, becomes a smoke screen for what actually happens once you start getting in shape. Somehow, you begin to feel and look healthier. Your posture changes because your self-confidence, not to mention your muscle structure, has returned to your being. Little by little you're toning up this package that holds all that you are.

Your investments at first seem monumental—the time, the exertion, the expense—especially if you're just doing it to please someone else. When you start realizing that you are doing it to please yourself and improve your physical being, the investments seem minuscule compared to the gains achieved. Every day that mirrored image becomes more attractive to you.

The sense of accomplishment, coupled with the endorphins released through the exercise, reverse the despondency, and provide a strength that indicates that you can still be the master of you, without having all those barriers for protection. The strength that your body attains can also carry over to your non-physical being, allowing for that journey inward to continue with the assuredness and the self-esteem gained from the achievement of success of the process of getting in shape.

Feeling good about you is the beginning, and for most people the easiest way to achieve that feeling is to observe the physical changes in oneself. Some people find that they have to work very hard to bring about noticeable changes, because years of abusing one's body cannot be reversed overnight. To combat years of zero exercise might involve a physical regimen of ten hours of gym time each week—without fail.

Treat it as a job, in which you're getting paid in phenomenal feelings about yourself and your accomplishments. Remember, you don't socialize at a job. Too many people join gyms and then spend most of their time exercising their facial muscles, and not working on the structure of their body. Don't get me wrong; gyms are great places of social value. They provide an atmosphere of people with a common goal–to improve their appearance.

It's also a place, where people feel uncomfortable at first. The worse shape you're in, the more uncomfortable you feel, but if you look around you'll see people who started right where you are today, who thought enough of themselves to overcome the fear of rejection, unworthiness, and apprehension of the work ahead, to get to the point where they are today. When you look around that gym, you need to judge whether these people have more capabilities to realize their goals in life than you do. What is obvious is that they have a commitment to improving themselves.

When she asked me how to set up the controls on the Stairmaster machine, since this was her first time in the gym, I mentioned to her that it would probably be a good idea to start exercising on less strenuous equipment. I told her that it took me awhile, on other machines, to build up my capability to get the most effective results using the Stairmaster. She told me that her problem was that she spent too much time "building up" to things, and not enough time actually doing them.

She appeared to be about 5'6" tall and easily weighed 200 pounds. She told me that she gave birth to another child six months before, and her weight had gotten out of control. After having her first child two years before, she had gained so much weight that she was embarrassed going to the gym. Her choices now were to stay home and feel bad about herself, or suffer the initial embarrassment and begin to get back into shape. Her point was that she wanted to get in shape as quickly as possible, so her embarrassment wouldn't last so long.

Well, I showed her how to use the machine and gave her some words of encouragement. She lasted less than two minutes, huffing and puffing, saying, "Well, that's a start— a little more each day and I'll get there." Over the next few weeks I'd see her on different pieces of equipment, working as hard as anybody in the gym. She was also doing aerobics and swimming laps in the pool. After a few weeks, I happened to be next to her on the Stairmaster again, and she told me how much "fun" she was having working out, and how she had already lost twenty pounds. She kept talking about her "diet" and "energy" as she was exercising; something I could not physically do. To me, I get out of breath walking up all those steps, and I really can't talk while I do it.

When I decided that I had enough of that grueling exercise and began to climb down, she asked where I was going, and suggested that I "push" myself a little more. I left to do some other exercises and watched as she continued stepping away while talking to the next bewildered soul who took my place on the machine. She seemed like a different person, no longer talking about being embarrassed, but

47

talking about how good she felt. At that point, if you saw her for the first time, you would still think she was overweight, but definitely in condition.

A couple of months later, I joined her in an aerobics class. She was no longer struggling to keep up as she had done before, although I continued to miss a few steps. The contours of her body had reappeared and I would guess that she had lost another twenty pounds. She was certainly different than a lot of people at the gym; she seemed consumed with getting in shape. I've noticed that most people who begin in that much of a similar condition usually spend their time riding the stationary bicycles while watching TV. Granted, their risk of heart attack, pulled muscle, or damaged joints may not be as great as a 200+ pound, 5'6" overindulged Stairmaster working body might have. But she accomplished all that she did, and now certainly has less of a chance of some debilitating condition affecting her in the future.

In all my "people" experiences at the gym, she was definitely an exception to the rule, and what an inspiration. Obviously, the first thing she had to do to accomplish her extraordinary feat was to face up to it. Then she had to have the ambition to drive her to do a little more each day, and the commitment to see each day through. It seemed to be a tremendous amount of hard work, but I guess with all those endorphins kicking in, it actually did become "fun" to her.

Although I didn't have the opportunity to talk to her about it, I am sure her whole life changed. She seemed so proud of her accomplishments, and couldn't wait to tell people how far she had come, along with always giving others encouragement and a "push" to continue. Getting in shape became her focus, and as she told me when she first began, this was her "job" whose payoff was going to be feeling better about herself.

Working out to get in shape is going to provide not only a conditioned body, but will begin the process of searching out and receiving the relationship your love needs to be successful. First and foremost, you are experiencing **commitment to yourself** (the first step in loving yourself) and are associating with other people who are committed. Granted, these devotees of physical fitness are not expressing an undying vow to another person for the rest of their lives, but it's comforting to see someone committed to anything nowadays, even if it is only the improvement of their own body.

It just shows that there are people of all shapes and sizes who have not given up on their dreams, and who, rather than sit at home and watch make believe lives on TV or read about it in a novel, are willing to take the steps necessary to experience it first-hand. It's also reassuring to observe others who are interested in self-improvement enough to dedicate the time and personal resources necessary to achieve an improved look. Many of these people have experienced the same rejection and feelings of unworthiness that you might have experienced, but through their self-examination, have determined that they can and will make a change in their lives. While it is only a first step toward total recovery, the gym subculture provides an indication of what can be accomplished through hard work, discipline, and commitment.

So many people I know, who have so much more physical potential than I have, just refuse to even make an attempt at getting in shape. When I observe them and imagine what they would look like being in better condition, so many times I see potentially very attractive people, who do nothing to improve. And, yet they will express anguish with me because they don't feel attractive. In many ways I can empathize with them because I have been there—not with their potential, but certainly with their condition. And, I know that we will never believe we can accomplish our goals unless we try. I was disheartened and I was lazy too, but eventually I tried.

I know now that the only limits I have are the limits I put upon myself. If I spend ten hours a week in the gym lifting weights and doing aerobics I can get in very good shape. I know because that is what I accomplished. I also know that if I spend three hours a day in the gym doing what I am doing now and swimming for an hour that I can have what will be the perfect shape for me. It's nothing more than a matter of dedication and commitment that allows you to reach whatever goal you want. It's the hard work multiplied by time that equals the various levels of success you experience. There is no magic or mystery or secret formula, and anyone can do it.

Sometimes, when it gets to be a chore, I think about what I was like before I began exercising and how terrible I felt, both mentally and physically. No matter how hard I push myself now, I know that it can never equal the feelings I had by not being in shape. So now I try to enjoy myself when I'm working out thinking about the improvement in my condition. I also try and find ways to actually make it fun when possible, and believe me, when you are in shape your life becomes a lot more fun.

> *Traveling to meetings around the country means that I don't have as much of an opportunity to exercise, as I should. While in Houston recently, I realized that I hadn't worked out for days, and it seemed that I had eaten and*

drank everything in sight. I had gained six pounds and felt terrible, and couldn't imagine how I was ever going to do exercise enough to lose this weight. Then on some nights of sightseeing, I stopped at a few night-spots that had dancing. Apparently, if you are a visitor to Houston, the people there are required to ask you to dance every dance.

I never thought of myself as a "dancer," but I do now. I have never danced so much in my life. Staying on the dance floor for over four hours provides a tremendous aerobic workout, without realizing you are exercising. But, what a great way to exercise! I had no idea. It seemed to be the best of both worlds—getting in shape and socializing. I lost the six pounds I had gained plus another two pounds by the time I left Houston, and had a great time in the process. Of course, while I was dancing, I wasn't eating and drinking. So, if you are shy and need to lose weight, head to Houston and dance the fat away.

Everybody has different body types, and some people look their best a little overweight, or a little underweight. Although, with all the problems of eating disorders brought on by a distorted self-image, it is best to ask family and friends for assistance in judging one's appearance. And, being in shape, for our purposes, really means being and looking **healthy**. It means, projecting a look that tells people that you are comfortable and confident with the way you appear to others.

While our physical nature has predisposed many of us to a certain body style, it may prove more difficult to achieve and then maintain a great shape. But, we really have to strive for getting in the best shape we can with what we have to work with. It is truly amazing what we can do with our bodies when committed to working hard. It just needs to be a continual process. As we become involved in a fitness routine, we will begin to notice changes not only in ourselves, but in others who also are working on their physical improvement—some who started out a lot worse off than we did.

Good Enough

Of course, there are some people who are not in shape and don't think they should or could get in shape to be the object of someone's attraction. They feel that being in physical shape should have no bearing on whether someone is attracted to them. That would be perfectly understandable if these people didn't themselves become attracted to someone because of physical appearance or condition. And, while I am not suggesting that a person's body shape is the most important attraction, it certainly is given consideration in the scheme of things involved in a selection process.

Then there are the people who go to the opposite extreme and are attracted to someone just because of their "looks", and then adjust all their other criteria to create a false image of who they think they need and want. So we have illusions created by those who find physical appearance as the most important attraction, and illusions by those denying the attraction of someone's look. And, the rationalization for either position is easy to come by. Many times the reason some of us find ourselves in that rationalizing position is because either we are too lazy to find that person that goes beyond our physical attraction to include all those other important attributes, or because we are too lazy to become attractive to someone else.

I guess what it comes down to is just to try to do your best, for yourself. While your appearance, in all probability, makes a difference to others, in reality it certainly must bear some influence with the way you feel. If you say it doesn't, you're not being honest with yourself.

Being in shape is not the most important quality a person should have, and probably doesn't even rank anywhere near the top of considerations as to whether a person's life is worthwhile. But, it is important from a marketing standpoint, as a broadening of a potential suitor base by attracting attention and improving self-esteem.

What we have to understand is, that if we're *Suddenly Single*, chances are that we have esteem problems. But the way to deal with them is not to lower our standards. **The way to combat a lowered self-stature is to build it up by gaining confidence through honoring ourselves with self-respect.**

We all want to be loved for who we are, and not just for the way we look. But it's the way we look that expands the opportunities for people to be attracted to our love, and who we are. No matter what our features display, our total look is enhanced when we are in shape. It's amazing what conditioning can do to the perception of the human body and the optimization of its appearance.

When a negative change occurs in a person's esteemed nature, confidence and assuredness, and the pride of presentation that these allow, the attractiveness of their love will be affected. Why? Because the value that they have placed upon their love seems to have been diminished. The package that held it didn't seem to cherish its worth. And, no, it's not because someone became older or lost their looks. It's because the package that held this beautiful love became unattractive—whether physically or emotionally.

Sometimes the product of love doesn't get seen through the package in which it is contained, because we even become too lazy to offer its expression. The attitude becomes systemic. It affects not only the conditioning of our bodies, but also the fitness of our love. Some things that are worthwhile, take an awful lot of work to accomplish. And while working hard doesn't guarantee success, it at least indicates an assumption of value of what you are working toward.

If the perception of love can change because of the apparent worth being placed upon it, then given time, love can also change, because the value placed upon it determines its success. Once again, if you think your love is worth it, then you need to work hard at it all the time, unless you're not being honest with how much you think it's worth.

Body Language

Becoming physically fit not only provides for a better health outlook but also provides the look of a better body; an indication of pride in oneself. For example, if you tighten up the muscles of your stomach, your chest looks bigger. If you make your chest bigger, your stomach looks smaller. If you improve your posture, your chest looks bigger, your stomach smaller, and so on. It's an illusion that eventually becomes reality.

People who are *Suddenly Single* many times don't have self-confidence, and are not self-assured, which means their heads hang a little lower than usual. Typically, their posture sags, and their muscles loosen. They sometimes appear defeated, or on their way to defeat. Their bodies sometimes seem to exhibit a miserable existence—sullen, cheerless, depressed. At a time when they desperately need comfort, their body language says, "Don't ask me, 'How's it going?'"

Our body's appearance and the language it professes, tells a story of not only where we have been, but also where we are going. There is a time for sympathetic ears and tears, but the beginning of the end of re-visitations to the past has to begin with the realization of self-worth. The best place to start is with your body language. In order to be loved, you have to be lovable. In order to be lovable, you have to love and respect yourself. Your body not only communicates its forlorn nature to others, but it also depresses and conditions the rest of your being to the acceptance of this burden. The place to start recovery is with your body and all the confidence it can convey to you and everybody else.

Back to the Basics

You need to start by taking small steps at first; walking before you run. Even beginning with just 15 minutes a day of walking can begin to change your life. And while exercising allows you to begin the process of recovery without any deep thought of strategies, walking would allow time for peaceful reflection, thinking of ways to improve your life and considering positive change. This is the time, when stress is being relieved, to get to know yourself better. To begin with such a mild exercise permits you to experience the introspection necessary to understand your thoughts because somehow everything seems clearer when you're walking. Maybe it's the endorphins, or just being alone with your thoughts, but it works.

Of course, to improve means to get better, to progress. To progress in your physical state requires a development that increases limits and necessitates pushing yourself a little more each time you exercise, until you reach a point where maintenance is the goal. Lifting five pounds before ten pounds and then twenty pounds before thirty pounds. Doing ten sit-ups before fifty and then seventy crunches before a hundred: swimming two laps and then building to twenty. Doing low impact aerobics before advancing to the intermediate stage and becoming flexible so that you don't damage your body so much at the beginning that you are not able to continue or enjoy future exercise.

The first yoga class I attended appeared to be made up of people without any muscle or joint constraints. They were warming up by wrapping their legs around their necks. At that point I couldn't even touch my toes. For the first time, I really felt embarrassed by my condition. In the regular gym, I was at least able to lift the weights and use the equipment to my own capability; maybe not as much or for as long as those who have been working out longer than I have. And in aerobics class, I could at least get part of the routines down and was able to last until the end of the class. But yoga was definitely a different challenge.

At first I thought that this class was just going to be meditation; where you sit around, contemplate, relax, and dream about getting in shape. I thought that this would be a good break, and that by meditating, my body would somehow become more flexible. And, of course, when I noticed the instructor and the absolute perfection of her body, I figured that I better start right away.

I knew I was not ready to get involved with anybody, and certainly was not looking at the instructor as a possible partner: Although, it would have been nice. I still did not want to look totally incompetent in front of her and the other, mostly female, members of the class. Needless to say, as the class began, I was totally incompetent.

I could not even do the seemingly easy parts of the warm-up exercises. My body didn't seem to want to go in any direction other than straight up and down, and after awhile even that became a chore. Throughout the class, the instructor continually took time out to come back and help me by pushing on my back, or assisting the bending of my leg, or providing me with instruction on the proper body position. It felt so great to be singled out like that. Right! I felt like the proverbial bull in a china shop. Of course, I was a lot bigger and more muscular than the little old ladies who comforted me with their smiles and comments that I was doing just fine. That hour of class was one of the most agonizing physical times that I have ever spent. And, it certainly didn't build up my confidence either. But somehow I got through it and, with the encouragement of the instructor, came back again.

I returned to this excruciating physical and mental anguish many times, for a number of reasons. First of all, that first class made me realize how inflexible I really was, and how important it would be for me, in my efforts to get in top physical shape, to be flexible. And then, I looked at the physical condition of those taking this class and saw the remarkably toned bodies of people that were probably well into their seventies, as well as that perfectly toned body of my instructor, which I have to admit was quite an inspiration. To watch her wrap her legs around her body and to lift herself up on one hand seemed miraculous. She told me that eventually that I would be able to do that; it would just take time and practice. Obviously, to achieve the look of her body and the capabilities she was able to achieve with it, took a lot of time and practice. It made me realize that to be in great physical shape was like a lot of things in life; it takes a lot of hard work and maybe even new experiences to accomplish success.

While I still haven't achieved that level of success, at least I have good intentions. And, since my traveling and my schedule hasn't permitted me to attend as often as I should or, amazingly, would like to, I still realize how valuable flexibility exercises are to my overall physical conditioning, and when I am able to attend, how much better I feel both mentally and physically after class is over. I also realize that I probably will never be able to contort my body in the positions that many of my classmates can. But I guess I will take what I have and do the best I can, and if my fragile ego ever needs a boost, maybe I can challenge one of these little old ladies to a game of basketball, with the hope that I am able to show them a thing or two.

You Are What You Eat

The extremes that we've put our bodies through, also probably involved our eating habits. Once again it will most likely take extreme measures to control and change this habit as well, but we can begin slowly and thoughtfully as we did with our exercise program, just as long as we begin soon. We certainly have been deluged with enough advertising about how to eat healthy to get in shape, and everybody now has a diet or a magic pill to take to get rid of unwanted fat or to improve the condition of one's body.

The truth is, though, it takes dedication and commitment to break those comforting eating habits that have brought you to your current condition.

People who have starved themselves because of the suffering they've endured, need to gain nourishment if they hope their bodies will respond to an exercise regimen. Exercise will increase their appetites, but with their limited intake of food, they have to be sure that everything they eat is good for them. Eating right will only enhance the way they look and improve their overall image. For those who eat too much because of the stress of their situation, the same solution holds true. However, these people need to cut down on the intake of food that is bad for them. This may all sound oversimplified, but it is amazing how many people will actually increase their physical activity and begin exercising, but will continue the poor eating habits that got them into their condition in the first place.

It has been proven many times over that too much saturated fat is bad for your health, and that certain foods contain chemicals and hormones that are put there to fatten up the products that we buy. And yet, we crave that sort of diet. Maybe if we just looked at it superficially, that those foods make us look bad, we will change our habits. If we came to the realization that everything from our complexion to the location of our fat deposits is determined to a large extent by what we eat, we might actually be inhibited enough to change those yearnings. Another tough decision. Do you give in to the wonderful immediate cravings of that delicious chocolate layer cake, or opt to give up on dessert after you've finished your spinach salad?

Immediate gratification usually always wins over the accomplishment of long-term goals. This is because we can see it, smell it, taste it; our senses bring it all together so that we can visualize how good it's going to be for us at that moment. It is difficult to visualize the negatives of our long-term actions when immediate gratification is right there. To be successful in the future, we must imagine the results of our actions today. We must create a believable image that will ultimately be pitted against the instant satisfaction of our behavior, in this case, what we eat. And, of course, we must start today.

I guess I can't diet, because I'm such a big eater. It's not just that I love to eat, it's that eating satisfies the nervous energy that seems to emanate from inside my body. Of course, exercise eats up a lot of the excess calories that I consume, but if I continued to eat what I was eating, all the exercise in the world wouldn't have helped me lose weight.

My normal blood pressure was 145/98, and that was after it was brought down from my thyroid condition. I was also taking high blood pressure pills and I had an artery that was 15% blocked. I wasn't feeling good physically or emotionally. Of course the two are complementary and were exacerbated by a failing relationship.

Now that I am by myself—as a temporary solution—my blood pressure is 120/65 without medication, my artery has a 0% blockage, I am never sick, and consider myself in excellent physical and emotional health. What has contributed to my healthy condition was not having to deal with a failing relationship anymore, and also having the capability to decide what the eating habits of the house are going to be.

I now eat and drink healthfully. I mention drink, because typically alcoholic beverages have little, if any, redeeming qualities. I do drink red wine on occasion, because of its positive impact on the condition of the heart. One drink that I can never get enough of is water. Water cleans the body of toxins. I never was able to drink much water before. Maybe it was because tap water didn't excite me, or even cold water stored in a pitcher in the refrigerator couldn't entice me to drink what I needed. Then one day I went to one of those discount food clubs and bought a case of 24 "sport" bottles of water. There is something about grabbing a 24 oz. bottle of cold water from the refrigerator. It becomes a replacement for the grabbing of a can of soda or beer, as we have become so conditioned. The fact that it is in a bottle and cold somehow makes it more attractive.

Then to make sure that I don't lose out on the fluoride content to protect my teeth, and also to save a little money, I refill the bottles after use with tap water and use them again. Of course I can't do that too much because of the threat of germs. I have now gone from drinking four or five colas a day, with all their caffeine, sugar and sweeteners and other mysterious ingredients, to drinking over a gallon of water per day. And believe me, I can really tell the difference. Whenever I travel and end up drinking lots of cola and alcoholic beverages, my body feels weak and fatigued, and my mind doesn't seem as clear.

Water also replaces the need to consume so much food. It's like a snack that serves some useful purpose. You can actually lose weight, the more water you consume. Of course, the key is to let it pass through your body and not have it be retained. One thing that retains fluids in your body, thus causing you to either keep the weight you have now, or put on more weight, is salt. It seems salt is found in just about everything we eat. Sometimes it occurs naturally, sometimes it is added in the processing of products, and most of the time we add it ourselves to flavor food. Salt consumption has also been linked to high blood pressure. It is amazing how, since I stopped using salt to flavor my food and watched the salt content of the food I was purchasing, not only has my blood pressure and weight dropped, but also the taste of my food has improved. Before, the dominant taste of the food I ate was salty, and I had a craving for that flavor. Whether it was meat or fish, salad or vegetables, the salt flavor actually dominated the taste of the food, and it was not as much an adventure eating different types of food as it is now.

Sugar is a lot like salt in that it occurs naturally, is added to products in processing, and is added by us to the food we eat. Sugar is also bad for our diet. While it seems to give us energy, it is also has been linked to diabetes, and when not burned up in the body through exercise and metabolic functions, it turns into fat. Every once in a while, whether because of nervous energy or mild depression, I buy an extra large bag or two of giant, double fudge chocolate graham cracker cookies. As a binge eater, they usually only last a few days. Of course, while eating them my nervous energy and depression increases, causing even more of a craving for these delicious treats.

Inevitably, after polishing off my supply of these fat-causing and sugar-filled cookies, I notice where they have gone in my body. It seems that somehow, miraculously, they have turned to fat and position themselves primarily in my abdominal area. They provide me with love handles at a time when I least need them. And, what's left over seems to deposit itself in my face and chin. Afterwards, I have to work out for weeks to trim down and diminish their effect. When

I went to the gym, I ended up comparing myself to those body builders with those "six pack" stomachs, to my "graham cracker" stomach. I then realize how much work and time it takes to rid myself of those few moments of "pleasure," and I say never again. At least until it happens again. Maybe someone will develop a non-fat, no sugar version of the double fudge chocolate graham cracker. But even many of those non-fat foods that beckon us contain a lot of both sugar and salt, trading off fat for calories, sugar that turns to fat, and salt that retains water weight.

If you follow all the dictums of those diets on the market, probably the only food that everyone agrees is valuable is water. It seems that everything else is out of bounds for one reason or another. I've been on high carbohydrate diets—lots of pasta, whole grain breads, with fruits and vegetables—where I had lots of energy, but if I didn't exercise quite a bit I would gain weight. I went on a high protein diet with lean red meat, turkey and lots of fish, especially tuna fish. It seemed that when I was working out, my body would get really toned and I would gain strength on this particular diet but would lose energy and thus enthusiasm for working out. My muscles would actually get bigger, but my body would seem to get bigger too, especially if I was eating a lot of red meat. I could imagine how the steers felt getting fattened up before the slaughter. I'm sure I was consuming the same hormones. There's also the possibility of liver damage if this diet is continued for too long.

There were the primarily fruit diets, where I would put a grapefruit, an apple, a kiwi, a banana, a mango, strawberries, pineapple, an orange, cranberries, and cantaloupe in a blender with ice. This huge drink would obviously satisfy my hunger for most of the day, and I would feel and look great with plenty of energy. The only problem I had was that even with plenty of exercise I could not lose weight. But, I really felt healthy. I guess it was just too many calories, and the sugar content of the fruit was probably more than I could burn up. An interesting point is that it seems the harder it is to peel the fruit, the better it is for you; the kiwi versus the banana, for example.

Another diet that I enjoyed, and experienced success with, was eating primarily vegetables. It would seem that I could go to a salad bar nightly, and eat as many vegetables as I could, without gaining weight. I would have to be very careful about the kind and amount of dressing I would add to my salad, though. Many dressings have just as much fat, sugar and salt as a fast food burger and counteract any benefit received from stuffing yourself with "veggies". Of course, there is the old stand by, olive oil and vinegar. Olive oil contains little saturated fat, no cholesterol, sodium or carbohydrates, and studies have indicated that it can be very beneficial to your health.

Whatever diet I try, if I don't include junk food and remain observant of what I am eating, I will lose weight and generally be in great physical condition. I have become conscious of the nutritional needs of my body and when I am able to provide a balanced fulfillment of those needs, I not only feel good, but also look good. It takes more time to carefully shop for and prepare healthy food than it does to drive through a fast fat food outlet, but the result for me has proven its worth.

One rule of thumb that I use is, consuming fat and things that turn to fat are what make me fat. Sounds simple enough, but it is amazing how many times in the past I couldn't put that concept together with my physical appearance. If I over-indulge by eating too many vegetables and fruits, I may not lose weight, but I will also not notice actual fat being added to my body structure. Since fat contains about twice as many calories as carbohydrates, and it's quickly converted to and stored as body fat, my weight seems stabilized when I chose complex carbohydrates, like fruits and vegetables, over fat.

I have found that the best way to rid myself of my occa-sionally bad nutritional habits and their fat content is to provide an equal amount of bingeing with nutritional foods and exercise. I usually go on an extremely high fiber diet, eating only fruits and vegetables and drinking lots of water. High fiber foods usually take longer to chew and stimulate the digestive juices that flow in your mouth and stomach. They also allow you to exercise your facial muscles more; in between eating I also chew a lot of gum. When I eat these types of foods, it seems that I remain full for a longer period of time, because the fiber absorbs the water and expands; like when you let a bowl of Extra Fiber All Bran with skim milk sit awhile. Of course, while eating this way, if I also do strenuous exercises like aerobics or lifting weights, I not only visibly reduce my body fat, but it seems evident to me that my metabolism seems to increase for a full day after I exercise. My mood is elevated and I am no longer subject to a depression or anxiety that makes me crave those chocolate cookies.

Instead of eating three large meals a day as we have been programmed to do since we were kids, try eating five or six of the right type of foods in smaller or medium quantities. This will keep the metabolism working while burning fat. When I eat three large meals a day I think my body holds on to that food, not knowing where or when its next meal is coming from. More frequent, smaller amounts allow the metabolism to continue to work releasing energy because the body doesn't feel threatened by starvation. Once again, it is the same with water. I learned in the Army that if your body does not receive enough water, it feels threatened that it might die and therefore retains water for emergencies. If you drink a lot of water, it not only helps to remove re-tained water, but also helps to moisturize your skin—just in case you need to be motivated further to the point that what you eat determines how you look.

It's a vicious cycle. The more you despair, the more you crave foods that contribute to your despair. The more you eat right and exercise, the less you crave those harmful foods and the more you want to exercise. When muscles are toned it seems so easy to stay in shape, probably because metabolism is increased and it becomes easier to burn up calories. You end up looking better, feeling better, and have a positive attitude toward maintaining a healthy lifestyle.

Do It Now

Everything worthwhile takes time, and the hard work associated with accomplishing your goals. You are not being logical, or honest, if you want results as soon as possible, and yet you agree to put off for a day, a week, or a month, the action needed to reach that outcome. *Suddenly Single* people are notorious for waiting at home for that miracle to happen. How realistic is that?

How much time and productivity is lost, waiting? Waiting is a lazy person's activity. It not only wastes time and delays the needed progress toward your goals, it probably affects the life of another person out there—the person searching for you.

Once again though, we demand immediate gratification. If it's not the food we eat or the body we seek, it's a person to love, or at least companions who can help imitate love. If we resign ourselves to the fact that it is going to take some time for us to get over our failed relationship, to get our lives in order, and then to find the near perfect recipient of our love, then we realize we have time to execute a plan. This course that we prepare, given that time, will allow for all that we determine we need to accomplish, to present that total package to the outside world. Granted, along the way, there are people we will meet while working out to get in shape, who may have a lot more in common with us that just the pride of improving their appearance. There will be people we meet in grocery stores who will also be reading the same labels we are, to determine what healthy food to buy to improve the condition of their bodies. Who knows, you can get lucky! But you can't get lucky waiting around for something miraculous to happen. **In order to win the lottery, you have to buy a ticket.** It takes an investment to have a justifiable hope of succeeding.

So the plan begins with commitment, and urgency—today, and we all know what is urgent. It's the same feeling you get when you're alone and you need someone there to comfort you right away. Now you have to translate that feeling to apply to your immediate goals. It's the same word with a different meaning and direction. Its pressing nature now becomes part of the plan toward self-improvement. With a well thought out timetable in your plan, the urgency becomes a positive aspect of your life, rather than a negative sensation. I emphasize well thought out, rather than reasonable, because reasonable allows for our own inherent laziness once again to enter into the equation of our plan.

Once the itinerary is set and the schedule is in place, and acted on, success will come. We start to make noticeable improvement, and can gauge the results along the way. We can get an estimate of how long our journey may be, and a projection of how our lives will benefit. This anticipation causes us to become excited about ourselves, and our outlook on life again. It causes us to translate those other feelings we had at the demise of our relationship to a different meaning. We become distressed if, at times, we cannot schedule the demands of our self-improvement plan. We become disheartened and depressed when the acceleration of our progress is slower than we predict. We get sullen when the endorphins of our absent labors are not present.

The terms of our condition are the same, but their direction has changed; now it's ourselves, not our lost love, we are thinking about. It's not how anybody else is going to make us feel better; it's about how we are going to make ourselves feel better. And the reason these terms are even still hanging around is because we realize how much our achievement really means to us. Once we start down that road to improvement, we feel value, we feel worth.

We begin to believe that the opportunities for us to connect with that one person who can admire what we have to offer are being enhanced, because we are being enriched. We feel better about ourselves. We've become more attractive, more lovable to ourselves, and more confident as to whom we really are. We find those barriers of protection coming down, allowing ourselves to be exposed without the constant fear of rejection and hurt.

The pride we discover is not in what we have become, but rather who we are; the person who has been concealed behind the shield of caution. We are not emerging as new and different people, exchanging our bodies, minds and emotions for a more capable package. We are blessed with what we've got; we're just accentuating the positives and diminishing the negatives, reflecting who we deserve to be.

Accessorize

While your reflection only provides a physical portrait, its display offers a perception of the character, the attitude, and the outlook of that very personal image. Everything mirrored before you creates an image that will relate to someone, the nature of your being. Even your hairstyle and your posture add to the story of who you are, or at least, who you appear to be. Even the accessories that you choose to complement your physical being and environment add to this judgment of this person you're observing as your mirrored image.

Would the clothes they wear matter? They would if a certain type of appearance mattered to you. Of course what they wear not only has the capability of accentuating physical characteristics, but also provides an insight into personality traits. While clothes could present a false personal image or do injustice to body type, they typically are viewed as a statement of attitude. While attitudes can change frequently at this stage of life, it can't hurt to dress with style or even just a concern for tidiness. And, would you appreciate it if their clothes fit over a fit body?

Clothes are just a part of the accessory formula that adds to the image we create. These additions that complement our physical being enhance the way we appear to other people and involves everything in our environment that offers a glimpse of our personal nature. It is with this view that we perceive others as they perceive us.

Now you can even imagine accessorizing beyond the clothes to the environments that people are usually observed. Would the car they drive make a difference? It might, if that was viewed as a measure of success or self-esteem. And, a car with dents and a broken windshield might indicate more problems then just not having the "right" car. At least to most people, a car should be clean.

A popular perception is that you can tell a lot about a person by the clothes they wear and the car they drive. While chances are, that a flashy dresser driving a sleek new sports car will certainly be noticed more than someone less stylish, some might feel that this person might be too stylish for a relationship. Also, these are just the sort of things that are "eye catchers"—things that attract perceptions and conjure up images of value and character.

If what you are wearing and what you are driving isn't getting you noticed, then you might want to spruce up a little bit. You are not what you wear, or what you drive, but I would be willing to bet that with most people, you could write a book about how their clothes and their cars reflect something about their nature. **When you don't yet have any other criteria with which to evaluate someone, the visual effects can determine your perception.**

There are some characteristics that, generally speaking, are truisms. Usually there is a preference that a person be in some sort of healthy condition; and I'm not talking about being buff or an extraordinary body that may indicate a preoccupation with the priority of one's appearance, but an acceptable shape. It may be because of physical attraction, or simply as an indication of pride in oneself. But, whatever the preference or inclination of attraction, certain basic standards generally provide for a minimum acceptance level of consideration. Common sense should always prevail.

Market Yourself

When businesses put up big, flashing neon signs, it's an attraction to their location; to let people know they're there. They can have the greatest product in the world, but if their customers don't know they exist, their products will never get sampled. In many ways that's what physical attraction is all about. You owe it to your love and its expression to be sure that as many people can visualize and experience it as possible.

When we go to a department store or grocery store to buy those objects of value, doesn't the packaging attract our attention? Isn't that what first draws us to try or buy different products? Billions of dollars and countless years of research indicate that packaging of products is essential to establish and maintain an attraction. When was the last time you purchased something in a plain brown crumpled wrapper over an appealing, desirable package? Which appeared to have something of value inside?

Keep in mind, that all that packaging research was accomplished to attract you to a product, which may be exactly the same as that product in the brown, crumpled wrapper. But, many of us will never know about that wonderful product in the sloppy marketing package. You don't need a graduate degree in marketing to understand the importance of the desirability of that mirrored image you are now facing. If your love deserves the chance of being experienced, than you better make sure that your package attracts somebody's attention. **While sustained product loyalty** comes from the perceived quality of the product, it is the package that gets the product sampled.

A Star Is Born

We will be creating a package that, while being noticed by others for its worth, will also create a sense of pride for us because of its improvement. We trust that what we find attractive is also what others will find attractive, and don't mind working hard to look better. We will view all this talk about not giving in to societal pressure about having the perfect body or the acceptable look as another smokescreen that clouded our self-improvement, and inhibited our capabilities. We understand that the way we look to others is many times the same way we look at them.

There is a reason that all these perfect looking people are on the covers of all these fashion magazines. It's because you and I wouldn't buy them, if we were on them. We like to look at pretty women and handsome men because attractiveness sells. Look at all of the products that are sold by these people. And they're not the only ones buying them. We're the ones being influenced by the way these products are marketed and who is marketing them. If clothes look good on an attractive model, I guess down deep we hope they will look the same on us. **We are more attracted to an appealing package** and hope that our appeal can become equally attractive.

While all of us are not blessed with perfect bone and body structure, why condemn those who are, while secretly wishing that we could be. We can certainly take what we've got and improve upon it. But that takes hard work and discipline, like a job does, with the pay being a more attractive you. For these alluring "cover" people, their looks are their job. They get paid to look attractive to you, and usually work hard to attain and maintain that appearance. We condone their efforts with the viewing of the movies, and the purchase of the magazines in which they appear and products they sell, and yet question our own desires to become desirable.

Why does everyone want to look like movie stars or models? It's because their look is accepted as good-looking by those of us on the outside looking in. We've even allowed some pretty ordinary looking people to capture our fantasies. Most of the time, it's because of the aura they project rather than their gorgeous looks. It's an aura of confidence; a success that we translate into beauty. Some of the most popular stars, those voted the sexiest and/or most desirable men and women alive, are rather normal looking people who somehow radiate compelling charm and invoke envy. Don't forget, we never see them when they wake up in the morning, or after they've showered, or have been up all night writing a book, unless of course it's in a movie where they've been prepared for our viewing.

We see them in movies, and publicity shoots, at the Oscars, or doing interviews. We see them at their best; a place that has taken a lot of hard work and discipline to achieve. These people should be an inspiration rather than a deterrent to our own lack of success. We can mold and shape our bodies to be at our best, and possibly be as attractive as the people appearing on the screen. While we may not have supermodel features, we can certainly enhance our body structure enough to arouse an interest that will go beyond those superficial necessities of attraction. We've proven it by those celebrities to whom we are attracted.

Without question, there are so many qualities more important within the human totality than the physical nature of our being. Once again, the shallowness of many a relationship based on only a pretty face has led nowhere. So many times, that's where our criteria stop. While, clearly the heart and mind should play so much more of an important role in the choosing of a partner for a successful relationship, it is however, as unfairly as it may seem, that exterior package that gives so many an attraction at first glance.

That attraction has got to start with you. That alluring look has to be first reflected in a mirror to you before anyone else finds it as tempting. It's the assurance that is gained from that image that enhances your attractiveness. If you feel good about yourself, others will feel good about you. **It's a transformation from self-consciousness, which is not very attractive to others, to self-confidence, which is.** It is that "self" that is going to determine to whom you are going to appeal.

Don't Worry, Be Happy

So, we've gotten into the best shape we can, and can now reasonably expect that people will notice us. If not for an appreciation of the way we look, certainly because of the pride we exude from the confidence in our physical selves. The next step is to project some of those inner qualities that have been hiding beneath the surface. That projection is our personality. Our disposition, distinctiveness, humor, and spirit, put a face to our character. This face becomes part of what others see, part of our visible identity. Once again, we must put our best face forward. And what qualities do we want to project? We must still maintain that we have to be honest, to honestly have hope of attracting that one person we so deservedly need. While we may not be happy all the time, especially after experiencing the hurt that we just went through, coupled with the excruciating exercise regimen and the departure of the steak, baked potatoes smothered with sour cream and butter (why is it that the only healthy thing on the plate gets thrown away: the parsley?) and chocolate cake from our diet; we must put on a happy face.

When we all previously agreed that someone would rather be with someone in shape than out of shape, the same holds true for personalities. I would think that most people would rather be with someone happy than someone sad, unless, of course as with the in shape example, there is an ulterior motive. The best expression of a happy person is their smile. I guess you can still be happy and not smile, but who would ever know? The object here is to let people know. Have a happy package, so that your attraction is enhanced. Many advertisers for products use bright colorful packaging, to not only attract your attention, but to convey a friendly, cheerful, even radiant atmosphere; everything a smile conveys.

Some people haven't smiled in a while, and a good sincere, happy smile, takes practice. Like with exercise, you've got to start today. The stooping and shrugged shoulders that the self-confidence and workouts have eliminated now must be done to the facial muscles. For many, your sad expression has caused the muscles around the mouth to sag and a permanent frown has set in. Just as the aerobic effect of exercise releases endorphins that make your body and mind feel better, thus encouraging more work outs, smiling causes a happier feeling that makes you want to smile more.

While I was daydreaming at church one Sunday, I was thinking that this would be a good place to meet a woman. I mean it would be great to meet someone who I was attracted to, with the same religion and maybe the same beliefs about love, commitment and marriage. And then, out of nowhere, walks in this woman with a little boy and no wedding ring. She stands right next to me and we exchange pleasantries. At first I thought, "Thank you, God", but as good looking and as physically fit as she was, I couldn't take my focus away from her frown and the sorrow expressed by her face. She just exuded sadness. I felt so sorry for her and spent the rest of the time in Church imagining what terrible things must have happened in her life to cause such an expression. Here she was, an apparently single mom, trying to bring up a little boy who didn't seem much happier then she was. She seemed to have the worries of the world on her shoulders, which in reality she probably did. I had seen that same look before on so many people I had met that had been bitter and angry for a long time and conveyed that they still harbored those same sentiments.

I thought that it would be nice if she met someone who could make her smile and wipe away that frown, but I knew that it wasn't going to be me because I wasn't attracted to her. The lack of attraction was because of her frown. I began to feel somewhat disingenuous and wondered why her facial expression was so important to me. I guess it was somewhat selfish, in that those of us Suddenly Single are looking for someone to make us happy rather than someone to perpetuate sadness. Maybe we need to think more about how we can help sad people become happy. After all, it wasn't long ago that I had worn a similar frown. I had forced myself to make the choice of portraying sadness or radiating joy, and I chose to express my happiness with my smile. One reason I made this decision is because I realized that people are searching for the security of happiness, not the complications of sadness. The other reason is that I wanted to be happy myself.

I found myself observing a woman who by most measures

would be viewed very attractive, and not being attracted to her at all. I began to realize that for whatever reason and consequence, the first and critical point of attraction for me, is a smile.

Of course, if you just go around and smile for no reason, that will also attract a lot of attention; negative attention. The way to practice smiling is to do and think about things that are happy. Go to movies, or watch TV programs that are fun. Read books and magazines that bring you joy. Hang around with people who have a sense of humor. The more you smile the easier it becomes. And the easier it becomes, the more sincere is its reason.

For some people there is nothing sexier than a great smile. When we look at those desirable stars who we see off the screen, they all seem to have great, personable smiles that seem to accentuate all the positive features of their faces. Smiling is like building up your chest so that your stomach appears smaller, or tightening your abdomen so that you chest looks bigger, or just changing your posture, so that everything seems proportional. It somehow makes your eyes seem brighter and your blemishes disappear. The posture of your face begins to change. Physically you look better, and mentally you feel a whole lot better.

Your outlook now portrays the expression of your attitude. It becomes the topping off of your physical well-being and indicates that you have arrived from your physical and emotional journey, to a place of enough confidence that allows you to smile. A smiling face creates an impression of not only a secure, happy environment, but also allows for a mystery of what helped develop that environment and how it is possible to reach such a special place.

As I reflect back over the years of my noticing, and being noticed by, the opposite sex, I realize that my prime motivation of attraction has always been a woman's smile. It has been as if it provided an opening to an introduction because of its friendly nature. A smile has always seemed to request a response or at least invited an exchange of thought. It let me observe and know that someone was either happy or happy to see me, or maybe both. I have been told that it was the defining expression that attracted women to me.

4

Journey Inward

Now that we've begun to accomplish the necessary steps to begin projecting a positive physical image, it's time to go beyond those concepts to formulate an idea of who we are. For all the obvious reasons, this projected image of our inner being should always reflect reality. While it may not be as easy to visualize qualities and traits as it was when analyzing physical condition, it is even more important to achieve an accurate portrayal of who you are. While all the attractiveness stuff presents us in an appealing package, it is all the ingredients included in that package that makes up who we are; ingredients as matchless as our DNA.

Many of these ingredients lie well beneath the surface, causing you to delve deep to uncover the real you—the you, only you can really know. This journey, while more difficult than merely getting your body in shape or changing your eating habits, is also so much more important to the discovery of who you are, and the future of your being. It helps determine your goals, and most importantly, assists in establishing the direction toward the target of your love. Of course, ultimately, it decides who the recipient of your love is going to be.

While you have begun to mold and shape your body through exercise and diet, analysis of your being will prove much more challenging to accomplish. There is no readily available mirrored image to observe or easy to visualize standards with which to compare. There are no labels to read or mechanical equipment to allow a mindless psychological regimen as your physical evaluation allowed. It's just dealing with your innermost thoughts; your ideals, principles, and beliefs, and eventually your feelings. It's nothing like the loneliness you've experienced, but it is very much being alone—with yourself. It is delving into the depths of your mind, the experiences of your memories, the feelings of your heart, and the substance of your soul. Wow, now that sounds pretty heavy! All of that just to get ready to start dating again? Well certainly, all that, if you want to do it right this time.

There are a lot of people out there who will be attracted to your physical being, because of the package you presented. Now it comes down to the product inside. It really doesn't do any good to just advertise that you have a better package than all those other products out there, although there are those who are only interested in the look of the envelope, and don't pay much attention to the words within. But who wants to attract people like that anyway, unless that's all you've got to offer?

The product of your love is worth so much more. Besides, where would their product loyalty be if they were just interested in you because of your physical attraction? As soon as a more appealing package came along, they'd be gone. We need to attract those who are going to have a clear understanding of who we are. Then, there are no surprises, regrets, misunderstandings or dissatisfaction along the way, so that their commitment can last a lifetime.

So now you have to change your focus from providing an attractive package for other people, to making your innermost qualities equally observable. **The purpose of creating the package was not to just attract attention; it was also to improve self-esteem and thus increase the number of opportunities for expressing your love.** Feeling good about yourself leaves a very attractive impression on those observing you. While this attraction may just be superficial, it will certainly provide a lot more attention to all your other qualities. There will be more people noticing more of your characteristics. That way you can be more selective and the people you are attracting can be more selective, which enhances the chance of a mutual admiration. No one should have to settle for just attraction. You really want someone who wants you for everything that you are, provided they can figure out who you are. Of course, that's something you have to figure out first. And, it has to be accurate; not the portrayal of who is being looked for by somebody else.

Considering the influences and impacts of the environment in which we exist, it will at first, be difficult to offer this accurate portrayal. We are certainly influenced by the relationships we've had in the past. Then there are the movies and TV shows that we equate with reality; the heroes, and leaders whom we admire. There are the others whom we have observed succeeding and those who have failed in what they tried to accomplish, and our conveniently-oriented lifestyle which has prompted us to make the decisions that are expected of us by our society.

Then there are those things that should be considered our strengths, which may be perceived even by us, as our weaknesses. And our weaknesses are many times glorified to be strengths in our society. It's confusing with all the pressures and influences, but we've got to be truthful with ourselves. It's the only way to succeed in the difficult task ahead.

As we've realized from the hurt of our past experiences, many times it may have been necessary to even be protected from the truth because of the pain it inflicts. It's one thing to tear down the barriers of protection from others, but it is even harder sometimes to do it for ourselves. While leading a happy existence, prior to problems in our relationships, our potential for being a good person was probably realized because it received a lot of attention. Since that time, other negative potentialities and feelings may have surfaced, because of the attention that we spent on them.

We may have hidden agendas that sometimes we don't even want to know or think about. Most people want to be considered good-intentioned people, even though deep inside some may have a predisposition toward bad intentions and for creating havoc in their, and others' lives. These feelings are occasionally brought to the surface when the desperation or anger of a negative experience presents itself. This exploration could reveal feelings hidden because they were never needed or exposed before: A side of a person that even they themselves have never noticed in the past. Self-awareness may not be all that's necessary to provide a starting point for these people's self-improvement. While for some, their reactions might seem perfectly normal considering all the hurt and pain they have endured, it wouldn't hurt for others to seek out counseling before beginning this journey.

Even those truly good-intentioned people sometimes allow false images of themselves and others to become their reality, because they so desperately want others to be what they need, and they desire so much to be what others need. That's why it is so important, at this stage, and every stage of your journey, to be sincere and straightforward. If you can't present yourself honestly, you have no right to expect potential mates to present themselves honestly. Any relationship that is not based upon the honesty of both parties is doomed to failure, necessitating more remorse and despair and another search, and so on. It is time to do it right.

One good thing about conducting this self-probe is that, while it is difficult to expose yourself, it is relatively obliging and forth right, because there is no one else to criticize, misinterpret, or judge. It involves only you, determining who you are. Of course, there may be times when it can get pretty intense, and at that point it would be good to sound out issues with someone else like a good friend, or a counselor. That point is reached when you find that you may not have the ability to sort out why you feel the way you do. For the most part, though, you are just conducting a survey assessing who you are today, so that the people you meet tomorrow will have a clearer and more honest definition of who you are. More importantly, you can have a better idea of who you should be matched with in the future.

For some people it may be a good idea at this point of their journey to keep a daily journal, writing down their feelings and hoped for goals. This journal should also include steps taken to achieve their goals on that particular day. Over time this will allow an assessment of progress and an indication of the relationship between goal accomplishment and feelings. While so many times we feel stuck in a stage of life, by accurately analyzing where we started and where we are, we will be able to change our perception that we haven't progressed. It is really amazing how in a relatively short period of time, we will be able to compare the current low stage in our life as being so much higher than where we began when we started making note of such conditions. That will give us the motivation to probe deeper and seek more.

It is by delving into your innermost thoughts, you'll express those ideas that are not usually expressed. Your opinions, which may have gone unexposed in your previous relationship, were perhaps not of major concern, or perhaps were too much of a concern and would have just provided more complication to an already complicated life. Typically they are the ideas that we keep hidden for one reason or another. Ideas or feelings that are sometimes not comfortably discussed with others might involve sexual matters, family concerns, and life experiences that trigger certain reactions or behaviors, or personal capabilities or disabilities. Even the clarification of values and associated reasoning becomes a subject of such varying belief, that it may be difficult to find someone with an equally involved understanding. Sometimes it seems almost as difficult to open up the sacredness of your being to yourself, as it is to share such a confidence. But, you must understand yourself before you can explain "you" to someone else.

As I first pondered the texts and syllabus for two of the courses I was teaching—Ethics and Human and Organizational Behavior—I realized that I was in a somewhat unique position to teach these subjects because of my personal and business experiences. Since these were both courses for students in the MBA program, these subjects certainly needed to relate to the business and societal aspects of the issues they presented, but clearly to me the personal relationships of their study were going to be the basis of my direction. In many ways both of these courses seemed interrelated because of the personal introspection that would be necessary to define for each student what acceptable behavior in each of these disciplines would entail.

Since I had already completed quite a journey in both business and society—with my political experiences— and had just finished a quite thorough self-analysis after my failed relationship, I felt very comfortable knowing the trip I wanted to take my classes on. But, no matter how much you think you know about yourself, new experiences always bring on new insights. While I learned a lot about myself from teaching my students, I also learned quite a bit about other people: how and why they think as they do, and more importantly, how very different some of us are from each other.

Something that I learned from my experiences in life, and that my students seemed to verify with their input, is that there are so many important valuable considerations that we don't think about until we are intimately confronted by them. This is primarily because we are so concerned with the daily operations of our lives that we don't have the time or inclination to delve into the complexities, or for even some the confusion, of analyzing our values and motivations. We rather become societal members with our ethics and behavior governed by and reflective of the rules and laws dictated to by the participating majority rather than individual conscience. Of course, if we didn't have rules and laws, we would have a chaos of individual anarchy. But, my point to them was, that we all benefited by thinking about who we are as individuals and how we can and should relate to others in our society as different as we are.

We all benefit when the individuals that we cross paths with everyday, have relationships with, and make decisions that affect our lives, take a journey inward and analyze who they are and what they believe. They then can understand that they are unique products of their genes, experiences and beliefs. That's when we all can figure out the rights and wrongs that make up our individual ethical code and hopefully get along better by understanding each other and ourselves.

We might not always make the principled decision or take the honorable action, but we will know what we believe to be right and wrong for others and us. That confrontation alone should make us more virtuous. Then we need to journey to why and where our motivations lead us and their relationship to those in our environments. This not only allows us to understand our behavior, but also with correction will permit us to justify it in the future.

Every aspect of our lives can change if we take the time to introspectively examine this individual who makes up our society, who works in our businesses, and who forms our relationships. It is each one of us who can make this difference for ourselves and those around us. It is this confrontation with ourselves that is necessary to understand who we really are.

While there were many valuable personal and societal insights that it seemed we all gained from these courses, the most valuable appeared to be one that involved the treatment that we deserve and the treatment to others that we deliver. It was a simple insight that concerned ethical behavior from an individual perspective. It allowed an evaluation from a personal sense of what was right and what was expected. And while, it sounded too simple to be equated with a conclusion of a Masters level course of study, it was simply, The Golden Rule: "Do unto others as you would have them do unto you."

Maybe a good place to start a journey inward is to first think about the benefits of doing what is right for you and others of your concern. It is then that you can truly express a behavior that reflects a comfort with who you are and where you are going.

It Feels Right

Our ideals relate to our morality and beliefs. At least, they probably should. We need to establish what is really important in our lives, and whether we are on the path to accomplishing goals that are meaningful. Life is too short to spend time on a road that leads to nowhere with diminished purpose as its vehicle of choice. We should live by our values, so that when we have to decide which path to travel, and who to travel it with, we'll know what we believe in, and then all the other decisions will flow.

Too many relationships are built upon the superficialities of societal importance, rather than being on the same life path. They are like huge trees blown down by strong winds. On the surface they looked invincible, but their roots didn't go deep enough. There wasn't enough there to hold them aloft. If we can't find someone who believes as we do, not only will we waste our time on the wrong path through life, but also our relationship will not be able to withstand the storms of its existence.

You have to honestly know what you believe in before you can ever interpret whether someone honestly believes as you do. If your purpose in life is more than speciously getting it over with, then you don't have time to spend it with someone who is going to help you waste it, or argue your way through it. **Time is your enemy when it is spent wandering aimlessly on ill feelings. Time is your best friend when it is spent creating joyous memories.** The duration of your life can be lived timelessly or occasionally, depending to a large extent upon what you believe, and the person with whom you share those beliefs.

What you feel is somewhat less tangible. Our beliefs and principles have a concrete base in our thinking, compared to our feelings, which sometimes are all over the place, seemingly without rhyme or reason. And yet our sensations are so very important to who we are, and to how we interact with others. Our feelings seem to combine all that we are, forming a spirit that is uniquely us. They seem to be an extension beyond the mere thoughts that we profess to others and ourselves. **Feelings accentuate every expression of our being, and become the adjectives of who we are.** How we feel affects our minds, bodies, and provides the sentiment of our hearts. Feelings seem to be derived from our souls.

Our feelings are so valuable to the understanding of ourselves, that we need to expect that a recipient of our love to at least feel as we do, which then provides the ultimate in communication. But before we can communicate our feelings in an accurate and positive way, we must first understand what they are and where they come from. Now is probably a really good time to analyze what your feelings are and from where they're derived because in all likelihood, you have just experienced almost their complete range in a relatively short period of time. Chances are, you have encountered the most recent negative ones alone. This may not have appeared beneficial at the time, but experiencing negative emotions so recently allows us to carefully observe them now.

It is certainly more comforting and worthwhile to analyze and understand our feelings, and their reasons, rather then thoughtlessly have them enter and exit our being without knowing the purpose as to why they are there. For some people, feelings are like strangers who come and go at will. These people become emotionally out of control, because they can't confront what it is they are feeling. To them, it is always more frightening to stand up and question something as powerful and unknown as a feeling, and the emotions it provokes, than to allow it to coexist without question. They think that not knowing is better than knowing. They justify that even negative feelings are justified, and the less we question and analyze, the fewer the problems and complications are awakened.

Slip Sliding Away

Not knowing the evolution of emotions can lead to uncontrollable feelings with little chance of getting a grip on the realities of the circumstances involved. It becomes like spinning out of control on an icy road, so consumed with fear and despair as to not to be able to take corrective measures. You become at the mercy of a condition whose motion and direction make no sense and offer little hope for a positive solution. You are not only frightened because of the possible outcome but also because of your inability to think and cope with the urgency of your plight.

So many of our emotions start out on a trip down that icy road and the danger presented is not from the condition of our path, but rather from our resultant reactions. By understanding your surroundings and environment, it becomes much easier to prepare a plan for those emotional ups and downs that will eventually cross your path and cause you to react one way or another.

Dangerous road conditions are just part of the normal journey when you're *Suddenly Single*. It really shouldn't be a surprise when you hit an icy spot now and then. It's when that spot becomes the imagined precursor of doom that we react out of reality. Our heart starts beating faster and our poor sad lives agonizingly pass before us. Our emotions are spinning out of control. In panic we do everything wrong. Like stepping on the brake increases the spin, our desperation prompts screams of anguish that enhance the despair. We turn the wheels of our direction every which way possible hoping that somehow we can once again be pointed in the right direction or at least calm the spin. Nothing seems to work until we crash or stop.

Hopefully, we haven't injured too many people along the way. And hopefully we learned that there must be a better way to encounter the motion of emotion. Inclement conditions are natural, normal occurrences on many paths throughout life. While we may sometimes be surprised by their appearance, we really shouldn't be shocked by their occurrence. And then, sometimes our emotions sneak up on us. It may seem for no reason or some minor occurrence that a feeling of sadness appears.

The key to coping and reacting reasonably is to become aware of your environment and its effects on your reactions and to know that bad feelings will occur from time to time. It's natural; it's normal. It's all part of the journey you're on. There will be times when loneliness will seem to want to drain you of your worth. Sometimes it will be anger that will request you lash out or frustration that causes impatience. This journey will venture on many roads of different companions. To be successful you have to trust that the conditions are temporary and passable if you are alert to their presence, thoughtful and reasonable to their concern, understand why they exist, and know that many others have passed through this inclement route before.

Before we can ever hope to control the intensity of these *Suddenly Single* emotions that exist within us, we have to recognize, and understand their origin. We have to think about our circumstances as we experienced these feelings; what caused them, and finally what made them subside. Of course, the best way to analyze is to allow for the intensity of your feelings to get quiet, so that you can look at them objectively. **You need to first put the fire out and then take the time to figure out what caused it.**

To understand our feelings is the only hope we have of eventually controlling them. To control one's feelings is to become their master; to think clearly without the burden of overwhelming emotions. This means dealing with our grief and our loneliness in a positive way that will lead to the realization that having even those seemingly terrible feelings, can lead to good things for good people.

5

The Ballet of Grief

What a terrible feeling it is to be grief-stricken. Experiencing the suffering and desperation of losing a companion and with it one's hopes for the future. A mind clouded in misery, a body weakened by torment, the constant worry and uncertainty, with no hope of resolution or normalcy in sight. The preoccupation with thoughts of deception and wasted time, of being used, and abused, of mistakes and the lack of expression of feelings, and of the loss of the communication that could have led to solutions. How do you cope with it all? How does anyone cope with it all?

Do you ever wonder why some people don't feel, or don't appear to feel, as grief-stricken as you do, even though they too have experienced the same loss? How could they not react with the same despair? How can they be so strong and seem so much in control of their emotions? Well, first of all, we all have a tendency to hide our emotions, mostly because of pride, and not wanting others to see us as weak. And while we sometimes question our own resolve to survive, we want it to appear to others that there is no question that we will. It is usually true that misery loves company, and while there is plenty of it out there, it is sometimes difficult to find because we are so good at masking it.

There is a tendency to want everyone around you to believe that you are better off now, before you actually believe it yourself. To admit your despair, expresses your failure. So, as a defense mechanism, you compensate by pretending that everything is all right, thus diminishing the chance to share your frustrations, and gain support from those who care. By pretending that all is well, you may even appear cold, detached, far from the loving, caring, and good-intentioned person you really are. Being honest with yourself, however, allows you to be honest with other people. There is nothing wrong with hurting or grieving over the loss of the recipient of your love; that's what good people do. The problem lies when it is protracted beyond a reasonable amount of time. That's what causes shoulders to shrug and mouths to frown.

Then there are those who truly don't feel grief-stricken about being single, suddenly. They're the ones who usually relish the notion, the freedom, lack of responsibility or commitment, or some other reason. The shame of it all is not that they feel the way that they do, because for them it is where they want to be, but that you might appear to be like them, if you are really good at masking your true emotions. You might feel that it doesn't matter what other people think, but it's going to matter to the one person who is looking for a soul mate to feel just as they do.

The best policy, once again, is honesty. At least let down those barriers so that you can trust yourself. The barriers to trusting others might still take awhile to disappear, but you have to first believe in yourself, in your goodness, before you can ever have the hope of trusting another again. You have to have faith that you are right, before you can be right for anyone else. And, if grieving is right for you, let it show—just make sure it is justified and reasonable.

Being grief-stricken is, after all, a natural consequence of an unbelievable occurrence. Unbelievable, in the sense that when you trust and share your love, you believe it will endure forever. It's like the death of a family member or friend. The longer or more intensely you grieve, the more you loved, and miss the person who died. When the relationship dies and the recipient of your love is no more, it is perfectly normal for good-intentioned, caring people to grieve. And, the intensity of your grief is a good way to judge and measure the true worth of your failed relationship. Grief is, after all, an intense emotion brought on by a loss. It is an expression of someone and something you miss. Its intensity and prolonged effect is subject to the importance that you place upon who and/or what you are missing.

What Does It Matter?

If, after becoming *Suddenly Single*, a person finds themselves missing being in a relationship, having a home, bills paid, and needs provided for, chances are that the most important thing was the economic security or homemaking provisions of that union. They find themselves grieving for a little while over that missed security or domestic help until they figure out how to replace it with someone else, or by assuming the responsibility themselves. That's what the relationship was primarily about to them, and it should be fairly easy to figure out what or whom it is going to take to replace it. While all grief has a self-centered characteristic, in this case, their new-found dependence on self becomes the primary reason for their despair, because when all else fails, they must provide for themselves.

If one finds oneself grieving over the missed companionship of the relationship, the talks, trips together, all the shared experiences of life, then the most important thing to that person was the company. They may long for a replacement, or replacements, to fulfill the need of being with someone. Their goal will be to find friends or a special person who can satisfy the familiarity and friendship that they miss. For them, if worrying about finding people with similar interests is their primary reason for grieving, finding a companion to replace what was lost in the relationship should help them deal with their loss. The person who deals with this despair cannot handle this distress alone. Their grief becomes more complicated, because they cannot provide a resolution by themselves; they need a companion with shared interests.

When the loss of intimacy of the relationship causes a person to grieve the most—the sexual interactions, the closeness, the romance, the sharing of secrets and feelings—that was what meant more to them than anything else. Intimacy is not as easy to replace as security and companionship. It requires careful choices and trust. How many people do we know who were so desperate for intimacy that they again made bad choices, choosing the first person to come along to fulfill their intimate needs, only to find out that their own desperation masked their criteria for trust? Intimacy requires much more careful considerations because it includes a bonding that can bring about a profound impact on one's future. The sexual nature of intimacy could also present disease or pregnancy, forcing a more permanent relationship than was planned.

The closeness and the sharing of an intimate relationship can almost be achieved through companionship, but necessitates more of a binding trust that does not exist between people whose primary bond is similar interests. Romance embraces the expression of intimacy, and awakens dormant emotions. The loss of this intimacy produces a much more profound grief because of the intensity of the longed for feelings. For some, it may be just as easy to find another intimate relationship, as it is to achieve security or find companionship. If they can deal with the prospect that this new relationship will grow and last for awhile, and preclude them from searching or being the recipient of a more permanent or fulfilling intimacy, then their longing will be satisfied.

There is quite a difference comparing the despair encountered between the loss of the security a relationship provides, the talks that companionship allows, and the sexual bonding and shared feelings of intimacy. And, while one may grieve in different intensities over the loss of security, companionship, or intimacy, other relationships can provide a replacement, causing the grieving process not to seem as intense. **There is then, a definite correlation between the meaning of the relationship and the intensity of the grieving.** A relationship that didn't serve more than those basic needs and could easily be substituted really isn't one that deserves a whole lot of grief.

When someone gives their love and commitment, and perceives these to be not only accepted, but also returned, they assume a lasting trust will always exist. When this type of relationship is destroyed, the intensity of the grief becomes overwhelming, because it is not just a basic need that is missing, but also an eternal sharing of love that is missing. It was a love with a future, a love that might have even been thought to be binding before God, and it was a love that denied the possibilities of another love, forever. With that love was a trust, a belief in another to believe as you do, a submission to the destiny of the relationship, a home with a family and even children, and probably a continuing history leading from struggle to success.

It seemed, to the grief-stricken observer of its demise, to be so much more than the security, or the companionship that formed its beginnings. It combined all the facets of intimacy into a ballet that, at times, seemed choreographed to last a lifetime. And then, at times, it seemed like its participants couldn't remember its movements or purpose. It was then that doubts surfaced, but the trust was always there. Not necessarily the trust that the ballet would always be perfect, but the trust that it was at least choreographed to last a lifetime.

The intensity of this grief stems from the realization that this ballet, entrusted with the sharing of the deepest feelings, and glorified by true romance, has played its final performance. To the grief stricken it's unbelievable, because the lasting love and the trust that it contained, wasn't everyone's perception of the relationship. To one, it would last a lifetime. To one, there was a oneness of purpose, and a loyalty of dependence. That's what they miss, and that's what they long for. That's why they are grief-stricken, because they never thought of planning for a final performance. Their partner was never really in the ballet; they were waiting for a better part to come along, and always planning for their closing act. Hence, their partner's grief is shorter lived and less intense.

What enhances the grief is the deception and the insecurity. Why plan, if previous plans had no meaning? Why search, if their previous partner, whom they trusted, could not be trusted? They become bewildered dealing with the chaos and disorder that now surrounds them.They admit somehow making the wrong choice before and wonder how to make the right choice, if one exists. They've somehow misread their loved ones and are faced with the dilemma of how that interpretation was allowed to happen. It seems all a mystery to them, how someone they knew so well could not share their feelings. It's this mystery, without a clear logical answer, which will provide a foundation for their grief.

They grieve for their loss, but they also grieve because of their perplexity. The apparent inequities of life, further fuels their confusion. How can someone who views a relationship as unimportant find security, companionship, and intimacy, while a person who values a relationship for its love and commitment can only find despair and anguish. These inequities exist of course, because people are different and have different purposes in life. Those with less meaningful objectives will find those objectives easily reached, and once again easily dismissed. Those with higher goals will have more difficulty achieving their mission, but once reached, because of its value, will have difficulty ever parting with it.

It may seem unfair to say, that those who place more value on their relationships, because of the love and commitments they behold, deserve more grief than those who don't have such values. **But to grieve thusly, is but a measurement of the capability to love, and what a wonderful quality to grieve over.**

That final performance of your last ballet may have been a very sad and dark one, but there is still hope for a bright future and everlasting performance. It will depend upon you having the faith to continue being committed to the belief that you will be joined by a partner whose promise is equally as valuable. The grief you experienced in your previous relationship will provide so much more of an appreciation of the importance of your capability to love. You must now get beyond the darkened grief for your love to experience another ballet. This time you must choose a partner who will also grieve if commitment to the performance is lost. In order to realize the true meaning of that bright rainbow of love, you will have to experience some rain.

It's Just Sickening

When I first met Ray, he had come to the legislature to administer brief treatments of reflexology to members and

99

staff, as a method of stress reduction. Massage therapists and even chiropractors who volunteered their services also came periodically to offer some relief from the trauma that our bodies endured from the long hours and pressures encountered. When Ray treated me with what appeared to be a glorified foot massage, not only did my feet feel better but the agonizing back pain that had been with me for the previous year had all but disappeared—without him ever touching my back.

I was not a big proponent of alternative medicine, but after years of traditional medicine without any relief other than pills to mask the pain, I was ready to try anything. Now, I had beneficial results from chiropractors or from massages in the past, which provided temporary relief, but nothing like this. For a few days my back actually felt cured.

After the legislative session was over, I visited Ray at his office for a full reflexology treatment. As he worked massaging my feet, he began to explain how reflexology works. It seemed straightforward enough, but being skeptical it was difficult to believe why it works. He began working with my hands and ears and was able to identify trouble spots within my body and even the causes and then treatment for alleviating all the stresses my body was enduring. It was like he could recognize ailments without my even telling him, just by feeling the nerve endings in my extremities that he was working on, and then cause their effects to diminish or disappear.

Needless to say, my physical condition began to improve, as did my temperament. I seemed so much calmer and relaxed. Ray then went from administering to my physical ailments to acknowledging that it appeared, once again through the touch of my nerve endings, that I had deep emotional concerns that were probably the root cause of many of my physical ailments. As he continued his treatment over the next few weeks, I came to realize that much of my anxiety had been released and replaced with a sort of tranquility. He specifically treated areas that he said dealt with depression, anger, and anxiety, all of which I knew I had, but none of which I expressed to him.

In my conversations with Ray since my treatments, he has told me of treating people suffering from the traumas of divorce to those diagnosed with acute schizophrenia. As a member of the President's Commission on Mental Retardation, I was intrigued by the potential of the treatment of those mentally disabled. I also became fascinated by the possibilities of what this treatment could do for those who were experiencing severe trauma brought on by the emotional distress of separation, since I had formerly believed that the only way people dealt with it was through self-analysis, time and sometimes even concealment. But, if this really worked, what a tremendous help it would provide to those who have difficulty coping with their despair. I thought that if a person can't think clearly because of all the pain they are experiencing, be it mental or physical, how could they plan to improve their condition?

So many people get stuck in a quagmire of despair that they can't think straight and deal with their circumstances. Even if this treatment only provides a degree of stress reduction, it would still be much easier for people to cope. If it could somehow alleviate the pressures of depression and anxiety, how much easier it will be for people to hope.

Whatever the reason for its success, after meeting so many people who were helped by this particular brand of reflexology, I could not question its benefit. It reminded me of a few conversations with people who were Suddenly Single who went to massage therapists, to not only relieve the pressures of their anxieties, but to feel the touch of another person. Men went to a female therapist and women went to a male therapist, not with sexual connotations, but merely to feel the touch of the opposite gender. Someone who was caring and interested in their well-being somehow made them feel better. There is more to reflexology than that. But, as becoming first lovable to ourselves in order to be loved, we must also be willing to care for ourselves to ever have hope of reaching the point of being comfortable searching for someone else.

Physical and emotional pain makes it so much more difficult to heal from the wounds of a broken relationship. The grief and accompanying despair and confusion hinder a vision for a tomorrow that was never planned. The trauma that seems to permeate your being needs to be dealt with before any hope of achieving some degree of normalcy and certainly before you can even begin to plan for future success. So many people that I talked with in this situation found themselves incapable of dealing with a positive outlook because of their condition. They had so much mental anguish that they couldn't think. All their thoughts seemed possessed by the negatives that had recently entered their lives.

Their depression became a place where they felt they were doomed to stay. Some had trouble even doing their work at their jobs, while others immersed themselves in their work so that they didn't have time to think about anything else.

They all mentioned how grieving at this time became the most time consuming part of their lives. Their physical being reflected and complemented their emotional anguish. They seemed exhausted all the time, even on those occasions when they had enough rest. Sickness, and in some extreme cases disease, followed the depressions and anguish that the body was absorbing. Their physiques deteriorated exacerbating the negative impacts on their self-esteem. They ached inside and out and lacked the motivation to seek out comfort.

It is so important at this stage of despair to seek out some comfort. A critical part of the process of healing is to try every method and treatment to relieve anxiety and depression, so that positive decisions leading to necessary solutions can be attained. Even a periodic relief from the anguish of physical and emotional ailments provides a hope that feelings of comfort will once again return as the standard of performance.

It is as we watch the performance of the ballet, that we realize the importance of the choreography that brings all the various elements together. But without the individual performer, who is able to utilize their mental and physical talents to their maximum capability, there would be no ballet. Their performance would be dismal indeed if they could not focus on their next movement.

6

The Sounds
of Silence

If a tree falls in the forest and nobody hears it, does it make a noise? Does it make a sound? Of course it does, because noise and sound are real and don't depend on the presence of sensual acceptance to exist. So many sounds that nobody hears, because to others there is not a sound unless they hear it. Even all those sounds around us that our senses don't recognize because they are so familiar.

We listen when people talk, if it's interesting. If it isn't, we sometimes drift away to more important noise. We listen for abnormal sounds that alert us to something out of the ordinary. We hear the washer, dryer, dishwasher and even the lawn mower for a little while, but then their noise disappears. We can even dismiss the sounds of cars, trains, and planes when we become so used to their repetition. Our senses become dulled to sounds that lack priority. Our lives have become so cluttered with noise that we often don't listen. All that chatter and clutter become inconsequential, because of all the important sounds that take precedence in our lives.

It's not that there is an absence of noise that creates silence, but rather, an absence of concern. Our own comfort levels determine what we want to hear, and what we want to tune out. The context of our silence becomes a conscious lack of listening. With all the noise around us that we choose not to hear, we adjust our senses to listen for silence. Sometimes we listen for when the spin of the washer or the activity of the dishwasher stops, or the microwave concludes its hum, or the lawn mower ceases its clutter. Other times, we place more of a priority on the silence of important things that surround us. When unconsciously listening to our little children play, we suddenly discover a lull in their noise, and are immediately alerted. When a baby stops crying or an elderly parent becomes abnormally quiet, there is discomfiture. There are sounds that are very comforting.

What does all this noise talk have to do with being *Suddenly Single*? Has much of the sound surrounding you disappeared? Are you hearing things that you never heard before? Have the sounds of silence become so deafening that you can finally hear yourself think? Does this sound familiar?

To be thrust abruptly in isolation, or at least to be without that one person with whom you could speak and listen to on a regular basis, presents a silence without comfort. Do you make a noise when you cry alone because of despair? Do you make a sound when you scream out by yourself in pain, when you are hurting? Does it matter if you're the only person listening, when you're talking to yourself? Like the tree that falls in the forest, you make a sound, but it doesn't matter, because nobody's listening, and, if nobody hears it, nobody cares. That is what's so hard about being alone and lonely—the silence. Others can't help you if they can't hear you falling. And while your situation is so desperate to you, the silence you hear is the absence of someone else listening.

It is not only the absence of sound when you are finding yourself alone, it's the awareness of sounds never listened for before. You find, that so many of your senses, thoughts, and feelings, were intertwined in your relationship, not allowing for an interaction with the minute details of your environment. The stillness of your new-found lonely surroundings is accentuated by noise that has advanced from the background, to now having meaning to your senses.

In your longing to hear activity, your hearing settles for the hum of a refrigerator, the blowing of the wind, the dripping of a faucet, the muffled engine of a plane miles above. You end up listening for those things of little consequence; the falling raindrops, the chirping birds, the voices from next door. You wonder why the dog is barking, what's happening to cause all those sirens and horns, and what are those people saying as they pass by your window. You become involved in an environment that was always there, but never noticed. Your attention was focused on a higher level of communication, not your mundane surroundings. You had someone to focus your attention on, and didn't need to be bothered by things of little significance. Now, you long to just hear the phone ring, or the doorbell chime.

These sounds of silence mean that nobody else is listening. You realize how alone you really are. Your once bustling home has become your solitary confinement. You begin to think that any noise, even the sounds of your failed relationship, must be better than this. You replace your partner with your own voice in con-versations, trying to figure out what went wrong. But, you learn that the comfort of thinking out loud when you are by yourself is diminished, when you continue to do so out of habit when others are present.

You realize that cooking for one is not even half as satisfying as cooking for two, and find yourself using the same amount of time, the same number of utensils, and at first, the same amount of food. You dream that it is all a dream, then wake up to the real-ity of being alone. The joys and hardships of your experiences don't have the same meaning that sharing them provided.

The circumstances of the past and plans for the future that took up so much of your time, are no longer discussed. And now, you have plenty of time to think. There was a time when thinking was a valued exercise, always limited by time. But now you have too much time: To imagine what might have been, to weigh blame, to speculate on suspicion, to contemplate the mysterious future and to ponder loneliness. Hearing yourself think at a time like this is what the silence of loneliness allows. It can become devastating to your well-being.

The Look of Despair

There is also a silence of vision and an emptiness of sight. People and things are missing from your view and you long for movement. Your surroundings seem to be manifestations of the dark and empty condition of your life. What you hear and what you see now seem so firmly connected. You can't say "good morning" and "good night" to someone you can't see. The personality displayed by clothes and belongings is visually silenced by their void. You are now looking out a window for an arrival that will never come, seeing an empty home that can never be filled, being beside covers laying flat and lifeless on a bed made for two. You long for the sights and sounds. You miss not only the sound of laughter, but also its accompanying smile, the cry of sadness and its accompanying tear.

The mirrored reflections, are now only you. You search for movement, but nothing moves, except the birds that were chirping, and the leaves blowing in the wind. You see plants dying and weeds growing. You notice empty spaces in closets and drawers, with missing and disordered possessions. You see no reason for the maintenance of yourself or your previously shared environment. You visualize things getting a lot worse before they will ever get better, and it seems every time you think you see a light at the end of the tunnel, it always seems to be a train coming the other way.

God, it seems so desperate and hopeless, and so justified for self-pity. The past is gone, but the sense of the past is still hanging around. The voids of sight and sound fill us with emptiness. We can now point fingers of blame only at the nobody who's there. We are alone, with the only choice to persist and prevail. But, to survive this silence, we must have faith that this is just a step along the way; a period of recovery that will eventually lead to being able to listen and be listened to, again. We eventually come to realize that while we are very alone in our space, there are so many others alone in theirs. We are all coping, waiting for time to pass and silence to disappear.

We were sitting around one day, talking about the profound differences that occurred in our lives since we had each become alone, through similar circumstances. Sue was the type of person who even in normal conversation would appear to always try to "out do" others with similar situations. Maybe, that was a problem she had in her relationship.

According to Sue, she had the most unfaithful husband there ever was. He was so unfaithful, that he appeared faithful, and swore to that quality until the day he left her for his long time girlfriend. She then had the worst divorce of anybody she had known. According to her, it was the worst time anyone could have, coping with being by herself for the first time in so many years.

When we talked about what each day was like, I began to understand that Sue wasn't exaggerating her circumstance.

She was just in such a desperate condition of despair, that she assumed that no one else could possibly be going through what she was, and yet, somehow surviving. She mentioned how she must be so much more sensitive than other people; how she must be so much more in tune with her surroundings, to have her senses be so affected by this change in her environment. She talked about how little things would conjure up tremendous feelings about memories, and about being alone. The simple comforts of being with someone, that she took for granted, she now missed terribly.

She used the word "frightened," when she related to the affect this new experience of being alone was having on her feelings. She worried that if her security was threatened, would there be someone there? That time she sprained her ankle and her husband had to carry her upstairs to bed because she couldn't walk; what if that happened again? When that strange car was parked in front of their house one night and her husband went out and chased two kissing kids away; she couldn't go out to check. Even that time she opened the cupboard and had that little mouse jump out causing her to scream and start shaking all over, and having her husband hold her and tell her not to worry; she'd never be able to sleep if that ever happened again.

For Sue, a sense of fear also accompanied all those other senses awakened by her new experience of being alone. But like the rest of us, she listened for sounds that she was used to hearing. She heard sounds that she never thought existed before. She missed seeing someone else, but now noticed movement of little things that never seemed to move before.

She longed to hear voices, and wanted to just be able to talk with someone. Now she just talks to herself. The phone that used to ring all the time with her husband's friends calling is now silent. She now just waits for it to ring. For a while even telemarketers got a welcome response. She listens to music for sound and to forget, only to have it force memories on her. She remembers who she was with when she heard that music before, and now its lyrics always remind of her present dilemma. She longs for the sound of a cough or a sneeze, the flush of a toilet, or the opening and closing of doors, to know that there is someone else there. The clutter and dirty clothes around the house, that evidenced her husband leaving his mark, is now immaculate and sterile. She is a very tidy person, but now yearns for someone else's mess. The too crowded closet that held all their clothes together including everything they bought for each other, seems plenty big enough now. She misses seeing his clothes next to hers. That meant security to her. Although, she did mention that if there was one benefit to everything that happened, it was getting that extra closet space that she always needed. I guess that's a "woman thing."

Sue agreed with everything that I had said and others had expressed to me about how our sensitivities are affected by our suddenly being alone. She also added how she missed the touching. The incidental brushes against each other, the holding and hugs, and even the casual touch of each other's bodies as they slept. She missed the distinctive smell of his clothes as she did his laundry, or the scent of his after-shave that permeated their bathroom. She even went so far as to bring up the taste of his lips and tongue as they passionately kissed. She started to continue, but I told her that I thought that was good enough, and that she probably included all the feelings of her senses that we all felt at one time or another. The longer we talked about it, the more we would think about how much we missed it. I think we both started to realize that certain sense deprivation could be alleviated right then and there, with each other.

What we also agreed about was that our current feelings of loneliness were more about being alone than being together. Sure, there were things we missed, but they were things that were just us, longing for someone else. The cravings we had could really be satisfied with the feelings and companionship that we would feel with another person in the future. In the present, I offered to bring my dirty clothes and scatter them around her house. And, then when she washed them, she could smell my shirts. Anything to help a friend. She thought I was kidding. But kidding aside, there is much that we could do for ourselves, to turn those present solitary moments, into times of being comfortable being alone.

It was encouraging for both of us to talk about our feelings, and to actually find humor in many of our experiences. A sense of humor is an essential part of the healing process. I think Sue realized, that she was not the worst-case scenario. There are many of us who feel obligated to continue our victimization even though we are alone, by permitting our environment to dictate our loneliness. Sue and I both made changes in our lives that recognize living alone as just an accepted state of being, rather than a condition demanding continued sensitivity to yearnings of the past.

It is still difficult living alone, but at least we both have friends who will ring our phone, come over to our homes to

share its sights and sounds, and allow us to talk to some-
body else besides ourselves. It is also comforting to know
that there is someone who understands and appreciates
the way we feel. The best that we could do is to encourage
each other that our condition is not as bad as it seems.

Create Encouragement

If we have faith, we have hope. Our hope becomes our reality
when we can look in the mirror, wipe away the tear, and put a
smile on our face. It's when we can turn up the music really loud
and the lights really bright; when we can turn the TV to any
channel that holds our interest, and it brings us joy; when we
can open our doors so that the isolated chirpings become the singing of the birds, and hear the whistling of the wind through the
trees. We can change our hope to reality by creating so much
sound by ourselves that we never have to listen for that refrigerator or dripping faucet again.

As I began to notice myself wallowing in self-pity, I realized I
had escaped from many of the things that had previously
brought joy and a sense of accomplishment to my life. These
were the things that didn't involve companionship or the in-
timacies of a relationship, but were rather involvements that
required just my own singular interest. As I looked back at
the times that I achieved a personal fulfillment even when
coupled in a relationship, I realized that that the only change
brought on by my current circumstance of being alone was
that I had more time for accomplishment.

Reflecting, I discovered that as a public official I was al-
ways able to serve my community and help people in need.
I received a sense of joy by giving my time and efforts to
people who desperately needed someone's help. I always felt

a deep sense of pride when I was able to achieve success, fighting on behalf of those whose rights were being denied or whose condition warranted assistance. Then, there was always a wonderful feeling of relief and satisfaction when someone's life was put back in order or somehow made more bearable because of my actions.

I began to understand, that while I may have at times felt my life was not worthwhile because of my lonely circumstance, it was certainly worthwhile to all the people I was helping. I realized that I became so mired in the concern for my own well being that I was beginning to neglect all those circumstances of other people's lives, who were a lot worse off than me. It was my own selfish ego that had brought about my isolation and the silence of my environment.

I, once again, became less concerned with what was going on in my personal life and more concerned with helping others in theirs. I was able to exchange the whimpering of my personal despair, for the strong voice I had experienced in the past, defending others. My time was no longer spent dwelling on the mistakes and choices of the past, but rather on the solutions to the problems of those I was helping. The clutter I was now surrounded with was not reflective of meaningless memories but instead, of purposeful actions required to achieve positive results. My focus shifted from making my personal and family life better, to assisting other people and families achieve a better life. The silence of sounds and vision were replaced by the deafening roar of a very busy life.

I was able to immerse myself in finding solutions to problems in education, assisting the disabled, figuring out how to cure health care, providing for more economic development, analyzing ways to reduce crime, and improving the quality of life of those people who entrusted me with these responsibilities. I soon found myself spending every waking moment, and even some when I should have been sleeping, thinking about solutions to problems, answers to questions, and planning for the future. I had lost what little time I had allocated for self-pity. I was now again experiencing the joy of fulfillment, and couldn't believe that I had ever thought of my life as not worthwhile.

While my position might afford me more access than others have to the interactions involved in helping others, we all have the capability to reach out and help even one person or one family. Every person has so much to offer to the lives of others; that's what really makes our lives so worthwhile. And, no matter how bad we think we have it, with just a little searching we can always find someone worse off. When you find yourself alone, there is always someone who is more lonely; waiting for comfort to arrive. When you find yourself in a depressing condition, it's really pretty easy to find someone else that has a lot more to be depressed about. And, when you find yourself crying out for help, if you can quiet that urge for a while, you can hear so many people with so many better reasons to cry for help than you. As the saying goes, "It is in giving that we too receive." My life has benefited so much, by just being able to leave the self-contained silence of self-pity, to reach out to those whose needs are so much greater than mine.

We can exchange our self-pity for self-respect, and begin to hear and see the beauty of life again. We can fill our empty space with things that are more beautiful than what was there before, and bring a new order to our possessions. All the weeds in our lives can be changed to grass and flowers. We can take possession of, and love, our homes and ourselves, again.With the doors open, the music playing, and the smile from our singing lips, those dying plants surrounding us will flourish, as they never had before.

This becomes a time to notice that our environment is something more than just clutter in our busy lives. All of the added experiences and responsibilities; the anticipations and expectations; and the problems and explanations of our previous relationship have now disappeared, except in the recurrences of our memories. There is now more time to reflect on the beauty that was taken for granted because we didn't have the occasion to experience it. There seems to be a compensation for all the disorder and confusion previously endured, a redeeming of the senses that now allows an awareness of what were formerly the insignificant beauties of life. Our view becomes focused on the details in our environment and the quality of the sounds that we hear.

We come to realize that "order" is not just a demand for service, but an integral part of the solution for improving the condition of our lives. When the clutter that exhibits our depressed state of being is cleaned up, we come to the understanding that there were many things surrounding us that contributed to our feelings of despair. We must rid ourselves of that which does not belong in our lives and does not add to the order necessary to function in a positive way. We organize our belongings, structure our environment, and plan for the future. We clean up the mess we have created for ourselves and remove all the garbage that blocks our progress. We find ourselves not only in a neater, more ordered environment allowing for more of our capabilities to show through, but we may find ourselves with new friends or maybe just alone. When we get rid of all that doesn't belong in our lives, we can start fresh and decide for ourselves what to accept and what to deny without something or someone blocking our view. Order and its positive outlook replace our clutter. We become encouraged to look at things differently; to look in a brighter light.

We become more introspective. We figure out what makes us feel better. Knowing that we are in control of our environment allows us the realization that we influence our outcome. We appear differently because our appearance makes us feel better. Our walk, our talk, the way we dress, and the way we live, exhibit a confidence that everything in our lives is in order. Everything and everyone around us, is there for a purpose; being there because they belong in our lives. We banish negative influences from our lives unless they can be redirected to provide a positive response. The order that we have created no longer allows dwelling on the mess of our creation, but rather provides an opportunity to visualize a happier life.

We cease watching TV as a distraction from our clutter and rather choose it for its substance and joy. We enjoy the shows that mimic our lives and lives of those we know. We laugh at others and ourselves on Seinfeld, Frazier, and Cheers. Sometimes we listen to music; happy and soulful music that in the past acted as a distraction from the hurt, now has a profound meaning to our lives conjuring up images of beauty, love, peace, and hope. We listen to rock 'n' roll turned up really loud and sing along to the Beach Boys, Simon and Garfunkel, Ricky Martin, and Santana, and for the moment exist in a time warp of a happier time. When we think of the saying, "Music soothes the savage beast," we now experience its meaning. Bocelli's "Romanza," or McLachlan's "Angel," can now soothe even the "savage beast" of the hurt of our past experience. We escape our lonely surroundings "in the arms of an angel," and somehow know we are not alone, because we have ourselves to begin to appreciate the beauties of life.

The silence of your loneliness will have been transformed to the sights and sounds of just being alone. The next step is to share those senses with those who will not only appreciate their beauty, but also value the person who made them aware that there are sounds in the forest that we all need to hear.

There is a story my niece, a nurse, told me about two seriously ill men, occupying the same hospital room, but separated by some distance. One man was allowed to sit up in his bed for an hour each afternoon to help drain the fluid from his lungs. His bed was next to the room's only window. The other man had to spend all his time flat on his back, without a view to the window. They talked for hours on end about their families, homes, jobs, and their involvement in the military service, and their travels. Every afternoon when the man by the window could sit up, he would pass the time by describing to his roommate all the things he could see outside the window.

The man in the other bed began to live for those one-hour periods where his world would be broadened by all the activity and color of the world outside the sterile hospital setting; albeit being described by his friend on the other side of the room. The window overlooked a park with a lovely lake. Ducks and swans played on the water, while children sailed their model boats. Young lovers walked arm-in-arm amidst flowers of every color in the rainbow. Grand old trees graced the landscape, and a magnificent view of the city skyline could be seen in the distance.

As the man by the window described all of this in exquisite detail, the man on the other side of the room would close his eyes and imagine the picturesque scene. One warm afternoon, the man by the window described a parade passing by. Although the other man couldn't hear the band, he could see it in his mind's eye as the gentleman by the window described it.

Weeks passed and one morning the day nurse arrived to bring water for their baths, only to find the lifeless body of the man by the window, who had died peacefully in his sleep. Saddened she called the hospital attendants to take the body away. Although the other man missed his friend, he soon asked if he could be moved next to the window. The nurse was happy to make the switch, rolled his bed over, and after making sure he was comfortable, she left him alone. Slowly, painfully, he propped himself up on one elbow to take his first look at the world outside. Finally, he would have the joy of seeing it for himself. He strained to look out the window beside the bed, only to discover that it faced the blank wall of a big empty building across from the hospital. The man called the nurse and asked her what could have compelled his deceased roommate to describe such wonderful things outside this window. The nurse responded that his roommate was blind and could not even see the wall. She said, "Perhaps he just wanted to encourage you."

We have to be encouraged, if not by others then by ourselves. We have to realize that this change in our lives has created an emptiness within us. While its sense manifestations might be the sights and sounds we miss, it is the void inside us that creates that hollow feeling. Something has left our being barren and seemingly vacant of desire and anticipation of the future. It's a hunger, not satisfied by food; a thirst, not quenched by drink. It's a longing to be fulfilled again, knowing that it may not happen in the same way again. It's a starving for affection, for caring and sharing. It seems so hopeless. Encouragement must come from somewhere.

We have a choice of looking at a cup which is terminally empty, devoid of the meaning of its existence, or a cup that is waiting to be filled with a new reason for its meaning. The emptiness can afford us the opportunity to start over, clean of the clutter of memories, with new and better experiences enhanced by the enlightenment learned from the past. The cup can begin to fill again with the imaginings of all the possibilities that can occur. It is our dreams after all, that will enable us to look beyond our current circumstance, to a reality that is just a period of time and some encouragement away. To dream of the beauty that can surround us should be all the inspiration that we need.

7

Anybody Else There?

Here we are, with all that grief and loneliness dwelling inside of us. All these seemingly terrible feelings waiting for the healing that will come from within us. The quick fixes that we are presented offer immediate gratification, but eventually only delay a real solution. The drugs, alcohol and sex provide an alternative to facing the pain of loneliness, but just mask the emotions that have to be dealt with in the future. Even those anti-depressant pills providing relief for those most desperate times, provide a depressing, delaying effect if depended upon for too long. So where do you go for comfort? Family, friends, and counselors can help you cope and maybe even sort out all of those confusing feelings. But, unless they have walked in your shoes, they will not have a clue as to how you feel.

Why does it seem that nobody understands? Maybe there are some who have had similar experiences, but without your honest request for help, they just don't know what to do for you. Of course, everyone has their own cross to bear, so why should your problems seem any more desperate or urgent, especially to those who have no idea what you are going through. How many times has someone told you to "get over it," "move on with your life," "forget it, he/she isn't worth thinking about," "start enjoying life"? As though your feelings come with an on/off switch.

They don't understand how your relationship was part of a plan forever, not one limited by time. At least that was your plan. But now you're expected to turn the off switch to the expression of your love, the memories, and the experiences of your lost relationship. Hardest of all, you're expected to do it alone, after the conditioning and commitment of your previous bond caused you to believe that these types of serious problems needed to be handled by the two of you, together. But, now there is just one with no shoulder to cry on, no advice to seek, and no company for your misery.

Sometimes we feel so isolated that our feelings seem to control us. It's almost like we internalize the mistrust we experienced with our partners. We no longer trust that we can manage or control our emotions. We give up and allow the circumstances of our lives to be dictated to by things over which we have no control, because we refuse to take chances. We wander aimlessly, waiting for that miracle to occur in our lives without having the necessary faith, either in ourselves, or in our God. Our problems seem so overwhelming that we make the decision not to make any decisions. Then we wonder why everyone has let us down, when in reality we let ourselves down when we substituted wallowing in our status quo for our faith that things will get better.

Real faith is never easy. We can say we believe in ourselves and God while normal life is going on. But when it comes down to those really desperate times, we tend to lose the faith that gives us our hope. Maybe it's because we feel let down by everybody, because no one's helping us solve our problems, or maybe it's because we had faith that we wouldn't have these problems, or because when we had faith before, we weren't alone to test its truly personal nature. Maybe we are becoming conditioned to avoid all those things that bring us pain, and have now included faith in that equation. It is due to this lack of trust that we allow ourselves to mire in a depression of our own making.

We feel alone and weak, suffocating in our self-pity. We dismiss all our talents and blessings as not being able to compete against the despair of our circumstance. We choose to isolate ourselves, not only in our surroundings, but also from the hope of our future. The answer, of course, is to have more faith—real faith; to begin to believe in our God and ourselves again when things are really tough. Yet so many times we are led to believe by others we know in a similar circumstance, that a belief in God is a limitation to our newly acquired single life. Many people at this stage of their lives drift away from their religions and their belief in God to help make things better. It's not just because they feel deserted by their faith, but because they now must spend their time preoccupied with surviving, and faith becomes a luxury and limitation it seems they cannot afford.

The time spent when coupled planning for a future, welcomed faith as part of this plan that promoted a positive outlook on life together. Religious beliefs and practices became part of an observant display of thankfulness and a belief that "the family that prays together, stays together." Many couples believed their faith was like the third leg of a stool—it gave stability to their relationship. And for those who believed that their union would be further blessed by God because of their observance, it became an essential part of its "being." Their prayers together would insure their future. But the prayers didn't seem to help at the time an answer and a solution was so desperately needed. So now the praying stops and the observance of beliefs is no longer needed. The drifting away from faith and religious participation begins.

For as long as I had known Grace and Bob, they had seemed to be a fairly conservative, church–going couple. They were always participating in church activities, especially those that involved their children.

After a couple of years of not seeing either one, I ran into Bob at the gym. We exchanged greetings and I asked him if he had moved, since I hadn't seen him or Grace, even at church. He told me that they had gotten divorced a couple of years before and that he had stopped going to church because it just didn't feel right, and he assumed it was the same way with Grace. He said he takes his kids on holidays, if they want to go.

Bob mentioned that before he and Grace had married, that they had hardly ever attended church, but began doing so after his first child was born. They felt as if their lives began to "settle down" and going to church seemed to play into that whole attitude. Besides he and Grace agreed that going to church would enhance the upbringing of their children, which was their main responsibility.

I began to feel uncomfortable listening to him tell me about why he didn't go to church—it was like he felt he had to give me an explanation even though he was only an acquaintance, and I was just wondering why I hadn't seen him, anywhere.

I sensed that he felt just as uncomfortable having to tell the story, but it seemed like something that he had to do. He continued explaining how he thought that by becoming involved in a religion and being an active, practicing member, would provide added depth to his marriage. He said he believed that his marriage would be blessed by his newly observed faith and the practice of his religion. To him, it seemed as if all the successful marriages that he knew of, would probably credit their religious associations with much of their success.

Well, it wasn't to be that way with Bob and Grace. Maybe it was because they felt their "practice" of their religion was enough. Maybe it was because the commitments, belief, trust and faith of each of them was never present in their prayers for success. Whatever it was, I could certainly tell by Bob's remarks that he was certainly disappointed that his marriage was not as "blessed" as he thought it should have been, and that there was no longer any need of obligation to continue in the "practice" of his religion.

I could certainly empathize with some of his feelings. When I first got divorced, it was difficult for me to go to church, not because I no longer had a need to, but because I was embarrassed. I didn't want to have to admit failure of a commitment in a place that demands it. I didn't want to be asked about the demise of a relationship from people whose success could somehow be related to their involvement with their religion. It was almost as though the failure of my relationship had transcended to the diminishment of my individual worth in the eyes of God.

But, I continued to attend church, partly because I was afraid that if I stopped that I wouldn't go back, just like the friends of mine with similar circumstances. The main reason I continued to go though, was because I realized that I needed the strength, understanding, and comfort that I thought it could provide me now more than ever. And, that's what I told Bob when he asked me why I still go to church. He did bring up the conflict of having the limitations of a religion burdening the freedoms and sexuality of single life. I guess that's why many single people stop going. Of course, if churches were just limited to people who don't commit sins, they would be pretty empty places.

> *It's also a shame to think that this sort of guilt might preclude us from meeting someone with similar beliefs at church.*

It is when we observe in others this same diminishment of faith that we are allowed its justification. If it seems everyone else in a similar circumstance has moved away from the practice and dependence on their beliefs and are not only surviving but also thriving—it must be a positive direction. And the limits having faith and practicing beliefs places upon a person, are certainly not something that someone newly single needs at this time of their lives. Unfortunately, many times that is the perception given by our societal environment; a perception that may lead in an opposite direction to achieving the hopes of ones future. To deny our faith, and its positive recognition of God, offers only daily survival, not future thriving. **If we can deny our beliefs and our faith when times are tough, maybe we never believed in them when times were good.** Maybe that's why prayers don't seem to be answered. And, to justify such denial because of the worries of being considered by others a single hypocrite or appearing not to have the strength to cope with life alone, is just an excuse for not believing. Those who really believe don't change because of changes in the circumstances of their lives. They may become disappointed by the outcomes of their choices or disillusioned with the faith or beliefs of others. They may even be embarrassed by the prospects of practicing their beliefs alone as an exhibition of the failure of a "blessed" union. However, their only hope of finding another who believes as they do, is to continue expressing their belief, rather than exhibiting an apparent denial.

Sometimes, when we're bogged down in despair and uncertainty, it's difficult to figure out if we have enough faith, because we seem so burdened with each and every day. But, we have to hope with the same convictions and commitment that we expect others to have with us. Only then will we experience the relief that hope can promise and that faith can deliver, and attract people with those same qualities.

We must also distinguish between the self-control—which allows us to limit our choices of emotion and action, the control of our lives— which directs us to plan responses and influence our environment, and those circumstances in life over which we have no control. Those things out of our control have to be left to our faith in a higher being. To have faith in ourselves however, recognizes capabilities and can match them with desired accomplishments. We discover how to limit and control our choices and eventually influence our environment by even planning for contingencies. It is the faith in oneself that allows the confidence to take control. We can then believe we have all that is necessary to achieve our goals including the will and commitment to see them through.

Real Faith

To help determine the intensity of this conviction and commitment, I'm reminded of a little story that I read many years ago. It presents a line that needs to be crossed, if you want to experience true faith.

> *A man goes hunting in the mountains by himself, as he had done many times before without incident. Just as he was ready to shoot at a deer, a bear appears out of a clump of bushes behind him. The bear had apparently been eating berries and was startled by the hunter. As the bear stood up and let out with a menacing growl, the hunter quickly stepped back, tripped over a log behind him, and dropped his rifle. Sensing there was no time to retrieve his rifle, the hunter began a mad dash through the forest, with the bear in hot pursuit.*

He came upon a steep cliff, and without hesitation began climbing down to a ledge, hoping the bear would lose interest and not follow. The bear began climbing down to the ledge. The hunter, realizing that the ledge was not big enough for him to escape the bear, began a desperate descent to a steeper area with lots of loose rock. At about the same time the bear reached the ledge, and was seeming to decide whether it would be in its best interests to pursue its prey, the hunter began to slide down the cliff. He came upon a tree limb growing out of the rock, and grabbed it, thus saving his life. He now found himself dangling precariously over a 200-foot drop into jagged rock, with the bear overhead, waiting for its dinner. The hunter's arms began to weaken, and realizing there was no hope of him solving his dilemma, began to cry out for help. Knowing his isolated location, he promptly faced the fact that no one would hear him, and that he would have to hang on until the bear left, if it ever did.

As dusk began to form, the hunter knew that his only chance at survival was through divine intervention. He thought, "I go to church, I provide for my family, and am good to my neighbors. I've always believed in God. Surely God will save me." He then began crying out for God to save him. There was no answer. He pleaded with God, expressing his faithfulness and beliefs. Still no answer and no help. He then cried out ever so humbly, "God, I know you love me, I know you'll protect me, because you know I truly believe in you." Just then a bright light shone from the heavens, and a comforting, Godlike voice echoed in his ears. "Do you really believe in me?" "Oh yes, yes I do," responded the desperate hunter. The voice echoed again, "Do you have faith in me that I will protect you, and care for you?" The hunter replied in a quivering voice, "Oh yes, I have faith, I've always had faith in you." Then the voice whispered one more time. "My son, if you truly believe, and really have faith, then let go."

Most of us would then respond, "Is anybody else there?" Sometimes we think we have all the answers, and that we are the only ones who know what's best for us. We depend on immediate gratification to determine which paths we take in life. Despair in our lives clouds our judgment, and allows such a high value to be placed on goals that have more of a relationship to our current condition than the future promise of our being. We have such an intense, desperate focus on our survival today, that productive plans for the future get put on hold with no schedule in sight. The mystery of the future doesn't allow us to let go of even the desperateness of the past.

We become stuck in a quagmire of present circumstance and a failed relationship and then when realizing we don't have the solutions, reach out for any helping hand that appears available. We reject truth, and in its place accept the false soothing hope we long for. We also continually listen for advice on where we need to be from others who have little idea of who we are or where we are coming from. This rut allows us to hold on and not let go.

We've allowed our societal mores to dictate our behavior and even our feelings. We've lost control of ourselves, because we've permitted our emotions to be exaggerated relative to what other people think of our circumstance. Our negative feelings gain strength from feeding on each other, sometimes in an uncontrolled frenzy that doesn't allow an accurate measure of the amount of grieving that should occur given the situation. We get so wrapped up in our self-pity that nothing can be done to help us; we lose our self-respect and the opportunity to have faith in ourselves.

The faith we should have in ourselves doesn't necessarily mean that we can solve all our own problems. This faith of self should be that we can recognize the problems that we can solve for ourselves and distinguish them from problems that we need help solving. This faith also should mean that we don't always understand what is in our best interests, as despair can cloud an issue, and that sometimes, immediate solutions have contributed to our past mistakes.

Sometimes, our desperation breeds more desperation. But we must have faith in our God and ourselves that somehow our goodness will be rewarded, and that deep inside we have the courage to wait, and become better. That's where our faith in God allows us to let go, to prove that we also believe in ourselves, in who we are and in the strength of our being, to have hope; oh, and of course, every once in awhile, we need help and direction.

Even though we think the answer might be to have another hunter or a rope miraculously appear, or have our partner change so that our relationship can be saved, to have real faith is to "let go." To put the decision in the hands of goodness, will produce a result that will be the best for us, and our future. Not the easiest, just the best.

Another reason letting go is difficult sometimes for a *Suddenly Single* person is because past experience may not have provided the solution of one's choice. To let go means to have trust, and if you're *Suddenly Single*, chances are, that is not your strong suit anymore. We have probably all heard the saying that if you love something, set it free. If it comes back to you, it's yours, if it doesn't, it never was. To refuse to let go, means to attempt to control the outcome. You think letting go will result in your finding out that you were not loved; hence your refusal. To finally let go, allows you to be sure. It all has to do with trust. After you find out that you couldn't trust anything but your instincts, you either become wary of trusting anyone again (if you couldn't even trust the recipient of your love) or you become wary of letting go again. The only beneficial solution, again, is to just be careful whom you trust. When you're desperate you may choose someone you **wish** you could trust, rather than someone you **know** you can trust.

Remember, if your faith and hope are fostered by your convictions and commitment, you will eventually attract someone with the same qualities, if you are open and honest enough with those qualities to be observed. It's when we give up that passion for hope that we settle for someone we just wish we could trust, rather than that someone to whom we could "let go."

Irony of Faith

It is again so very important to understand that, in that state of despair, confusion reigns, and sometimes faith in yourself and your God are tossed aside in favor of a return to normalcy. You pray that everything will work out for the best, which for you means back to where it was. You pray for your relationship to survive. You then hope that your partner feels as you do. You pray that the love of your life will return. You hope for a miracle and you are sure what is good and right for you. However, it takes two good and right people to make a relationship successful, and you grieve that your partner doesn't have those same definitions. You ache when your prayers are slow to be answered. Then you doubt when the answer is not what you prayed for.

In the beginning of your relationship's demise, your prayers were only about the relationship's survival. When your commitments to that union were spurned, the hopes and prayers for the best were actually beginning to be realized by you and your God. Subconsciously, back to where it was, was not a place you wanted to be. You deserved better than that.

Once again, we must have faith that sometimes our prayers are answered not always the way we hope. In all the bewilderment and disorder that surrounds the pain we suffer, many times we cannot understand how this is happening to us. We cannot comprehend with all our faith in others, ourselves, and God, how we can be treated so badly and left alone. It seems so contrary to be punished for our faith, and to endure the heartache of loneliness, alone. And yet that seems to be the irony of faith. Somehow, some way, something unknown is occurring which will reward goodness by providing what is right.

The endurance of time spent alone is really a lengthy learning process rather than a punishing sentence. But in the throes of the confusion of despair, who really cares at that point about getting an education? Eventually though, what we learn after working through the chaos in which we find ourselves, is that if we keep our faith the best will occur. And while it may seem that our ordeal was spent alone, there were others walking similar paths; there were others observing our pain; and there were others praying for our best. Our despair only allowed us to see our solitary selves, without noticing all those walking along beside us. We become so burdened by the weight of our condition that we refuse to allow our faith to carry us through the most despairing of our times.

Let Go of Yourself

So, is there anybody else out there who understands the despair and desperateness that you feel? Is there someone who could use this understanding to help you deal with your pain? Well, there are plenty of us who have been through the same or similar experiences and are looking for others to share our misery and validate our expectations. The only chance we will ever get to meet however is for each one of us to "let go". Letting go, not just of our past failed experiences, but also of the barriers of deceit that we erect for protection.

As was mentioned previously, sometimes we deceive others, and ultimately ourselves, when we pretend that all the hidden turmoil has produced little effect on the circumstances of our lives. We end up creating an image to others of a person in control and not bothered much by the negative events occurring in their lives. That would be great if it were true. Yet that attitude and presentation doesn't evoke much sympathy or empathy, if that is what is desired.

I remember Susana and her story, and how I felt little sympathy for her. Rather, I felt admiration. She had honestly taken control of her life and showed me a sense of purpose that I wished I could have experienced a year before. Then I wouldn't have had to **crave the sympathy that self-pity demands and rather just searched out the empathy that someone understands.**

The affinity that she and I experienced resulted from truthfully sharing our stories and our feelings. Neither one of us was seeking pity from each other, but needed an assurance of understanding that so many others in similar circumstances need. It is when we disguise our expression that we mask any opportunity for someone else to understand what we are going through.

This barrier to the expression of the reality of our feelings, not only affects how we appear to those observing us, but may also adversely affect the portrayal of another's justifiable feelings. We have a tendency to learn from the appearance of people who have similar experiences and sometimes mimic their responses as the way we should act. Or, most of the time we judge our own capabilities from another's apparently honest response. We have observed other couples seemingly expressing a non-stop joyful existence, and we're offered a comparison of the imperfect relationship we were experiencing. We have noticed the carefree lives of our friends and acquaintances, even when they were faced with similar situations to ours, making us feel diminished in our capability to cope. We see happy, surviving people all around us, even though families are crumbling, divorces are skyrocketing, and relationships are becoming meaningless. We constantly compare ourselves to those who seem so much better off than we are. Our judgment is based upon how other people appear. So many times we are deceived.

When I first met John, he was going through, what was becoming to my trained eye, a "typical" divorce. It featured diminishing communication and commitment and the willingness of one partner, in this case his wife, to move on. While he claimed he didn't understand why it all happened and that he wanted to stay married, John seemed to be coping very well with his newfound single life. As a matter of fact, he seemed to have it made. He would go out every night meeting friends at bars, dancing, going to parties, traveling all over the country, having a great time. Friends of his, even some married ones, appeared envious of his plight and wished they could experience his enjoyment of life.

Every week he was with a different woman and enjoyed the intimacies of marriage without the long-lasting responsibilities. It seemed he was on a constant chase through life and was enjoying every minute of it. He also didn't appear to be suffering from any ill affects of his divorce. I must admit that even I began to question the painstaking process I had just gone through to deal with all the issues that were presented to me. He had made it through his divorce without a scratch, and from all appearances may have even certainly benefited by it.

While I was convinced of his happy lifestyle, I was not persuaded that it would have been best for me to equal his experiences. I guess I believed that I was more thoughtful, more feeling, more responsible, and more concerned about my future. But, I also had a lingering doubt that I was weaker, more incapable of dealing with my circumstance, and more damaged by my experiences. It was when I realized where I had come from to the place I was, that I understood that the path I had taken was clearly the right one for me. I had dealt with all my issues and knew who I was and where I was going. It was now time for me to be happy.

John was presenting to us all a different method of coping. He was happy from the beginning. I likened him to a racehorse breaking from the gate, running full speed in the race of life. The only problem was that he didn't have any training. There apparently was no thought given to the plans for pacing himself to finish or for winning the race, if those were even objectives. But it was impressive watching him perform and he had everyone convinced that he knew how to win the race.

135

Occasionally, I would join the race with John. I, however, felt perfectly trained. Then one night, he came over to my home to pick me up for a party we were both attending. As I was finishing getting dressed, John sat in the living room and noticed a draft copy of this book and began to read it. By the time I came down to leave he had skipped through some of the chapters. He had tears in his eyes and told me that he felt the same way I did. He expressed how difficult it had been for him dealing with his divorce and starting over. He said that he felt lost and grief-stricken and didn't have anyone to talk to about his feelings. He wondered why I had never talked to him about the things I had written in this book. I told him that I didn't think he had the same feelings or thoughts that I had. He said that he felt insulted.

John's a great guy, but I guess I really didn't think he had feelings. He presented to me, and everyone else he encountered, a contented and satisfied lifestyle. He missed out having the conversations of understanding that we all need, to deal with what we are going through. He didn't receive the immediate comfort that we can get from someone who has been there, when our lives seemed to be turned upside down. He hadn't taken the time to figure out where he was going and how to get there. He was lost, but disguised it so well no one ever offered to help him find his way. It wasn't because he didn't need help, comfort, and understanding; it was because he gave the appearance that it wasn't necessary. And what about all those others out there, who saw John's actions as solutions to their problems. They will either have to disguise their misery to make it appear that they too are coping, or compared to John, they will feel like failures. Or what about someone like me, who knows that the process of healing is going to involve some pain, hard work, and even depression along the way. Compared to the disguised happiness of John, one can certainly get more depressed about being depressed.

Feelings need to be expressed truthfully if we are to have any hope of finding others out there who can offer us help and whom we can help. We don't have to walk around all the time express-ing our despair and depression, but we do have to "let go" of the deceitful disguise that there are no problems. Everyone has prob-lems. If we could all be truthful about the difficulties we face in our lives, not only would we be able to comfort each other, but we wouldn't be judged so harshly when we compare ourselves to the perfect lives of those we observe. We need to deal with our or-deals from an honest and fresh perspective so that the deceit of the past has passed and the truth marks a new beginning.

8

The Past Has Passed

How long are we supposed to live in the past? How long are we supposed to grieve over the death of our relationship? As we previously discussed, for each one of us the answer is going to be different, depending on what kind of value that relationship had in our lives. To grieve over someone we love and miss who has died, is a grief of fond remembrance that can have a lasting, positive impact on our lives. To continue to grieve over a relationship that provided, to some degree, a waste of your time, will just allow for more wasting of time. To extend the anguish over a partnership that included mistrust and despair will just bring more of the same. To prolong to sorrow over a failed union that, at times, made you lonely even when you were together, will just exaggerate your current loneliness.

After I got divorced, I crossed paths with the Pastor of the church I attend and mentioned to him what had happened. He suggested that I go to the next "singles club" meeting that is held once a month at the church. He thought that it would be a good idea to meet with other singles who had been placed in the same situation that I found myself.

After a few months, I decided to give it a try and went to the singles meeting. I was surprised that there were only six people there and found out that none of them had ever been in a committed relationship before. I stayed and talked to them for a little while and came away realizing that they had no clue as to what I was going through or even what my issues were. Since they had never been in a relationship, they didn't have memories, good or bad, with which they had to deal. I left feeling more alone than when I arrived.

A few months later I attended a lunch with the Bishop from my church and he brought up my Pastor's suggestion and asked how everything turned out. I explained to him my disappointment with the meeting, and that while I realized I haven't led a very sheltered life, that I was surprised that these people had gone through much of their adult life without a relationship; even with such a small group. Of course who knows, maybe they were better off not having the memories that I had. He suggested that I give it one more try, and attend a singles meeting that was held each quarter that included all the churches in the area. He felt that not only might I gain something, but that I might be able to contribute something to the lives of those in attendance. Even though I felt that it would either be a waste of time or could possibly make me feel worse than I already did, I agreed as a favor to him to go.

When I arrived, I noticed that there were about fourteen people; the youngest at least twenty years my senior. I started to make an excuse that I was at the wrong meeting when one of the ladies recognized me and asked me to stay for their meeting. I reluctantly agreed.

This meeting began, as all their meetings did, by going around the table and introducing themselves and telling a little story as to why they were there. Since I was new I got to go last. It started with one of the ladies describing how she had been married for fifty-two years before her husband passed away from cancer. She described the last few years of their life together as one of the most loving, caring stories I had ever heard. The next story was from a man whose wife had also died of cancer. They had gotten married late in life and had "only" been married twenty-eight years. He said that he and his wife "packed" more into those twenty-eight years than most people could for fifty years. Next was a lady whose husband had died of a heart attack at the beginning of a prolonged vacation. They had been married for thirty-six years and were finally getting around to seeing the whole world together. He died in the first country they visited. She said she was hoping to convince some of the members here to go with her to finish the trip so that he could see through her eyes the rest of the world. And so, it went on and on with each story more heartfelt and each memory still vivid in their minds. The length that their marriages lasted ranged from twenty-eight years to fifty-four years.

It was then my turn. I looked around the room and saw all these teary-eyed people having just expressed what seemed to be their life's experiences and memories always intertwined with a sharing partner. I explained the reason I had tears in my eyes was not because of my memories, but rather because I was so happy for each of them to have been able to share the love and commitment for all those years. I explained that I thought I was coming to a meeting where we were all going to be comforting each other with stories about how terrible our relationships were, and how we needed to forget and move on with our lives. Instead, I offered, that I sat there in total admiration when listening to the stories of people who were so lucky to have been with someone who contributed so much to their lives.

I told them that I was there to continue my process to forget, while clearly they are so fortunate to have memories that they must remember.

I learned a lot that day. Needless to say I was even more depressed as I thought about why that couldn't have been me telling a story about being married even twenty-seven years. And, the memories: why couldn't that be me talking about good, loving, committed remembrances of time sharing with a partner whose separation occurred at the finality of the vow "until death do we part?"

Well, unfortunately it's not me. And while, there are some people who sometimes need to remember some of their memories, I for one needed to forget.

The past is now just memories; some need to be remembered, some need to be forgotten. Sometimes, we dwell too much on the memories that need to be forgotten, and don't remember those that we need to learn from. To move on, means to not worry about the past, and focus on the future.

When we are *Suddenly Single,* it is sometimes hard to forget those past, failed memories, because they are so recent, and they encompassed so much of our lives. We become consumed and obsessed with problems and solutions of that past relationship that don't matter anymore. We analyze what went wrong or think about what might have been. We dream, we wish, we regret and we constantly revisit.

We're like new farmers who, when plowing their field, are always looking back to see how they did, only to find out that by doing so, the field they're plowing is crooked. They soon learn that in order for their field to be plowed properly in the least amount of time, they must stay focused on the field ahead. All that's being plowed up behind them is the useless, barren last year's crop. Of course, you have to analyze it before you begin plowing to get all the bugs out, but once you start plowing you should never look back. It's always tempting, but it's just a waste of time and effort and usually causes you to get off course. When you determine that there is no possibility to rejuvenate that barren crop, it's time to plow it all under, never to be seen again.

When a relationship is over, it really doesn't do any good to maintain false hopes; it just delays the healing process. Memories are reminders of the past. To proactively live in the present and hope for the future, you have to stop looking back. I found the best way, is to remove any reminder of the past that can possibly be eliminated. It's best to give away or dispose of items of joint possession rather than have them as reminders. Pictures and mementos of a happier time will always be there as a provoking reminder of the past. Some people think it is part of their history, and need to keep them to cherish that happier time. I think it affords us an opportunity to revisit an ultimately bad experience.

You never have to worry about stumbling over something behind you.

Obviously all relationships have their moments and even years of happiness, but over all when you look at where you are today, alone with your love, you may have been better off if those few pleasant memories never existed. If you truly feel that way, you need to plow them under, knowing that you are capable of experiencing good and lasting memories with someone who will understand and appreciate your love.

143

We all have a tendency to somehow subconsciously wait for the good part of that person, who caused us to become *Suddenly Single,* to return. We do this by not replacing things that left with them; by not learning to take care of ourselves by replenishing what they contributed to our lives; by living in an environment that maintains rather than moves on; and by not seeking new relationships and opening ourselves up to others. **We're afraid of closure, because it finally admits failure.**It's about time we started cutting our losses. Chances are what happened to us was going to happen eventually, and we regret losing those precious moments in life. To waste more moments constantly remembering them is just wasting more productive time. Not wasting time was what made Susana's story so remarkable and ideal. It's a shame so many of us don't have the courage and confidence to do what she did, when she did it.

Not looking back sometimes means forgetting about a person's existence. Viewing furniture, appliances, clothes, knickknacks, and even wedding gifts, not as mementos of a past relationship, but rather as things that weren't yours, and that you never really wanted anyway. You need to replace them with things you do want, that reflect who you are, and not who that other person was, or even who that couple was. All of a sudden you will find yourself in a better environment, one that espouses your tastes. You might even find that the environment you created is a lot more pleasing to other people as well.

No matter how hard we try to relieve ourselves of the associations of a past relationship though, there will always remain sparks that will ignite memories. Whether it's the children, homes, jobs, places, people, movies, or songs of past remembrances, those associations will always be there. Hopefully with a diminishing effect as time goes on. In most relationships, there is enough around to remember to cause a glance back at the past now and then. It's when that glance becomes a prolonged stare whose focus precludes the imagining of a future, that time is wasted and hope is delayed.

When lives are intertwined and consumed with each other, it seems that every aspect of daily living somehow involves the other partner. When one partner leaves, a void occurs that gets filled with daily memories. For some relationships, that might mean that almost every minute of everyday could bring a lonely person some remembrance of the past. Big things and little things trigger thoughts that, whether positive or negative, dwell on the past. If you were to make a list, there are probably hundreds of things you could encounter on a weekly basis that could conjure up images of past experiences with your mate. The key is to lighten the load of those encounters by visually removing as many circumstances for their visitation as possible.

Glancing back occasionally is normal and sometimes unavoidable. Dwelling on the past by refusing to relinquish items of provoking memory is obsessive, and foregoes the promises of the future by living in a time that has passed.

Before I first met Marie, I was told by a mutual friend that she and I had a lot in common. What my friend really meant was that we were both divorced.

We first met in a coffee shop and talked for hours. I guess in some ways it was because we both longed to talk to someone who had an understanding of what we had been through. I was at a point in my life where I didn't want to relive my past experiences, although Marie was almost pleading with me to tell her every detail. While I was not much help, it seemed all her questions to me were related to something that happened in her relationship. And, then she would go on and on about her husband.

She would ask me questions like, "Did you travel together a lot?" and I would give a brief answer. She would then proceed to tell me all the places she and her husband had been to, and the positive and negatives of each trip. I could certainly understand someone who had just been divorced needing to talk to someone about their recent past experiences, but Mary had been divorced for over two years.

Mary seemed really nice, despite her obsession with reliving her failed relationship. Besides, I thought that once she got it out of her system, we would probably begin to talk about other things. As a matter of fact, the next time we went out, we went to dinner and only half the time was spent with her asking me questions to get to an explanation of something that happened in her marriage. The other half of the time I could tell that she was interesting and interested in me. She then invited me over to her house for dinner, and what a great dinner it was. I am sure her ex-husband is losing a lot of weight.

While I was over her house she asked me if I could change a light bulb in the ceiling that hadn't worked for over a year. She said that she didn't have a ladder, and if she fell off the chair while stretching to change it, that no one would be there to help her if she was seriously hurt. I got her assurance that she would help, should that happen to me. During my six hours at her house, I tightened a loose hose coupling that had been leaking water for over a year. I put a spare tire in the trunk of her car that was sitting in her garage since her husband left, and I connected a wire to a speaker of her stereo system that she had been listening to in mono since she could remember. I certainly didn't mind doing any of those things. Quite frankly, it felt kind of good.

During our conversation, I learned that when her husband left that she got the house and all the furniture, all the silverware and knick-knacks. She had all the mementos of all their traveling together sitting in various places around her house. When I mentioned that I had also been to a couple of the exotic places she had been, she proceeded to show me the pictures of her and her husband at these marvelous locations. She did say that she only kept the pictures of the "good times". The chair I was sitting in was a chair that they brought back from a foreign country because they both fell in love with it and had such pleasant memories attached to it. It began to get a little eerie. I was beginning to think that everything in her house was just like it was while her husband was still there. When I tactfully questioned her about it, she admitted that sometimes it's sad, but that they are just memories and it can't hurt to remember every once in awhile. It was more like a museum, and she was remembering every minute of every day. She was stuck in the past and was surrounded by things that caused her to dwell on her current circumstance.

I invited her over to my home for dinner, advising her that when she came that I really didn't want to talk about the past anymore, just the present and future. I told her that my home had just me in it. It was newly painted, both inside and out. All the old furniture, games, bikes, knick knacks, dishes, silverware and beds were given away to people less fortunate than myself. The only pictures anywhere in the house were those of my "immediate" family and me. Everything was new and reflected me. As a matter of fact, I would rather have an empty space waiting until I could buy something, than to have a bad memory be sparked by an item from the past.

We had a really nice, kind of romantic, candlelit dinner. We talked about things we'd like to do and places we'd like to go. She really loved my house and how I fixed it up. She said it was amazing, but that it really did reflect me. Very rarely did the subject of the effects of our past relationships come up, but when it did, it was okay. It was always a brief glancing back, rather than a focus of much concern. When Mary left that night she asked if it was hard for me to completely change my surroundings. I told her that of course it was, but that it was absolutely necessary for me to move on to a happy future unburdened by the past.

I saw Mary a few more times since then, but we gradually lost touch with each other. She sold her house and moved to the other side of the country. I heard from our mutual friend that she met a really nice guy and that they were traveling all over the world together creating future memories.

Those of us who desperately want a relationship to work will many times relinquish parts of our own personalities to enhance the position of our partner. We value their judgment over our own, only to find out after the relationship ends that we were right all along. People start complimenting your choice of colors, when all along you thought you were colorblind. New friends applaud your designing capabilities, when all along you were told that you couldn't mix and match. Strangers rave about the way you dress, when you thought you had to depend upon someone else to evaluate your appearance. It's then that you realize that what you really needed was a relationship that allowed you to express who you are, without fear that your capabilities would be looked upon as threatening.

That's what this time alone will allow, to express "who" you are. What you find attractive will be found attractive to someone who has the confidence in themselves to permit you to be yourself. But before you can live in the present, and look toward the future, you have to get rid of the past. You have to remove it from sight in every way that you can. You have to change the direction of your hope from what could have been, to what can be.

Your friends and family have to, once again if possible, just become yours. Your possessions have to belong to and reflect you alone. The wonderful places you have visited should be remembered for the sensations that they provided just to you, so that you realize you can experience things by yourself or with someone else. All those romantic moments of the past should be an indication to you that you can be romantic with someone new. You should feel confident that the good times could be repeated with a new person, who appreciates who you are.

It's Not My Job

Now, those of us who are co-dependent types have some added difficulties; chiefly, not admitting we are co-dependent. In the past we have relied on someone so much to accomplish tasks that complement our lives, that we have no one to turn to for help when they are gone—not even ourselves. A co-dependent person, for example, has all of his laundry piling up, waiting for it to miraculously get washed, dried, folded, and put away. He has an ever-increasing stack of shirts and pants waiting to be ironed or for the button fairy to magically replace buttons that have fallen off. Of course, the reason he can't find anything, is because he didn't put it away. For some reason, he feels like he doesn't have those capabilities in his repertoire. Others have difficulties deciding if having the oil light flashing on the dashboard is something that warrants the car being serviced. She may have also watched the lawn grow into a jungle, because she couldn't figure out how to start the lawnmower. She may also be willing to live her life before the sun goes down, because she doesn't think she has the capability to replace the bulb in the recessed lighting. It's not like the co-dependent's partner always did the laundry or the oil change. It's just that in relationships with dependencies we tend to **subordinate our own responsibilities and capabilities to require complementary task obligation.**

It's somebody else's job. If that person is no longer there, it's another reason to dwell on our victimization. In reality, many times, it's because we had depended so much on that other person, and had given so much of ourselves to them, that we don't want to "plow under" their obligations to us. Other times it's because we imagine their worth or demand an unfair obligation to our own well-being. It's just another way we look back, instead of focusing on our future and making our current environment better. It's just another way we have to hang on—as victims.

> *My friend Bill told me how he ran into some friends of his ex-wife who told them how she wasted her time when she was with him and because of him now has to struggle through life. It was a story that we all hear a lot of nowadays with all the divorces occurring and the need to express and blame one's failure on someone else.*
>
> *He told me that when he first met her, she had dropped*

out of college after barely making it through high school. She had numerous short-term jobs that offered little promise and usually had to work for her family to provide herself with a living. After they married she began working with Bill at his business. For a while she was a good worker who enjoyed the challenges of Bill's business as well as the security and stature of being the owner's wife. But then things started to change and her efforts at work began to diminish, she lost interest and blamed the business for not paying her enough.

Since she had always expressed an interest in going back to school, Bill encouraged her to do so and even helped her in her schoolwork once she was accepted. Of course, school became an on and off venture eventually ceasing because of all of her other responsibilities including the diminished effort spent at work. Bill, being fairly well educated, understood not only the hard work it took to achieve an education but also the commitment necessary to see it through. While he didn't see his wife as having those same capabilities, all he could do was encourage her to continue.

As their marriage was in the process of breaking up, Bill's wife pondered the possibility of having a child to which Bill was ambivalent. It wasn't that he didn't want children, it was because he was worried about the level of commitment his wife would have to a family, especially one that was experiencing problems. He asked her for some time to stabilize the relationship and to be offered some assurance that it was going to last. Shortly thereafter, Bill's wife left him, went to work with her family where she met another man and Bill and she were subsequently divorced.

Bill admits he made a serious mistake getting involved with someone he knew had a problem with commitment in anything she tried, but he is thankful that it happened sooner than later in his life. And of course, he also imagines what would have happened if he had ever agreed to have a baby, and is thankful for his decision in that regard. But to now be told that it is his fault that his wife didn't receive an education and that she is stuck in a go nowhere job, or that her biological clock is ticking and because of him she still doesn't have a child, just infuriated him. Of course, Bill was now complaining about how his wife not only left him but also his business, which was now too difficult for him to run and was failing because she left.

When I explained to him about all the similar stories I had experienced from both men and women and the role victimization plays when people need to explain their plight in life, he said he felt better. I even went so far as to explain that by him telling me this story, he was portraying himself also as a victim, and that in reality he should have known what he was getting into when he first met this woman. He and his ex-wife are both where they are today because they put themselves there. Usually the only victims in stories like these are the people that they are being told to—with the exception of the people who felt compelled to pass along those tidbits of information from Bill's wife. These spin doctors of victimization will sooner or later be complaining as to how they were placed in the middle as a messenger. Everybody eventually gets to be a victim.

We all needed to depend on someone we loved, and chances are the reason we're in this situation today is because we couldn't.

But, what a wonderful thing it is for two people to be able to share responsibilities and dreams. Sometimes it even results in more accomplishments than either one could provide independently because of the factors of encouragement and time constraints. In reality though, we should be able to accomplish as much or more than we could in our past relationship because of all its problems. Chances are that it's just going to take more time and incentive.

In a way, our co-dependency is nothing more than a conviction that we can't live without the other person, and when we're together we view it as a reason for the relationship to exist. It stifled our initiatives then, and will continue to smother our ambitions as long as we believe that we can't do it alone. The strength of a relationship lies in the capabilities of two individuals who recognize their differences, admit their shortcomings, acknowledge their proficiencies, and applaud each other's qualities. They need to allow that if they had never met each other they would still achieve.

Do we ever wonder if we'll find anyone as good for us again? Of course we do, and how foolish that is. We were in a comfort zone that sometimes ignored discomfort. But when we start thinking that we won't be able to find anyone as wonderful as the previous imagined love in our lives, we are really admitting that we are not worth very much.

Be Better

In a relationship that you assumed to be loving, you wanted to believe that your soul mate was the most caring person there was, although there were times when that person was the least caring. You thought that he/she was physically attractive because you had no reason to desire someone else. You just knew your soul mate was intelligent, so that you depended upon and trusted his/her failed opinions. No one could be more fun, until the sense of joy was not shared. That person was your best friend, until other friends became a lot more important than you. You thought you were loved, until you realized that love was limited in time.

Will you ever be able to find anyone as good again? Will you ever be able to find anyone better? Deep inside, we all know the answer is yes. To admit that however, you have to plow straight ahead without looking back. It is then you will find that there are more caring, smarter people who, through their feelings and joy, can bring you happiness. There are people whom you will find much more attractive and who will recip-rocate your adulation.

In all honesty, we have to admit that there are so many people better suited to us than our previous partner. Yet we remained as long as we did, stuck in a relationship of imagined perfection, contented by "This is as good as it gets." How disappointed we were, but how lucky we are.

There are those who do not allow themselves time to think about how lucky they and their previous partner are not wasting each others lives anymore. Their primary concern is how to repay any disappointment and heartache they feel they have suffered. They have become stuck in anger. To them the demise of their relation-ship has become a win/lose proposition. Typically, their self-esteem is so low that they believe the only way to build themselves back up is to first drag others down to their level. They plot and wish for all the wrong things.

They keep getting deeper in the hole of desperation and

depression, because they're obsessed with revenge. The tools that they use to accomplish their goals range from the alienation of their children and/or friends, to exaggerated or untruthful rumors. They remain as concerned with the progress and daily events of their former partner's life as they were when they were together; all the while, hoping for bad news. They continue to hang on to this failed union because it is the only function left to them in their relationship; albeit a harmful function.

All that idle time spent thinking of ways to get even is just wasting more valuable time. They need, instead, to plow it under, and look straight ahead. "Vengeance is mine," sayeth the Lord. All this revenge stuff should be out of their hands, but to those who feel that somehow justice must be served, the best revenge is to do better; be better.

There is a fine line between seeking revenge and propping up our self-esteem. We all would feel a lot better if we could immediately find someone better looking, smarter, more successful, and more talented than our previous association. It would be to show others that we can do better; a superficial gain, but it would also help our ego. However, that's only a temporary fix. We really need to show **ourselves** that we can do better, by finding someone who is loving, caring, appreciative, and understanding.

We need someone who makes us happy by being happy, who shares with us in good times and bad, someone who is trustworthy, and who will give us the security of always being there. When we find that person, we will have done better, and because of their qualities, that person will in our eyes be more attractive than any one else could ever be. And, that can then be our revenge.

There was a line that Jack Nicholson says in the movie "As Good As It Gets" that sums up in one sentence the woman I know that

I want and I need. It is when he professes to the woman he loves that **"You make me want to be a better person."** To me that says it all.

I remember when I first saw Fred, after about seven or eight years of losing contact with him. He and I had been good friends and went to graduate school together. I recalled how hard he studied and worked at his job and how devoted he was to his family. He had a bunch of kids and he always had one or two of them with him wherever he would go.

When I asked him how he and his family were doing, he answered that he was divorced and didn't get to see his kids anymore. When I asked him what had happened, he said he would rather not talk about it. I was shocked and couldn't imagine what could have caused such a situation to occur. After we talked for a while, Fred felt comfortable enough to explain that his ex-wife had been telling people that he had left his family because he was having an affair with a younger woman, but that it wasn't true. She said that to make him look bad and to cover her own guilt. It was Fred's wife who wanted to get the divorce, because she said that she wasn't in love or attracted to him anymore. Even though Fred thought that she was cheating on him, he tried to stay married for the kids.

He told me how bitter the divorce was and that it took almost two years to become final. During that time Fred had to run his business and take care of his kids, whom he had more than half the time. It was then that Fred met a younger woman who offered to help him at work and also care for the kids while he was at work. It was a

*platonic relationship to start and Fred felt this woman
was like an angel sent from God to help him survive with
all the responsibilities he had.*

*Apparently, the divorce turned more than just bitter, and
allegations and rumors were flying all over the place. Fred
said that this was just his ex-wife's way of trying to get the
house, the business, the kids and enough child support to
take care of them all. That was exactly what had happened
when his ex-wife's mother got divorced. To complicate matters, Fred's ex-wife had taken quite a bit of money out of
the business causing him quite a bit of debt. Eventually,
Fred paid her a settlement, offered to pay her a child support he couldn't afford at the time, agreed to joint custody
of the children, and received the failing business and a
house in foreclosure in return.*

*After the divorce, Fred worked even harder at his business
and eventually was successful enough to begin to pay off
his debt. He was then amazed how the relationship with
his ex-wife improved. Fred had even bought her equipment
for her new business and when that business began to slow,
he helped her get a high paying job. Fred's life had gotten
better and there was no reason for him to hold a grudge.
He had a good relationship with his kids, he was involved
with a woman whom he loved, and his business was slowly
becoming successful. At that point he actually felt sorry
for his ex-wife.*

*I thought there had to be more to the story than that since
he doesn't see his kids. Fred explained that his kids don't
want to see him anymore. He told me that he had gotten
married again and shortly thereafter his ex-wife started*

157

telling people that Fred married the woman that he left his family for and wasn't giving her enough money to live. I had more questions and concerns as Fred had to leave with the promise that we would see each other again.

Well, I saw Fred again when he came up to the Legislature to visit me. We went out to lunch and I explained to him that I was concerned how someone so devoted to his family, could have lost everything. How was he able to cope? Fred told me that he copes by letting go of the past and looking to the future. It was really hard, but it was his only hope.

He told me of how his ex-wife became so jealous of his life; of the woman living in the house that she used to live in; of his young children calling his new wife their mother; and of the success in his business. He explained how she lied to the children and brainwashed them to believe that he had done something wrong. She implied to them that they had to make a choice and how they chose living with her and never seeing him and his new wife, even though he offered them no such choice.

When I asked if jealousy could cause a mother to do that to her kids especially since she ends up with more responsibility, he replied that she didn't do it to her kids, she did it to him. Besides, she gets more child support when the kids are all with her. He said that she made a terrible mistake when she got divorced, because she thought that she was going to get everything and that he would be the failure. Her revenge was to take away the one thing that really mattered to him and the only thing she could take away— his family.

The effect of this revenge is extreme and so is the way that Fred is dealing with it. He said after years of court battles; years of crying sleepless nights; years of the depression of despair; and years of wondering how his children are growing up; he has decided to move on and start his life over. Although he believes he will never see his children again, he doesn't wish anyone any harm. He said that's why when people ask about his family, he says he would rather not talk about it, because all he wants is to be left alone to begin again without the constant memory of his loss.

He glances back but doesn't dwell on his situation anymore. He thinks about his future, and dreams of having a family again. When I asked him how a father could do that, his answer was, "It's the only choice I have."

The longer we dwell on the past, the longer it affects us, and the longer it keeps us bottled up in our despair. It deters us from our mission of finding the hope necessary to escape our circumstance and survive. It is so hard though, to leave a past that embodied so much meaning, to seek an unknown future. It is when we recognize that it is the only choice, because there are no other choices, that we can finally decide to leave our past behind. Given the situation, it is the only decision that allows for a hopeful future without the burdens and torments that mask the true feelings of our being. Our love needs to be expressed before we can have any hope that someone will find it. The problem lies when we permit it to compete in the same arena for the same time with the past.

We do better by becoming better-not bitter. Bitterness masks our good qualities, and makes us look like someone who can't let go. How attractive is that? Well, one of the best ways to judge your appearance is to analyze how other's similar characteristics appear to you. Can you imagine how it sounds when someone constantly expresses deep hurt and resentment? Who wants to get involved with a farmer who's always worried about last year's crop, when the seeds of a new relationship are just sitting there, wasting time, waiting to get planted? Bitterness and resentment inhibit your capability to have joy. We really can't have it both ways. The choice is between anger and joy—a frown and a smile.

Moving on, beyond the past, allows a new beginning. It's not that the past has not provided valuable lessons to begin life again, but it becomes a burden when it occupies time better spent. To move forward takes time and a commitment to a brighter outlook filled with the wishes and dreams of a new adventure. If all there is to hope for is what has already occurred in life, a dismal future awaits. Potentials and opportunities cannot be visualized, when looking back at a lost future. What was lost, can, and in many cases should, be regretted. It is when that regret embraces anguish and despair, and whose span of time delays progress, that it becomes a competitor for improvement and growth.

The wasted time and hurt feelings are just some of the many experiences that life beholds. They are now part of a history. The only place that they can now exist is in a memory. The hope for a future past, filled with today's joyful memories, depends upon the ability to forget. **A positive vision for tomorrow cannot today exist with the obsession of negative yesterdays.**

9

How Long
Does It Take?

This process of dealing with the past, coping with your emotional environment, and analyzing and reconstructing your mind and body is going to take some time. If you do it right, you'll be able to express the "you" who has been hidden beneath an exterior conditioned by emotional, psychological, and physical barriers. You will then be able to heal just about all the wounds that you've experienced. But it does take time. For most of us it will take at least one year and one day, to have a fresh beginning—**to reach the other side**—although we continue to think we can do it sooner. But hasn't impatience provided us with all kinds of associated problems before? It takes at least a year and a day to go through all the experiences that you shared as a couple; to meet with all the friends and acquaintances; to attend all the meetings and organizations, to revisit those places you've been together; to engage in the activities that you shared; and to announce to your world that you are single again—suddenly though, it may seem to them.

It is going to take a while to confront the past, and bury it behind, as you move on. There is so much to reflect upon, eliminate, forget, and finally deal with. It's going to be like erasing each step of a self-compiled list off a blackboard. Every day there is going to be someone else you run into who's going to ask you the same questions about where your "other half" is. Every day you're going to be able to erase another name. In the beginning it's going to be time-consuming and painful, because you will feel compelled to make excuses or offer detail, and try and explain how something like this could ever happen. You'll express anger and hurt. You'll try to explain it to death to those who express disbelief that something like this could ever happen to such a perfect couple. But as time passes you'll realize that the excuses and detail really don't matter except to those who are closest to you, and they knew all about it the first few weeks of your uncoupling.

The anger and hurt will, with the passing of time, subside. The explanations will become shorter when you realize that people understand, through their own experience, that when it comes to couples, nothing is as it seems. Long before the year is up, you should be explaining the demise of your relationship with just the shrug of your shoulders, perhaps a little smile, and, "it just didn't work out." At that point, it's not going to be that you're hiding your true feelings, but rather that you've already confronted the past and realize that you're dealing with the present.

Some couples only have a few friends and acquaintances, while others have hundreds that they associate with. There are social friends, neighbors, fellow workers, club and organization associations, parents and teachers of kids at school, as well as family members, and all kinds of people who become intertwined in their lives. There are those who didn't have much meaning in the relationship, and there are those who were deeply affected by the breaking of its bond. In some cases, many of these people are going to have to choose which friend to keep or which one to give precedence. Sometimes, it will depend on which story they believe. In some cases, there is no choice to make because one of the couple has also left friends, who also feel abandoned.

We've seen situations like this so many times that it has become the norm rather than the exception. But it is going to take time to sort through all the people who were a part of your life. As with everything that you have to go through at this time, it will get easier with practice. Eventually, before the year and a day is up, you'll have had enough practice and confidence and healing to just blame everything that happened on El Niño—or the alignment of the planets, or Y2K, which usually provokes a laugh and lets you know you're getting over at least the anxiety brought on by your despair.

Every Day Anew

It's still going to take a full year to go through and experience by yourself all the holidays and special dates that you were used to sharing. From Thanksgiving through the Christmas holiday, New Year's Eve and of course, July 4th, alone, will give Independence Day a new meaning. Then there are the birthdays and anniversaries, Mother's Day and Father's Day, whose joined celebration are no more. Even the little things that provoke a notice of change, like the seasons, may provide memories that will have to be confronted.

The feelings that the cold of winter brings will somehow be different. There will be memories of skiing, football, coats and sweaters, snuggling by the fire, watching the snowflakes fall, and cuddling while on a walk or in a chilly bed on those long nights. Now the environment will somehow seem colder and the nights longer. This will be an especially harsh season because the focus of giving is so evident. The joy of Christmas seems to have been stolen by a grinch who refused to share its celebration. Then the injury suffered at Christmas has the insult of New Years Eve added to its repertoire. The realization of loneliness reaches its peak when a dream night for couples presents a nightmare for singles. The goal becomes to somehow just make it through. The coldness seems to encompass the entire environment.

Then the springtime feelings come; the flowers blossom and the trees bloom. You'll be reminded of tennis, golf, gardening, shirts and slacks, walks in the park, spring cleaning, and the sun that used to brighten your days a little longer. But now it doesn't seem to matter if the flowers blossom that much and the spring-cleaning gets put off for another season. But, you'll be thankful you survived the holidays and maybe have hope that the longer days will begin to provide relief from the long nights of winter.

Summer embraces you with its heat and its passion. Everything's in full bloom, the grass is green and growing, schools are out, there's swimming, baseball, vacation, concerts under the stars, barbecues and parties. There are t-shirts and shorts, the glasses of wine in the spa, the bodies exercised and tanned, and the days are as long and as bright as they can be. Yet, now, past passion has disappeared along with the coupled vacations. At least the fireworks are an experience of celebration rather than as an expression of a failing relationship. The grass has to be mowed, there's more time to spend by yourself and there is someone else in the spa sipping wine. But, the longer days provide an inspiration to go outside to find someone new.

Then, there are the feelings of autumn; visually displaying it's resplendent color. A relief used to be felt, as the days got cooler. It's a time to finish up, close out summer and prepare for the winter. There are last minute trips. School is starting. Shorts give way to jeans and slacks, and even though leaves are dying, it seems like a new year is beginning with planning for the year ahead. But, the colors of dying leaves don't have the same beauty now, alone, and to some become nothing more than dying leaves. Those last minute trips become a scouting adventure for a place to take someone new, or to find someone to warm up with in the winter.

The seasons stay the same, but the feelings will be different. This first year alone may provide sadder memories than the year before. But, like the leaves of the trees in autumn, it presents a confrontation with the death of the memories, and the planning of a new beginning.

This first year needs to provide closure to the relationship, so that confrontations to the past don't linger. Since you're going to feel miserable going through all those holidays and seasons and special dates anyway, you might as well deal with all the other past experiences at the same time. Eventually, you're going to have to attend those same meetings and functions that you used to, go to the same stores, visit the same schools, attend the same activities. You need to confront people, places and things with your new beginning, to erase everything on that blackboard of the past.

Of course, during that first year you also will be well on your way to achieving the physical condition you seek by maintaining an exercise program. You will have promoted a change in your eating habits that will have provided you with a healthier appearance and outlook. And, with the notes you are taking along the way you will have a comparison that will show how far you have advanced since the start of your recovery.

Your life has changed. The sooner you exhibit that change, the sooner you will be able to have memories of a new past. You can't look forward and look back at the same time. You must stay focused, or the present, that becomes tomorrow's past, will just be a series of crooked rows plowed by a farmer who didn't learn at the beginning of his field, to put his past behind him.

Confrontation with the past isn't all bad. Sure, it provides memories that aren't all that pleasant to deal with, but it also provides a sort of closure. You're not going to have to worry about that first experience again. It's the beginning of dealing with people as a single person again. The next time they see you they won't be surprised or shocked. Each time you see them, they'll think less of your past relationship and more of just you. It's the same with places.

The first visit incurs memories of a couple, but the next visit is just yours. Eventually, the memories are of just you and maybe even someone else. It's the same with things of your environment. Some of your possessions and the space in which you live can also conjure up thoughts of the past. If you change your environment to something new that is just yours, and get rid of those things that provoke bygone images, those sad, daily remembrances will disappear. Your environment then just becomes yours.

While I was at a legislative meeting in Washington, D.C., I attended a reception for all the participants. At that reception, I struck up a conversation with Martha about some of the issues we had heard about that day. We talked for about an hour and then went to the planned dinner and talked for a couple of more hours. As usual the conversation drifted to personal lives.

Martha lived in D.C. and worked for the federal government. She had a pretty good job and had worked her way up over the ten years she had lived and worked there. She had come to D.C. with her husband shortly after they were married, when they both had been offered jobs with the government. Almost three years ago she and her husband had gotten divorced. We really didn't dwell on our previous relationships, but rather discussed what it was like being single again. We each had some pretty interesting insights, experiences, and humorous stories.

I could tell Martha was a very thoughtful person, who spoke softly and seemed to have a clear understanding of what her life was all about. She mentioned that she didn't date much since it appeared that D.C. had more women then men and that most of the men where she worked were married. She didn't like to go out to bars, but she and some of her girlfriends went out to dinner occasionally.

When I mentioned that I was writing a book about being single, she was very interested in my thoughts and experiences and, in particular, how long it took some of the people I had met to get over their divorce. The conversation was becoming very interesting, but dinner was over and it was getting late, so we agreed to meet the next day during the conference. She also invited me to her home for dinner that next night so that we could talk some more.

She lived in a very nice town home, which was decorated very comfortably with, what I was to learn later that evening, all the furnishings she had when she was married. She had never moved and had kept everything the same as it was before her divorce. It reminded me of a couple of other women I had met who were surrounded by their memories.

During and after dinner our main topic of conversation was why I thought it takes at least a year and a day to get over a divorce. She had mentioned that after almost three years she was still not over hers. When I talked to her about how sometimes our environment causes us to constantly

167

revisit the past, she said that she thought about that, but made the decision that she was comfortable doing what she was doing and living where she was.

Martha loved her job, even though it was just a few blocks away from where her ex-husband works. She was the one who found the town home that she and her husband lived in, and it was in such a nice neighborhood that she was sure she could never find anything like it again. She was the one who decorated her home and felt comfortable with its environment. There was not very much that she would want to change about her surroundings, even if she could.

Her major complaint about her life was that she felt isolated. When she first got divorced, she dreaded going to work to face her co-workers and would leave early and would never socialize. She still doesn't go to places for lunch or dinner where she and her husband used to go—most of which are right near where she works. She never goes to social events because of the possibilities of running into her ex-husband or people who are going to want to know what happened to them. When she goes out for dinner now, she always requests that she and her friends go out of D.C. for that same reason. For almost three years, she has taken a cab to a grocery store outside her neighborhood, because she doesn't want to see neighbors and acquaintances of her and her husband at the grocery store she shopped at for seven years.

With all the glorious activities that go on in Washington D.C, on the holidays, Martha never goes to fireworks displays or the Christmas tree lighting, or for that matter hasn't even had a tree herself for the past two years. With all the museums and traveling art exhibits, there is so much to do in D.C. After talking with Martha though, I realized that I had experienced more of D.C. in the past two years then she had, and I live two thousand miles away.

When I first met Martha it appeared that she was a woman who really had her life together. After getting to know her however, even in as a short a time as it was, it seemed that she was barely hanging on. What she was hanging on to was the past. She couldn't bring herself to face up to what her life had become. It wasn't that she was waiting for her husband to come back, as is the reason so many other people keep their surroundings the same. She just lacked the courage to face the fact of her divorce, deal with the past, and create new experiences. She was stuck for almost three years. She wasted almost three years. Now, whenever she starts to start over, it is still going to take her at least a year and a day to get over her divorce.

The first year is going to be really tough, but we all have to go through it. The actual first step to recovery isn't really as difficult as it may seem. Thinking about that first step, however, is really unpleasant. Unfortunately, or fortunately, depending on your attitude, the only place to begin is at the beginning. Every day that you are able to experience the memories and put them behind you is a day closer to the cessation of your pain and the beginning of the future. Each day that you hide from the stress of these confrontations just prolongs and intensifies the fear of their challenge. Each hurdle that is erased provides an exhilarating sense of accomplishment, knowing that it is finally over with, and that your next experience will be that much less intense.

Temporary Solutions

It is important to realize that a conscious encountering of recent memories is not the easiest path to take. Human nature being what it is, we will have a tendency to take the most obliging direction. The easiest path is one that many of us have chosen before, and in all likelihood has placed us in the situation we are faced with today. It would seem a lot less troubling to not have to face the despair and loneliness of this first year alone by immediately finding another relationship. Anything too easy, however, is usually not worth having. If you've experienced that before and are now reading this book, you know exactly what I mean.

Poor Fred. I saw him a little over a year later and he had gotten divorced from his second wife after only three years of marriage. I rationalized with him about how difficult marriage is without having to go through all he did. I thought the issues with his first divorce and the jealousies of his ex-wife, coupled with his kids deserting him, must have been very depressing. Sometimes you get so consumed with the problems left over from your first marriage that it is difficult to focus on a second marriage. That's why so many second marriages fail.

Fred admitted that that may have been a contributing cause, but in thinking back, he realizes that this most recent failure began after his first divorce. He was desperate because he had his business to run and his kids to take care of. His previous wife had divorced him because she wasn't attracted to him anymore. He longed for help and needed intimacy, since he hadn't been intimate with his previous wife for the last two years of their marriage. Then came along the first pretty face offering to help him.

He didn't have time to consider substance; he was just desperate for help. Besides, he wasn't going to get married again. That "pretty face" helped him with his business and kids and somehow everything and everybody survived.

There was also a mutual sexual attraction, which allowed him to feel good about himself again. Over the years he thought he had grown to love her, and when she suggested that after all these years of helping him that she should at least have the hope of marriage, he agreed. He thought it was the right thing to do, even though at times her character, commitment and dependability came into question. He thought he owed her that.

Well, she left Fred because she said she wanted to experience the freedom of single life again—a life she missed out on most of the time when she and Fred were together. But, Fred knew from the beginning that she wasn't the type of person that could be committed to a relationship. He knew that ultimately, what would have been best for him was to tough it out by himself until he got his life in order. He just needed the confidence in himself to know that he would eventually meet a woman that could be the love of his life. He got involved in what he thought was a temporary relationship that lasted too long. Now all those years are wasted and he is right back to where he was after his first divorce. Fred is sad about his current circumstance and the missed opportunities for love, but committed to getting his life in order, and taking his time in creating his future.

It would be so nice to not have to endure the loneliness, and to have someone to talk to, and cuddle. It would be great to not have to experience the memories alone, to share your feelings with someone who can listen and care. It would be wonderful not to have to suffer the despair of daily living, and the added responsibilities and decisions alone. It would certainly be nicer and easier to find someone else right away, but chances are, it won't be better. The first good-looking, friendly face may appear as a savior in your time of need. When we're in desperate need we don't have time to look around for someone with substance. As with everything else in life, we need and we need now.

Not facing who we are and all that we can become, alone, just delays that inevitable journey toward success. If we immediately rebound from one relationship to another, our partnerships will always be based on fulfillment of urgent, short-term needs, while our long-term promises and dreams get postponed. It becomes a measure of who we really are, and whether we view ourselves as worthy of the wait.

Some people just can't live alone. They've been involved in one co-dependent relationship after another and feel that they can't make it on their own. They experience low self-esteem because of their previous relationships, and they actually believe that they will not be able to find anyone as worthy as their previous partner, even though their past partner wasn't very worthy. For them it takes a lot of courage and support to tough out being alone to deal with their issues and to provide the time necessary to search for the recipient of their true love.

So many of us have hung on to relationships that waste time and miss opportunity. It becomes a routine rather than a commitment. We continually wonder if there is someone out there who may provide more meaning in our lives, but we are afraid to take the chance of being alone. We settle and delay the chance of moving forward in our lives by becoming stuck where we are. These impermanent relationships just postpone the healing process, and sometimes even worse, cause us to miss out on somebody who might be permanent.

I was introduced by a friend, to a waitress at a trendy restaurant in town. He told me that she was a former mortgage banker who was "absolutely perfect for me." When I first met her, there was little doubt in my mind that he was right. I went back to that restaurant every chance I could to see her and talk to her, although our conversations were always limited to chitchat, because she was always so busy with her job. We never really got to know much about each other, but I at least thought we were both attracted, and had the opinion of a mutual friend that we were a match.

Well, to make a long story short, when I asked her out to dinner so that we could have the opportunity to get to know each other better, she replied, "I would really love to do that, but right now I have a boyfriend out of town, and I don't think he would appreciate it if I did." Becoming somewhat bolder, I asked her if she planned on marrying him. She said that she didn't think so, at this point. I gave her my card and told her to call me if she just wanted to go out and talk sometime. She never called and I don't see her anymore.

In a way I admired her loyalty to a boyfriend that she probably isn't going to marry, but I keep thinking back to how important timing is in our lives. I think of so many people met on my journey who said that they had hung on too long. It wasn't just the wasted time they regretted, but the lost opportunities who passed them by. I look at myself and my choices, and think about the people I could have been with, and maybe even the love of my life whom I never got to know.

Now, I'm not arrogant or even self-confident enough to assume that situations I experienced were cases where women shouldn't be wasting their time, because I could be the love of their lives. Maybe they were just being friendly. But I got the impression that maybe they were like a lot of people I had met who would rather have a bird in the hand than have to search the bushes. It's when the bird leaves the nest that you wish you would have started your search a lot sooner.

When I mentioned this encounter with the waitress to my sister, who happens to be my best friend, confidant, and adviser to matters of the heart, she became upset with me. It was her opinion that it was wrong of me to pursue someone who I knew had a boyfriend, no matter how temporary I thought the relationship. She thought that instead of considering my own circumstances, and what I imagined to be the future of this young woman I was pursuing, that I should put myself in the shoes of her boyfriend. How would I feel if someone was eager to exaggerate the temporary status of a relationship I was in, just to get a date because of an imagined more permanent relationship? And, I was reminded that it did happen to me.

She felt that it is the choice of the woman to decide whether she wants to continue in a perceived temporary union, and that after her decision to leave, is when it is appropriate for me to become involved. Her point was that many people waste their time being with someone who will not prove to be the love of their lives, but that is a decision that only they should make, without outside interference or encouragement.

> *As we were being told that our plane was delayed again, I noticed this very stylish, attractive woman standing next to me. I don't know what came over me, but I looked toward her and blurted out, "I hope that they have the decency to give us*

extra snacks." She started talking to me about all the delays she had experienced, that she was also booked on another flight that was leaving in a few minutes, and that she should probably take that one. We talked some more and realized that our final destination was the same. I was going back to Santa Fe; she was coming for a visit.

She then decided that she wasn't going to take the other flight. We somehow got on the topics of economics, sociology, our philosophies in life, and personalities who espoused those beliefs, and we seemed to agree on everything. Then we started talking about politics. It turned out that we had the same heroes and philosophies there, too. She was definitely my kind of woman. The thought actually crossed my mind that this was "too good to be true." I began hoping that they would cancel the flight just so the conversation wouldn't end—it was that good. Then they announced boarding and we continued talking as we walked onto the plane. I couldn't believe all that we had in common. Then I realized that we wouldn't be sitting together and I thought how stupid I was to not ask her, while we were at the gate, if we should get seats next to each other.

She was seated at the front of the plane, and I was at the rear. After everyone was seated she looked back, noticed that the seat next to me was vacant, and came back and sat next to me. We continued to talk nonstop. Just before we landed I asked her whom she was visiting in Santa Fe, and she said that it was her boyfriend, who was also visiting on business. What a downer that was. I had already imagined us having dinner together, sightseeing, sitting on the plaza talking, and introducing her to my fellow senators. What an imagination!

175

Needless to say, I was dumbfounded. I finally meet some-one who I can really relate to, and she too has a boyfriend. I knew I then had the choice of telling her that I would like to see her again, or of never seeing her again. This time I put myself in her boyfriend's shoes, and just wished her well on her visit. As we were leaving the plane she did ask me if I ever got to Orange County, and I told her all the time. That would have been the perfect opening for me to ask her for her phone number, had it not been for her boy-friend. As we departed the plane she introduced me to her boyfriend, whom I thought didn't match her personality, but maybe I was just grasping for some hope. She asked me if I needed a ride home, but I declined. So close and yet so far.

Being Suddenly Single is always a struggle between hope and despair, confidence and its lack thereof, and wishful thinking and reality. I am getting closer though, and with time and a little luck, maybe the next crossed path I en-counter won't have a boyfriend.

When I told my sister of this latest encounter on the plane, I thought she was going to compliment me on how I dealt with it. Instead she was disappointed again. This time because she thought it was fate bringing people with so much in common together. I think it also might have had something to do with the fact that my sister also lived in Orange County and listened to the same talk shows that this woman did. But the reality that I initiated conversation with this woman, after making sure she wasn't wearing a wedding ring and not knowing she had a boy-friend, meant that I had crossed no line of impropriety.

According to my sister, when this woman asked me if I ever got to Orange County, she was apparently letting me know that the relationship with her boyfriend was just a temporary one. And, of course, if she didn't have a boyfriend, she would have not had a reason to visit Santa Fe and I would not have met her. All of this reasoning and explanation led me to believe that these impermanent relationships not only waste time for the people in them, but also send confusing signals to those of us who might present a more long lasting offer.

Another point my sister made was that at the dating level there are different degrees of commitment. There are those who recognize up front their temporary status which allows that it will not be forever. And, there are those growing and learning relationships that take time to develop and could eventually last forever. You certainly don't want to become involved with a person who jumps from one relationship to another in either case. To become involved with a person who is interested in breaking up a relationship for their own benefit, is also a mistake, since that will just cause future concerns.

Needless to say, "temporary," whether as a perception from within or outside a relationship, presents a confusing guide to all those involved, and ultimately causes missed opportunities. While it may be difficult being alone, at least you have a more capable environment to find yourself and someone else in the future.

There is another side to the problems caused by forming temporary relationships. My friend Bob, who was recently divorced, became involved in a situation which seemed to be one of these win/win deals, for everyone involved. As a student of human nature, I wasn't so sure.

Bob who is a good looking guy approaching 40, liked to go

out country/western dancing with his friends on Friday nights. One night he met Suzy, and they really had a good time dancing with each other. The next Friday night, they met again and spent most of their time talking but still enjoyed the dancing that they did. Suzy was a very sexy looking lady, who had been divorced for many years, and Bob guessed her age at not much over 45.

At Suzy's invitation Bob went home with her that night and they exchanged pleasantries and intimacies. Before he left to go home, she asked him if he was dating anyone special. He told her that he wasn't, and didn't want to get involved with anyone. He liked to go out with different women for different reasons.

She then asked him if he had ever dated someone for just the purpose of having sex. He replied, "Not intentionally." Suzy then explained to Bob, that the only thing she was really missing in her life right then, was having sexual fulfillment. Maybe she and Bob could have a casual sexual relationship, and maybe even go country/western dancing every once in awhile. She assured him that there would be no strings attached, and that she didn't mind him going out with other women as well. Bob said that he would have to think about it. Not thinking with his mind, as he should have, he ended up, of course, agreeing.

Bob invited me to go dancing, on one of those Friday nights. I reluctantly agreed, even though I didn't know how to dance country/western. Bob assured me that there were plenty of women there who would be more than happy to teach me. Besides, he wanted me to meet this woman he was seeing.

*When I met Suzy, I agreed that she was a very sensual look-
ing lady, and she looked somewhat older than Bob. We had a
good time, although Bob never got to talk to anyone new, or
even some of the women that he knew, because he was with
Suzy all night, and she was definitely clinging. The next day
he asked me what I thought about her, and I said that I
thought she was really nice. When he mentioned that I probably didn't think she was his type, I honestly told him that
was my perception, but his decision.*

*Bob then related the story of their special kind of relation-
ship, mentioning that the sex was terrific, there were no
strings attached, and that the best part was that he could
also go out with other women. When I asked what other
women he was going out with, he informed me that he
hadn't been out with anybody else since he met Suzy. He
said he just didn't have the time. He said that the amazing thing was, that they don't really have that much in
common, but between the sex and the dancing, that took
up all their time together.*

*I guess it was my wry smile, pensive look, or maybe the
shaking of my head that prompted him to ask, "You don't
think this is a very good idea, do you?" I told him that it
might be all right for him, but if it was me, I would be
thinking that I was too consumed with fulfilling one of
my needs and might be missing out on satisfying all the
others with someone else. He mentioned that I shouldn't
forget that there was also some dancing going on. I also
mentioned that typically, after a while, there will be
strings attached. It might be different in Suzy's case,
although, she did seem to be somewhat possessive of him
that night.*

179

Since he was already spending all his free time with her, he wasn't experiencing the freedom to date other women that he thought was the best part of the deal.

Bob felt that maybe I didn't understand that it was just a short-term arrangement, and pointed out that according to Suzy, her friends thought it was perfectly all right and a great idea. I explained, that for her friends it might be, because Suzy's getting everything out of the relationship that she wants or needs, and that if he feels the same way, fine. I felt that most people, because of their natures, could not handle that type of relationship. I knew I couldn't, and would worry about the real agenda, if the woman I was with said she could.

Well, Bob proved me wrong, and for the next few months saw Suzy frequently and exclusively. That is until he met another woman who was more interested in going out with Bob than staying home and having sex. But, that was okay with him, because he was starting to get burnt out with all that sex, and of course, the dancing involved. When he told Suzy that he couldn't see her as much, she became upset and mentioned that she thought that they had an agreement. He explained that he wanted to date other women, and that he would still see her occasionally. She told him to forget it; it was either all or nothing. He chose the nothing.

For the next month, she called him at home pleading with him to reconsider. She called him at work, even though he told her that she could never do that. When he didn't answer his home phone, she left urgent messages. She went to all the bars and nightclubs he was known to frequent, asking his friends if they had seen him. When she finally reached him, she suggested that they just see each other occasionally with no strings attached. He told her that he couldn't do that anymore. She became furious and continued the pursuit. Fortunately, while all this was going on he had moved and was also required to be out of town with his job. Eventually Suzy gave up. Bob likened the end of his adventure to the movie "Fatal Attraction." He never admitted that I was right, and I never said, "I told you so."

He made a decision to keep busy so he didn't have to think about being lonely, and seemingly had all his needs fulfilled by going out every night and dating different women. His many new friends didn't remind him of his failed marriage, and his old friends knew enough not to help him remember. He is coping by not dealing with it.

Bob is just delaying his healing process though, and it may take him a long time before his life is set in a place where he is ready to begin searching again. But, he will be able to begin when he is ready. Of course, he has to be careful about some of the decisions he makes. He certainly won't be thinking about his past problems while he is busy correcting his current mistakes. It would be so much better though, to make the right decisions. He may not be moving forward, but at least he won't be losing ground.

For those who choose to tough it out by themselves, rather than seek the false sense of security of a temporary relationship, that first year alone needs to be more structured and busy; provided it's involved in a process of healing. **To keep busy just to forget, postpones memories for another time.** It's a time to measure not only what, but who can provide the assistance and positive reinforcement necessary to mend the wounds of the past.

Those family and friends can be depended on for support and comfort, unless they become a continual sounding board for all the issues of the recent separation. Searching out new people and experiences that can only provide a method to forget, just postpones the inevitable. It is rather those, who will only not force them to remember, who will provide dependable relief. The real comfort comes from the realization that someone understands and cares about their pain. They're the ones who know that, at some point for healing to occur, there has to be a relief from the memories of the past. New friends don't offer those remembrances. They're interested in who you are now and where you are going. They take your mind off past entanglements and offer a focus on the present. New friends of both sexes allow interchanges that probably hadn't been experienced toward the end of a relationship. They offer intimate, and intelligent conversations, joint interests and caring and sharing; all without the commitment or pressure of romance. These new friends are not there to replace or to defer responsibilities; they are there to help you not be as lonely.

> *I don't recall having a lot of friends while I was in a relationship. Sure, there were the old friends who lived out of state, and the friends that I would see occasionally at the legislature, or have a chance encounter with. But I never had any real close friends that I just hung around with. I was always too focused on my relationship. Maybe it was because I thought I was with my best friend and really didn't need anyone else. Maybe it was because I was so busy that I didn't have time to socialize with anyone else.*

I now have more friends than I have ever had in my life. They are so different, which makes my life very interesting, and so enriched. The only thing that they probably all have in common is their sense of humor, and even that is so different with each one of them. I guess another thing they have in common, is that they are all good people; caring and giving people.

Every possible interest that I could have can somehow be participated in or complemented by one of my friends. We go out to dinner, play golf, play tennis, go to movies, concerts, travel, go to parties, and we double date. We play games, sit around and talk, and help each other out in business. We work together, and we work out together. We deal with our present, dream about the future and help each other make plans for both.

Each friend has different interests, which allows me to stay busy participating in diverse activities. Strangely, at least to me, most of them are women. Not all of them, thank goodness. Some are married and some are single. Some are younger and some are older. Some I talk to every day and some once a week. Some live where I live, others in different states, and even some in other countries. They are all good friends and wonderful company. They are also the types of friendships that could even be shared in a future relationship, because we care for each other and will be there for each other's happiness. We've been there for each other before.

While co-dependent types are more apt to search out instant gratification, all of us are prone to the effects of loneliness, and will tend to seek companionship to alleviate them. It would be great if we could find friends to provide at least the companionship. Then there is a lessening of the sense of urgency to alleviate the effects of just being alone. We have to be careful, not to get romantically involved, until we deal with the issues of our past and "who" we are in the present. A year and a day is a long time not to get involved, but if we visualize our time alone as being fulfilling and productive, it will make more sense.

Piano, Piano

There is a lot more to deal with this first year than just confronting old issues. As you begin to move forward improving your life, every day becomes less painful than the day before. There are new issues and new experiences that somehow have no relationship to the negatives that have just happened in your life. Not only are there new friends to associate with, but new places to visit, new job opportunities, new activities and interests. Physically, there's the new you; every day changing, every week improving, every month becoming more confident. You'll have a new look to be proud of. You will have also discovered the inner you during that first year. You finally get to know yourself and the goodness that dwells within. It will be a "you" who is finally able to blossom forth, no longer burdened by a bad relationship.

There are the new expressions of a body, mind and soul; feelings of joy replacing despair, trust emerging where deception existed, and confidence flowing where fear resided. Your surrounding environment looks different. Your home, clothes, car, and all those things that you changed, express your tastes. There will also be the attitude that becomes an expression of freedom.

There is so much that can be accomplished in one year and one day that will dictate who you are and who you will spend the rest of your life with. At first, it seems like a long time, but after you get into it and see the distance you have to go, it sometimes doesn't seem long enough. For those of us who have the courage and the commitment, there will be ample time to do what must be done.

It takes at least a year to forgive yourself and others and to re-place old memories with new. It takes that long to substitute hurts with joy; to change despair to hope; and to restore your commitment to love. Just one extra day can't do it all, either. But that one-day, after that worthwhile year of accomplishment, will be the new beginning and its reward will be the opportunity of sharing of your love with someone who has waited all year for you to appear.

You will appear as if emerging from beneath a waterfall with your negative aura being erased, allowing for freedom to begin again—on **the other side**.

There is an old Italian saying that they use in Venezuela, that describes an attitude toward accomplishment. It presents a sense that great achievements just take a little more time. It is *"Piano, piano, si va lontano;"* little by little you can go very far.

185

10

Physician Heal Thyself

We learn, in the most difficult times of our lives, what we most enjoy in the best times. To experience mistakes, and the heartache and despair that are their companion, without learning is just allowing for more mistakes. But learning, especially from those errors in life that seem to drive your sprit lower than it's ever been, can in the long run offer more benefit than you can ever imagine. All those important things of life that we so many times take for granted, can be missed and longed for because of their value that is only now realized. Sometimes, the best way to discover joy is to experience sadness; the best way to understand integrity is to encounter mistrust; and the best way to appreciate the importance of sharing love is to experience its loss.

While it may be comforting to assume that life is totally out of our control, it might be worthwhile to examine our effect on our environment, as well. As professed in our legal system, it would be beneficial to examine our own contributory negligence to the failure of the relationship.

We all want to be able to blame someone else for our current predicament, and in reality there is probably reason for blame. The longer we dwell on pointing fingers somewhere else however, the longer it is going to take us to improve ourselves and increase our self-worth. It will prove to be, once again, a waste of valuable time. We must learn from the mistakes we made, no matter how minor we feel they were in the failing of our union.

Figure out, not so much what we could have done to save the relationship, since at this point will likely prove counterproductive, but rather what we could have done to just be better, ourselves. Not to dwell on the past, but to learn for the future.

Those we point fingers at are gone. They should have no more influence on our lives. We allow them to continue to be negative factors in our lives by reminding ourselves of the hurt and pain they caused. They need to be taken out of the equation of what happened and what's going to happen to our lives. That usually just leaves us on the other side of the equal sign.

We need to use our past mistakes to figure out why we behaved the way we did. There are usually plenty of excuses out there that will minimize our responsibility, and that's okay, because some of them are legitimate. Bad behavior, however, should not be excused. The NEW recipient of our love will not deserve that. And while ending a relationship over a cup of coffee is an example of extraordinary behavior, the use of a "handy pistola" or similar conduct would be an example of bad behavior, under any circumstance.

> *Mark was a business associate of mine who was good looking, had a great sense of humor and personality, and was smart and very athletic. His wife equally matched his attributes. In public they appeared great together.*
>
> *Every once in awhile, Mark would have mood swings becoming very quiet. When I asked him one time if there was something wrong he said he was having problems at home. He mentioned that he and his wife were having problems, and whenever they had a disagreement, he would get so angry he wouldn't talk to her for weeks.*

He said he tried not to allow his personal life to spill over into work, but sometimes it was unavoidable. When I asked him if he considered counseling, he told me that he didn't believe in exposing all your problems to a stranger. Besides, eventually they start talking again and everything seems all right for a while.

After about a year of ups and downs in their relationship Mark confided to me that he found out his wife had an affair with a married man. He said it lasted about a month, but that she denied it ever having happened. He said that their marriage had now disintegrated to the point that neither one would speak to the other, and they would avoid each other as much as possible. After about six months of this, Mark agreed to go to a counselor. It was there that his wife admitted to having the affair. Mark was devastated and couldn't believe that his wife could hurt him as badly as she did. His wife appeared equally remorseful, but at that point the marriage could not be saved.

It was years after his divorce that Mark finally met his match. They seemed perfect together. Mark really seemed to regain all the happiness he had lost. After about six months of dating, they had already talked about getting married.

At a party, I happened to ask Mark's fiancée how they were both doing. She said that meeting Mark was the best thing that ever happened in her life, and that he was really a good person.

She mentioned how she really enjoyed being with his friends and family. She then asked how we all got along when we worked together. I told her that it was really enjoyable, and that whenever we worked together we always made sure we had fun. She asked if when we had a disagreement and Mark got angry, did he ever stop talking with us for a few days. She said that has been happening lately to her.

She and Mark never got married, and when they broke up, he said it was because he could never trust a woman again after what his ex-wife did to him. When his friends suggested that he go to a counselor to deal with his feelings and relationships, he said that he didn't need a counselor because there was nothing wrong with him.

The best way to determine bad behavior is to visualize a life with a different person; a person not void of faults, but a nice, normal (normal, not perfect) person, with no hidden agendas and a commitment to love as strong as yours. Visualize an honest, caring person, who has needs and wants and who will experience ups and downs and have problems like we all have: A person who will encounter pressure and require compassion now and then.

Take this seemingly normal relationship and determine if your actions will reflect your previous mistakes and actions of your failed relationship. Figure out what makes you tick and react the way you do. Find out why—and it may take some professional help—you react to some situations that you find threatening or offensive, or why you don't react when other circumstance present themselves. Before you can explain to someone else who you are, you need to understand yourself and what motivates you to react to circumstances in certain ways.

It seemed finally, that I had met my match after years of hoping, and praying, with a little bit of searching thrown in. It was one of those chance encounters that I had experienced quite a few times before, but the difference was that now there was ample time for us to get to know each other.

It was at a convention with thousands of people in attendance that we crossed paths crossing a street. We smiled at each other, exchanged pleasantries and talked for a little while. We met that night for dinner with a group of friends and met the next night at a reception. From that point on we were hardly ever apart. We went for walks and danced the night away, and talked until the wee hours of the morning. In a few days we knew how special we were to each other. The next day after the convention she came to visit me, even though we lived in different states. The next week I went to visit her. And so it went on that way for five weeks, until I sent her a dozen roses the day after I left her home. She wasn't at work to receive them for two days, without offering an explanation. The next weekend I didn't hear from her at all, but received an e-mail a few days later asking how I had been. At that point I responded that I didn't think I could trust her and never wanted to see her again.

In my conversations over the next month with a few friends, mostly women, it was pointed out to me that I might have overreacted or at least acted hastily. I then called her and left a message for her to call me if she was still interested. She called back that night as if nothing had ever happened, although she did mention that she thought my message was rather strange and just assumed that I had found someone else. We agreed to give our relationship another shot and planned to take a trip in a couple of weeks to a resort for a few days and maybe even try to get together that weekend just for a day or two if possible. The

191

day before the weekend, I had finally made arrangements for my trip, only to be told by her that she already had plans. Once again I was ready to break off the relationship, but realized that maybe I was expecting too much and to rather go with the flow and see where it takes me as suggested by my friends.

We went to the resort and were having a great time. I had never felt more comfortable with someone and each experience seemed so much more worthwhile being with her. Everything seemed perfect except when she had a little too much to drink. I told her that I had experienced being embarrassed before by similar behavior in another relationship, and that I had hoped out of consideration for me that she wouldn't drink so much. It wasn't just her drinking that caused a major problem as much as it was her lack of memory, her reactions to me, and her abusive tone that were caused by her drinking. Eventually, one thing led to another and I began thinking that I was not only being embarrassed in public but was being hurt by someone I cared for. I went on the attack and lashed out at her in an attempt to be as embarrassing and hurtful as she was. That was the end of our relationship and I never saw her again.

Immediately after our confrontation, I realized that once again I had overreacted. I also realized that I was not only admonishing her for her behavior but also for behaviors that occurred in another relationship long ago. I had lumped her transgressions together with those that I had experienced with another person whose behavior caused a relationship to fail and deemed the same result was surely evident. I became exasperated when I realized that I couldn't control the actions of someone that I viewed as acting unacceptable. I felt my feelings were being diminished because they were not being matched in intensity or concern. I was demanding in return, all that I felt I was giving, from someone I had in reality, just met. We hardly knew each other, and yet, I was deep in a relationship that to her was just beginning. She had entered my life at a perfect time for me, but maybe it wasn't a perfect time for her. Of course, to me that didn't matter, because I was self-centered enough to think that no matter where she was, she should be at the same place I was. Because she wasn't, meant that she was taking advantage of my concern for her happiness, which was an expression of my falling in love. It was actually this feeling of love that betrayed me and caused me to be so demanding, bringing with it the seemingly overreaction to her treatment of me.

I have placed so much value on the love that I have to give, which I certainly believe is justified, that I feel deceived when it is not reciprocated; and reciprocated at the same time it is being offered. How realistic is that? Well, I'm sure that it very rarely happens that way. And, when it doesn't, I don't give it a chance. It also seems that during my involvement in a relationship, that I believe I appear to be of perfect motivation, but through analysis after the relationship ends, I find myself at least as imperfect as my partner.

This story in my life doesn't have a particularly happy ending, but rather an ending that provided for a valuable lesson. I now know the "what" and "why" of my behavior. I also realize that while the root causes of my overreactions may be the sincerity of my feelings, the demands of reciprocity must be tempered or they will never be allowed to be experienced. And, the "all or nothing" approach to a relationship usually results in nothing. Partners in a relationship don't have to grow immediately together, just as long as they grow together eventually. I have learned that not only must I still openly express my feelings, but that my only expectation should be that my partner expresses their feelings to me, so that I know whether or not we have a chance to grow eventually together.

We all have idiosyncrasies that we need to think about and deal with, so at least we can understand the cause of our behavior, and at best, change with the help of a new partner through communication. However, before we can ever hope to totally heal the wounds caused by someone else, we must first heal ourselves of those self-inflicted wounds buried deep in our being.

11

Who Do You Think You Are?

Beyond just wanting someone, anyone, to comfort us in our time of need, we have a pretty good idea of what qualities and characteristics a person should have to best match up with ourselves. We know from our experience what worked and didn't work. While it's never a good idea to generalize when dealing with individuals, a pretty good indication can be obtained as to what type of person would provide the best probabilities for a successful relationship. While physical attraction may be important, and intellectual compatibility might be necessary, and spiritual beliefs could prove significant, finding someone who feels as we do is crucial. It is crucial not only for us, but also for the person we are seeking to share love with. That way, when matches are made, it will be with two people who react with emotion in similar ways.

After Peter and Heather dated for about a month, her father died. He had lived in another state, and since his divorce from Heather's mother, he had remarried and started another family. Heather had gone to see him every summer when she was younger, but as she grew older the visits became less frequent and finally stopped.

She mentioned, rather matter of factly, to Peter that her father had died and that she was going to the funeral. According to Peter, there were no tears and no regret expressed. When she returned she told Peter that she felt out of place at the funeral, since she was the only person from her family there. She mentioned that her father's new family seemed to grieve quite a bit and must have loved him very much. There was no emotion coming from her at all. Peter was curious about how she could react that way, but was told that it wasn't that big a deal since she hadn't seen him in so many years. The subject of her father's death was never mentioned again.

Peter remembered becoming emotionally spent over the death of his mother when he was a young man, and how much he grieved whenever an aunt or uncle died, even if he hadn't seen them in quite some time. He was very sensitive in that way and felt that a role in his history, a part of his family, had been taken away. He always missed them and grieved accordingly. But maybe, because of the relationship she had with her father, it was different for Heather.

Peter told this story to me as he was explaining when he knew that he was going to give Heather the divorce she wanted. It was when his father died. He died in Peter's arms and his wife just stood there without a tear, without a word of consolation. She knew Peter's father very well. They were friends and seemed to enjoy each other's company. But, no emotion at all.

At the time, Peter longed for someone to hug him, to hold him and tell him that they were there for him. It seems no matter how grown up some people get, they still need the kind of comfort they received as a child. But there was nothing, just a blank stare.

The best way to know that someone understands your grief is to find someone that grieves like you do. And, relating to joy and sadness really requires a sharing of those emotions. This emotional compatibility allows for the communication necessary to feel the moods and experience the spirit. It provides a oneness in the understanding of disposition, tendencies, and temperament. It gives reason to emotional experience. In the successful realities of relationships, however, it makes up only part of what is necessary to feel like each other. It is the sensitivities to things like honor, pride, compassion and ultimately love that will provide the complete equation of feelings that determine whether equals will match. Those feelings go beyond emotion to a person's character to become a view of life. When you find the person that feels and sees the same view, you've met your match.

In this search for your soul mate you must understand that for you to find the right person for yourself is not enough. To ensure that the right chemistry exists to form and hold that continuing bond, you must be your soul mate's right person, as well. If the fulfillments only flow one way, you've wasted not only your valuable time and effort, but also someone else's.

Love doesn't happen with attractions, infatuation does. Love happens with shared feelings that grow from the commitment of two people. The energy that they create in this accomplishment is beyond anything that an individual can produce. Visually, it would appear as two forces flowing toward each other, and when meeting, blending to create an explosion of feelings—love. So, no matter how many of your needs are fulfilled by this other person, unless you can provide an equal flow of fulfillments, there will not be the blending necessary to promote love. As deeply and desperately as you want to share your love, it would be a mistake, as you probably already know and have experienced, to share it with someone who doesn't feel, who doesn't love, like you do.

Know Thyself

So, how are you ever going to know? Well first, you need to be honest with yourself. You need to know yourself, so that when that person, searching just like you, finds you, you'll both know what you have found. In other words, when two people with the same intentions meet in all honesty, they'll know if there's a chance that they are meant for each other. The same values and the same criteria are going to be used in each of their evaluations.

It is therefore, just as important to decide if you are right for someone else, as if someone is right for you. It's not only fair and reasonable, but it's critical to providing an environment where your love for each other has a chance to grow and prosper. Too many times people assume that if it's just good for them, it's good for the relationship.

That kind of selfish attitude can only succeed for a little while, until the other partner realizes that their concerns aren't being considered in the scheme of the relationship. The explosion of everlasting love can never occur under these selfish conditions. Of course, we could always change, or cause someone else to change to fit our criteria. Oh yeah, and I'm sure we've all been successful at that in the past. People, who are *Suddenly Single,* could easily belong to a Changers Anonymous group. There are many things that we believe we can change about ourselves, but it would be foolish to even think that we can change someone else.

Change The Oil First

Even changing ourselves is difficult at best, not because there isn't enough desire, or experience, or even sufficient help, but due to habit. No matter how hard we try to alter who we are, unless we understand ourselves, we cannot honestly even decide whether we want to change, or what to change. We must first figure out who we are. We then need to find out where these qualities and behaviors are rooted in our being, and how they got there. Then, we should ascertain what we cannot change, or refuse to change, and what we have the capability to change, and want to change.

Of course, it is important to conduct this analysis prior to meeting up with a future soul mate, so that you know who you are when someone conducts their own examination of you. It is also important to know at that time, not only what you want to change about yourself, but what you **have** changed about yourself, and that takes time. It's like selling a less than perfect car and telling someone that if they buy it, you'll get it tuned up, change the oil, correct that pinging sound, fix the wiring, and check it out so that it runs perfectly. Someone would be crazy to buy a car without having those things done first to see if it improves the performance. And yet, there are people out there who are desperate for accessible transportation, who would believe that what you promise is also what you can deliver. Sometimes, there are things that you just can't fix. **The road to the relationship junkyard is filled with good intentions.**

The only fair solution is to fix what you can first, so that you know exactly what you're selling and buyers know exactly what there going to get. That way, your desperation to sell, and their desperation to buy, doesn't become the reason for the contract. The term "as is" should have an even a greater meaning when applied to people. "Caveat emptor"—buyer beware.

Before you even consider putting a car up for sale, you need to visually and mechanically figure out what you are dealing with. You need to check it out for any body damage, and whether or not fixing it may make it more attractive to a potential buyer. You know that the first impression is important, and making it look good on the outside may be the easiest change to make.

Then you need to take it for a spin, with a careful observation as to any faults that exist that you might have just become used to over time. Of course, every car that has been around for a while performs differently. Sometimes it performs the way it does because that was the way it was designed and manufactured. Sometimes it behaves different from similar cars because of the way it was used and the terrain it experienced. But, you have to determine how well it is running, if you are satisfied with its performance, and whether somebody would want to buy it. Now, if you're not completely satisfied, there is only so much you can or may even want to do. The value you place on it will determine the kind of buyer you will market it to. **We can't always get what we want, but we can usually get what we deserve.** But, above all, being ethical demands that you be honest with a potential buyer, so that they know exactly what they are getting.

Selling a car and selling ourselves to the potential buyer of our love may seem like a simplistic analogy, but the basic principles have to be there for both to provide for a fair and successful "sale." Since we have previously dealt with how we can improve our marketability through the change of our physical appearance, let's now look under the hood.

What Appears To Be

While it may seem easier to limit our examination to our flaws, since chances are that's what others and even ourselves typically highlighted in the past, it would certainly serve us equally to examine our positive qualities. Being *Suddenly Single* may cause you to perceive a decrease in your real value, and diminishment of your worth. It may prompt you to confuse your strengths and weaknesses. That's why it is important to look objectively at your qualities, removed from the subjective causes of your feelings. While your goodness, trust, caring, and integrity, may have allowed you to be vulnerable to hurt, it is just those qualities that will allow you to experience and share joy. While your anger, resentment, suspicion, and fear may have permitted protective barriers to provide a shelter from pain, it is just those feelings that will bar you from the future of shared happiness.

It is sometimes beneficial to observe in other people those same qualities that you are exploring in yourself. Do you find people with all those "strengths" of anger, resentment, suspicion and fear, attractive? How easy is it to observe appealing qualities behind the barriers created by those "strengths"? What kind of future do you imagine this person will experience? What kind of future do you imagine this person's mate will experience?

When you encounter someone who exudes goodness, do you think that person can help make others happy? When you find someone you can trust, does it make you want to share the dreams of your life with them? If you notice someone always sincerely caring for others, don't you imagine a person who will care for you and you for them? Sure, these people open themselves up to hurt. But chances are, if their qualities are noticeable to you, they haven't allowed themselves to be frightened to raising barriers of protection because they also possess another key quality—courage.

When we succumb to the fear, are controlled by the anger, hang on to the resentment, and live with suspicion, we are just letting everyone know that we don't have the courage to show how good we really are. How important is it to figure out what really are our strengths and weaknesses? Well, that would depend whether or not we believe that the person searching for their soul mate cares if their future is going to be filled with open happiness or closed despair. Will that one person we have been waiting for, buy into where we are today to determine if we're worth pursuing for tomorrow? If we allow our strengths to be equated with negatives, and our weaknesses equated with positives, we will probably attract people with the same view, or maybe, somebody who pities us and wants to commit their life to this project of change.

My friend Barry told me how he was set up on the blind date from hell. He should have known, because this woman matchmaker friend of ours filled him in ahead of time on who he was going out with. The first thing she said was that Patty—the date from hell—told her that she took her husband for everything he had and that she was working on having him lose his job. She said that Barry didn't have to worry about Patty dwelling on positive memories of her ex-husband, because she took all his belongings and pictures in the back yard and burned them, and then took the ashes and dumped them all over the inside of his car while it was parked at his job. She also said that Patty called the police and reported her husband had abused her, while fortunately for him at the time of the alleged abuse, he was in the emergency room getting glass removed from his scalp from a mixing bowl she threw at him.

Barry asked why he would ever want to go out with someone like that, and our friend told him that she was absolutely beautiful, had a great shape, was passionate and wanted to start dating again. While she was a very strong-willed woman, she had a great personality. She was very successful in her business, had a take-charge kind of attitude and would probably be a lot of fun and interesting to date. Besides, all those things happened a year ago. She was a lot different now. Her husband was a real jerk and probably deserved the way she treated him. Our friend advised him to take it easy with her and he could probably turn her around.

Well, Barry not wanting to let any opportunity to slip by, especially with the dating drought he was experiencing, decided to give it a try. He had been through a rough divorce himself, with his wife cheating on him and stealing his savings, so he could sympathize with her anger. But he too had been divorced about a year, and couldn't remember the last time he expressed any anger or resentment. After a few months of harboring all that resentment, he decided that he was going to wish everybody well and move on. So maybe Patty had reached a point of similar desire.

They decided to meet at a bar, which was probably a bad idea, since the nervousness of their first meeting caused them to drink too much. No doubt she was beautiful, but the more she drank, the uglier she talked. When she asked Barry about his divorce, he said that he would rather not talk about it. She then started talking about "you men" and "your younger women", and "you never want to talk about it." Even after Barry mentioned that his wife had cheated on him, she still continued about how untrustworthy men were.

Then she proceeded to tell Barry all that she had done and was continuing to do to her ex-husband, and then asked him if he wanted to know why. When he said "okay," she told him how her husband had an affair with a younger woman. Barry tried to lighten things up by saying, "Is that all he did?" Well, needless to say she came unglued. She begin screaming at the top of her lungs all kinds of nasty things directed at Barry, whose words "I was just kidding" were never heard because of the uproar. He pleaded with her to please put down the margarita pitcher that she was waving menacingly in front of his face. The bartender, waitress and customers were all stunned with no one making a move to come over and calm her down. She slammed down the pitcher, yelled at Barry, "You're all the same and you're never going to get any of this," with her hands pointing to her body.

She stormed out of the bar leaving Barry sitting there stunned. He sat there for a while absorbing all the stares and whispers from the other tables in the bar. He then began to think what might have happened to his car in the parking lot, and thought at least she didn't know what kind of car he drove. Maybe she just did something to that Jaguar convertible parked next to his.

Upon arriving home he immediately called our matchmaker friend and told her of his encounter with the poltergeist. She said that she had just gotten off the phone with Patty. Apparently, this was the first date that Patty had been on since her breakup and she has been stewing in resentment for a year. She admitted that while her behavior may have appeared a "little extreme," she felt the insensitivity of Barry to her ordeal warranted such a response. After our friend explained that Barry had more or less gone through a similar traumatic experience, and had let go of his anger a long time ago, Patty apologized. She said that Barry was the first man that she was even able to talk to about her divorce, and that the anxiety of doing so, coupled with all those margaritas, just sent her off the deep end. She told our friend that maybe she could make it up to him in the future by having him over for dinner.

When Barry arrived at my house to vividly describe his twilight zone encounter, he made me promise to shoot him before ever letting him go over to Patty's house for dinner. He kept muttering something about making sure they test the ashes for his DNA. I have been told quite a few stories about how someone's anger and resentment have turned off a prospective match, but Barry's story was certainly an extreme case. As he was describing his date with Patty to me, he said that when he first saw her, she was one of the most physically beautiful women he had ever seen. By the end of the date, he said he was sure he was with the most unattractive woman he had ever encountered. "Beauty lies in the eyes of the beholder." So it is how we are portrayed to others, rather then how we appear to ourselves that will determine our attraction.

So, now we understand how our observations allow us to see how we are being observed. It's like self-oriented comparative shopping. Of course, just because we understand what is being observed doesn't mean that we have the capability or even the desire to change the perception. We may find that the qualities we exhibit are there by the design of our birth, or were manufactured by our upbringing.

We're Full of Soup

To know "who" you really are means an exploration to the deepest recesses of your being to figure out where you came from and how you developed. For those who find difficulty with developing clearly defined observations, it is always best to invest in a professional, to sort out any hidden issues or motivations. Whether or not you can or should be changed can only be determined once an analysis of all the various interrelated aspects of your qualities and characteristics have been considered.

To begin this journey, the best place to start is at our beginning. It begins with our design, our genes, our DNA. That's what makes us unique. Our genetic makeup determines who we start out to be, and in many cases who we end up with. In the beginning, we are only products of our parents, and in deference to scientific consideration, we are like the ingredients of a ladle from pot of alphabet soup. Sometimes we get more of certain letters than others, and sometimes we get more letters.

While each ladle is different, the recipe for the soup is clearly a family recipe, handed down from generation to generation. That ladle of soup from that particular pot will be unlike any other scoop from any other pot. There may be similar recipes out there, but the closest comparison of your "scoop," will have to come from the same pot. How does all this help us figure out how and who we've become? Or is it as my Aunt Millie used to say about my strange concepts, "It sounds like you're full of soup"?

To find out, we need to first look to our parents to see what their recipe was. Who were these people, these contributors to those different letters of our soup? Well, they had strengths and weaknesses and displayed certain qualities. They had their own disposition, inclinations, aptitudes, and temperament. If we grew up with our parents, we were given a glimpse of their unique personality, their psyche, their spirit, and their soul. And while sometimes their initial contribution seems diminished through time and experience, they will always be the designers of our being.

It must be understood that this design is not necessarily an equal composite, although it could be. The determination of your genetic makeup comes from which one of your parents contributed what letters to your ladle, and sometimes even their individual contributions when mixed together spell out words for you that aren't in either one's vocabulary.

Let's look at these people, from the point of view of what they meant to us. We must always remember that there are so many other factors that have been added to determine our current being, but as we have observed in others and even ourselves, sometimes we can see that "he's his father's son," or "she's her mother's daughter." It's the characteristics that have been inherited that we're interested in right now, albeit they commonly blend with the learned behaviors that we were taught growing up with our parents.

When I began my own self-analysis, both my parents had already died. My mother died at too early an age for me even to remember all the details of her personality. My father died more recently, and with much more vivid and profound insights from which to draw.

I remember my father when he was my age, from when I was a kid growing up to early adulthood. He was a hard worker, dedicated to his wife and family. He was a strict disciplinarian who decided what the rules were to follow, and if you broke them he got really mad and you were punished. In today's society, his punishment toward me would definitely be called child abuse. He had a temper that lost control whenever he lost control of whoever or whatever he was dealing with. His rules delineated clearly the difference between right and wrong, with specific highlights given to respect and honor. He was a tough guy who wasn't afraid of anybody or anything. No matter how difficult a problem was, he would somehow, some way find a solution.

His love of his wife and family were extraordinary, and the devotion to those he loved had no limits. He gave so much, but also demanded in return. His demands were focused on what he felt he had a right to expect, given all that he provided. While all the loyalty, love, and respect seemed fair, every once in awhile, the demands seemed extreme and controlling. When I look back, I see my father as a man who had to be in control, not just because he deserved it, but because he was so responsible, he feared that the dreams he had for us all might disappear if he weren't.

His love and devotion to his wife began when he first met her and didn't leave up to the time of his death, 25 years after she died. He prayed for her every day and didn't fear death, because he truly believed that he would be with her when he died. What kept him alive all those years was his devotion to my sister and me.

Growing up with my father was an observance of the absolutes of authority, respect, the honor of family, and the benefits of a strong work ethic. These are things that I could have learned from him, but over time realized there was a genetic compatibility. In so many ways, it wasn't just what I observed that formed who I was, but rather what I was inclined to do with the benefit of that observance.

Our later years together provided me with a mentor and best friend who taught me the lessons of life. He had mellowed in those years, and never lost his temper. I guess his thinking was that when you've lost the most important thing in your life, why bother getting angry at all the little things. The real lesson was, to take what you've got and make the best of it; to take who you are and be the best you can.

When something negative would happen that he couldn't do anything about, he called it "water under the bridge," and would say that if you can't retrieve it, let it go. And then he would always say that when something breaks, "don't just fix it, make it better." Sometimes, I think he changed his attitude, not just because of his experiences, but because he wanted to give an example to his children about what was important in life. He showed us that he could take the inclinations that he passed on to us and, even at his late stage of life, change the few that needed it, for the better. Maybe my father observed in me some of his tendencies and changed those few he needed to correct, while I'm sure the others made him proud of who he was and what he passed on.

And we did learn by his example. Early on, I learned to control my temper and to always think before I act. I first had to recognize that I had a temper, and then figure out where it came from. It was clearly a letter from my father's contribution to that cup of soup. The inclination that it sprouted from however, was not necessarily bad. My father was a very demonstrative, emotional person, which was okay until you hooked it up with frustrating anger.

The inclination was a passionate response to negative stimuli, but what I observed in my father and myself was an emotional outburst, justified because there was no thought of consequences or morality associated with it.

209

> *When I realized that by not thinking before I acted was stupid, hurtful, and just caused me more anxiety because of the resulting consequences, I began to think. Because of habit over time, I now never lose my temper. I do still however, allow myself passionate interaction, but always in a self-controlled, thoughtful setting.*

I realized that we have all these predispositions and tendencies, that through habit we can either foster or diminish. I also realized that **what we do habitually will eventually determine who we will become.** When we have a genetic inclination to harmful behavior, that is reinforced through observation and fostered by habit, we have to change the habit or allow it to determine who we are. Of course, first we have to recognize that it is harmful, and we can do that through the same observation.

There are so many things in my father's ladle of soup that appeared in my cup. I saw inclinations of honor, respect, hard work, discipline, passion, temper, authority, persistence, daring, and a host of other strengths and some weaknesses in those letters he passed on. The letters that shined the brightest though, were his tendencies toward commitment and love. I learned their expression from observing his life, but their intensity had to come from within.

> *Of course, my mom's ladle was equally as full, but unfortunately not as observable. She shared so many of my father's inclinations that I am sure that is what attracted them to each other. It was almost like they were two peas in a pod when you examined her inclinations toward honor, respect, love, commitment, and especially the value of family. There were always both sides of their families at our house all the time. She had a wonderful sense of humor and we used to love to make each other laugh. Once when*

a neighbor lady came over and was bragging about the good grades her son got, especially compared to mine, I came in and said something funny. My mother grabbed hold of me and said, "Here's my little clown." She told me that we both knew how smart I was, so we didn't have to show off to other people. She didn't have to show other people either—there wasn't a pretentious bone in her body.

She was very proud of herself, though. She was extremely intelligent and always had the confidence to express her opinion, in a soft spoken, slow, thoughtful tone, on a regular basis. She was also proud of her family and always let us know that. She always dressed stylishly and made sure that we always looked our best. That was probably more a result of being poor, when she first met my father, and being proud as a wife and mother, than from any genetic inclination. She was so appreciative and so grateful to my father for all that he provided that she even let him believe that he was in control, while she was the foundation of our family.

She had a fairness and reasonableness about her that, while sometimes counterpoint to my father's rigid enforcement of rules, always provided a sense of forgiveness and understanding. It was her compassion in her last years that taught us that to just feel sorry for other people wasn't enough. As a volunteer in a veterans hospital she communicated with men without arms and legs, who were blinded and diseased, that they could still laugh and be happy.

Before she died she thought that she had it all. A devoted husband, good kids, a close extended family, a happy and beautiful home and a sense of purpose and accomplishment.

She gave us those letters from her ladle and then allowed us to observe, for a little while, how to make life worthwhile.

Now that I have grown and am trying to look back to figure out the difference between what I learned from my parents and what I inherited from them, it comes back to the difference between inclination and observation. My observation lends itself to a learned behavior that selects from alternatives leading to a preference. My inclination rather, is a feeling, an emotional perception, and an intuition that is the preference. So when we talk about the importance of finding someone "who feels like we do," chances are we can begin with our parents.

It's All Relative

Genetic research has provided us with an understanding that there is a predisposition toward many conditions because of the genes of our parents. If either one had heart disease, or cancer, there may be a pretty good chance that we are prone to get those diseases as well. If either one had vision, or hearing difficulty, or problems with their back or bones, chances are we will be visited by those same maladies. And of course, if they were pretty healthy and lived long lives, the odds are good that we'll be healthy and live a lengthy life, as well.

Keep in mind that it is beneficial to know your predispositions, because many times those negative conditions can be delayed or reversed with proper care if you choose to increase the quality of your life. It is all these tendencies, and more, that you are looking for, so that you can begin to observe the patterns in your life, and understand their origins.

Genetics provide a scientific methodology to determine what is inherited, and while many traits appear inherited, they could have been learned through parental and/or sibling influence. Of course those that are inherited should provide a "feeling," a yearning for a preference, rather than reasoning or learning selection. But, to simplify our examination, we should still consider them both inherited, since that influence could appear just as strong as a genetic transfer. Even the "inheritance" of some physical characteristics may fall into this category, when you consider how many people begin to look like their pets or spouses.

Let's still assume though, that our physical nature portrays many of those more observable attributes that we inherited; the shape of our nose and face, the color of our eyes and hair, the size and contour of our bodies. Our other inclinations, while not as noticeable, become more apparent as we examine ourselves. We begin to suspect more than experiences and exposure as the reason for our conditions.

If you have a problem being overweight, and it seems like you've spent an entire lifetime dealing with it; if you smoke, are an alcoholic or have another addictive disorder; if you're short-tempered, anxious, or prone to depression, you may have inherited some of these from your parents. Your being an introvert or extrovert; your intellectual capacity and creative capabilities; those special talents dealing with music, art, and writing; athletic proficiency and hand/eye coordination, probably were inherited too. If it's possible, you really need to observe your parents to figure out if certain conditions inherent in them have been transferred to their son or daughter. At the very least, you will have achieved an understanding of what could have been inherited.

Of course, one of the best ways to analyze what you received from your parents is to examine, if possible, your siblings. Observe their tendencies. Are they similar to yours? Then start matching up their personalities and characteristics. Check out their mannerisms, delve into their peculiarities, define their qualities, expound on their virtues, and distinguish their habits. What you are probably going to end up with is an explanation of your gene pool. While experience, your environment, and other people who have influenced your life have had a big part in your personality, you will begin to notice familial similarities that you will surely be able to identify with those letters of soup from the parental pots.

If you saw my sister for the first time, you would immediately say that there was no way that she and I could be related. I'm tall, and she's short—well, compared to me she's short. She has dark brown hair, and I have light brown hair. She's modest and reserved, and I'm self-assured and outspoken. I'm impulsive, and she's reflective. Even when we were growing up, she got good grades, and I got bad grades. She was mommy and daddy's little angel, and I was the most mischievous kid in the neighborhood. At first glance, it appears our ladles got mixed up at birth.

When I began to analyze her qualities for comparisons, I had difficulty finding any faults. I had to go back to when we were kids and she was always tattling on me to my father. I began to believe that I got stuck with the ladle with the few faults of our parents in it.

When I further thought about who she is, I was so proud and so thankful that I came from the same cup of soup that she did. At least I have hope. She and I are so similar, though. While we have had so many different experiences: different successes and failures, different accomplishments and achievements, different friends and acquaintances, different jobs and educations, and so very different marriages and families, we somehow ended up so much alike. And since we live so far apart, it's not because we see each other all the time, or talk everyday on the phone. Yet somehow, we ended up agreeing on every issue we talk about.

We have the same passions and compassions in life. Whether it's our politics or religion, our morality or social conscience, we not only think alike, but we think alike for the same reasons. We both have the same sense of humor, and the same sense of family, and honor and respect.

People who know us recognize that we are our mother's and father's son and daughter. And, without a doubt, we learned a lot from our parents. But, while physical appearance may be deceiving at first glance, we know what we inherited from our parents. When we look into each other's eyes, we see the mirrored image of feelings. And when we observe each other's smile we feel the happiness of the accomplishments of a mother and father.

To even better judge your inclinations, you need to question your other relatives. What kind of relationship do your parents and siblings have? What have their family lives been like? Are they honest, trustworthy people with integrity? Do they practice honor and commitment? What are their passions and compassions, their beliefs and truths? How are their temperaments? What are their strengths and weaknesses, their accomplishments and failings? How do they deal with habits and addictions, acceptance and denial? Are they proud of who they are, and are you proud of them?

In all likelihood, if you can identify yourself with who they are, you are probably proud of them. If for some reason, you are not proud of who they are, but recognize yourself in their traits and inclinations, it's time to figure out if you can change so that you can be proud of yourself.

It is imperative that you deal with who you are, and if necessary, who you want to be, and be satisfied with a result before you begin your search for the recipient of your love. To ensure that you both know who you are both getting, it is important to expose your origins to a potential soul mate, so that they can fairly view your past, and the prognosis for your future. And, of course, it is critical for you to thoroughly analyze where, and from whom your partner came, and all the inclinations involved providing some assurance that they will "feel" just like you.

A Learning Curve

While the inherited characteristics appear the most difficult to change, their influence can be diminished through time and experience. The more we learn on our own, the greater the ability for individual growth. New traits and qualities, mannerisms and habits now appear. We have the opportunity to become, not only more individual, but because of our interactions, more societal as well. We are influenced by our peers, our heroes, our lovers, and our friends. We are affected and prompted by our movies, television, and radio. We are persuaded by news stories and commercials. We are constantly learning and changing, although we always feel the pull of our inherited inclinations.

Now that you have a pretty good idea as to your gene-related tendencies, you can now observe the "who" of the creation of the new you. Your mirrored image is probably the best place to start.

Ask yourself those same questions that you asked of your parents and siblings. Since this experiential time of development and learning is far more dynamic than the period influenced by inherited traits, these queries should also include who you want to be. This is so because, while any change is difficult, change from exposure should be easier than change from genes. Of course, just including who you want to be in this analysis indicates a disposition to change.

Dealing with all the qualities and behaviors expressed as result of genetic transfer will allow you to observe how you are different from that ladle of soup. Now you need to determine if you need to change any of those differences by examining what you learned to become. What kind of relationships and families have you been involved in, and were you satisfied with your participation? Are you a person of integrity, who is honest and trustworthy, valuing honor and commitment? Do others view you in that same way?

Your questions need to include, your beliefs, and your expressions of those beliefs. What are you passionate and compassionate about, and are you fulfilled in that regard? How do you relate to people; do you have a bad temper, and are your reactions out of proportion to the situation? How have your strengths and weaknesses been related to your accomplishments and failings? What new style, way of life, habits and/or addictions, have you acquired? Are you able to recognize acceptance and denial and deal with each with reason? What are your priorities, and what fulfills you the most?

What are your most immediate needs, how did you achieve them in the past, and how do you think you'll accomplish them in the future? And of course, how have you changed from your genetic design? These questions, and those you directed at others, will tell you where are you headed, and where do you want to be.

After you've looked in this mirror of self-analysis, determine your desired companions in order to get an even clearer view of who you are or who you want to be. The people you admire or are comfortable with, who provide you with a sense of identity, are good role models. In many ways, your closest friends can be who you are. You may enjoy the same activities, have the same intellectual capabilities, abide by the same beliefs, or share the same virtues. Your relationship with them can be as deep or shallow as your individual natures demand. To really understand you, look to your best friends and ask the same questions of them that you asked of yourself and your relatives.

You now know not only who you are, but how you appear to others. You can now begin the process of determining change. It's a difficult project, but not making a decision to change, is a decision in and of itself.

The Art of Change

It's ironic that one reason that the concept of change becomes so difficult is because we have been conditioned by our society to believe that it is so easy. Billions of dollars have been spent on books, videos, infomercials, seminars, and other products and techniques that promote physical, emotional, and psychological makeovers.

These products claim they can help change who we are, what we look like, how we feel and think. All we have to do is pluck down a few bucks and follow the conditioning regimen of a formula and "poof," we're a new person. However, it is so much more challenging than that because of all the influences of our tendencies and inclinations, our experiences, exposures, and relationships.

We don't prepare for the turmoil that change presents, and when we confront it, it seems more difficult than we had imagined, and therefore many times we abandon it.

Withdrawing can sometimes prove more costly than if change had never begun. And, if we think we've changed, and are not content with its result, there's a good possibility that we've not only wasted our own time and effort, but other people's as well. It is therefore crucial to attempt to adjust only those parts of our lives that we know we can and want to commit to for the rest of our lives. That will certainly limit what we can change, but it will also avert **creating a temporary fix, that can lead to permanent despair.**

Change has to occur because we love ourselves, and want to be better than we have been. It should never be attempted just for the reason that someone else will love us—there isn't enough purpose or commitment there. It has to be a fulfillment, whose goal is being satisfied in its uniqueness. What's "best" is going to be different for all of us. Change to become the same as everybody else should not be our goal.Changing to enhance the life of that unique individual inside us is really much more realistic, achievable and rewarding.

To be triumphant, the pressure to change needs to come from within. As when we began our exercise regimen to improve our "look" for other people, only to find that we were really doing it to feel better about ourselves. To be as successful inwardly, we must have the same conviction. Nothing important is ever easy. And like healing, what we learn to change in the most difficult times of our lives is what we can most enjoy in the best times. But we have to recognize failure before realizing success. We have to feel pain before achieving comfort. We have to endure doubt before experiencing faith. Only then will we have the strength and courage to change to who we want to be.

Once again, even minor changes and adjustments in our lives will be difficult enough, without expecting to change someone else's life. And it is never a good idea to attempt to alter you or anybody else to achieve a sameness of being. While it may be crucial to be paired with someone who feels the same as you do, it is equally important to recognize that there are similarities and differences that can both provide the enhancements necessary for all the achievements of a complete relationship.

With all the genetics, exposure, and experience that make up the personal environment of each one of us, it would certainly be counterproductive to deny the individuality of others and ourselves. Especially while sorting through what got us to this point in our lives, and who lies ahead in our future. People of different parents, backgrounds, races, religions, intelligence, and gender will have received an education in time and experience that will provide them with an expression of who they are. In so many ways, that expression will be different for each one. With luck, with the person you share your love, there will be a few important ways it will be the same.

12

Which Planet Are We From, Anyway?

There has been so much written lately about how different men and women are. It is almost like they were each species from different planets, as is portrayed in so many self-help books and readings today. It seems like we've gone from assuming that everyone should act, feel, and relate the same, to the formulation of a complex and complicated over analysis of the genders. We've gone from one extreme to another, and the breakup of marriages and relationships continue to increase.

To understand who we are and with whom we are destined to be, we need to continue on the road to understand where we've been, and why we are the way we are. First of all, we have to accept and recognize that men were created differently than women, in certain ways, for certain purposes. And, stereotypically, men and women are portrayed as behaving differently. But we know that this isn't always true.

To further understand the motivations and feelings of two individuals in a relationship, it is important not to over simplify, but rather to achieve a basic understanding of the diversity, without delving into complex equations that assume that each gender fits a certain criteria, devoid of little individuality. Basically, the genders are different, but beyond that, our genetics, environment, experiences; our minds, our hearts and our souls, result in people who cannot be lumped into gender-defining roles.

Man was created and developed as the protector, the hunter, the provider, the father and the husband. His job primarily was to provide security and a standard of living to his woman and his family. His prime behavior exhibited strength, leadership, decisiveness, and a sense of duty to his family. The pressure and success of this responsibility was rewarded by love and having other needs taken care of by his partner. As long as he provided for the needs of his family, he could be assured his responsibilities were fulfilled, and that his partner would provide for his needs.

Woman was created and developed as the gatherer, home provider, the nurturer, the partner, the mother, and the wife. Her job was to maintain the home for her family. Her prime behavior exhibited understanding, organization, support, nourishment, and comfort. The pressure and success of her responsibility was rewarded, by knowing that she and her family would be loved and cared for by her partner. And, as long as she provided for the needs of her family for which she was accountable, she could be assured her responsibilities were fulfilled, and that her partner would provide for her needs.

Now, that's really basic. As a matter of fact, that's really primitive, according to the society we live in today. But that's where it all starts. It's the disparate responsibilities that we have to our relationships that used to, and in some cases still do, define the difference of the genders. It's a distinction that God promoted, and the Bible encouraged, as the way to ensure a successful relationship. But, times have changed, and we as a society have deemed that equality in a relationship can now be defined as sameness of responsibilities.

That basic, primitive defining of the genders, explains a basis for established behavior patterns of men and women. It can probably be used as a starting point to figure out why some men tend to be more aggressive when it comes to business—the hunt, or when it comes to sex or physical activity—the release from the pressure of the hunt. Men, generally seem to be able to focus on a few, very vital components to survival. It can also be used to explain why some women seem to be so much more focused when it comes to the many details it takes to maintain the home—the gathering; the nurturing. It could also reveal why women are often more interested in intimacy than sex. They want to feel that their man is more concerned with their well being than just relieving the pressure of the hunt.

Generally then, on this really basic, primitive level, we can see how certain behaviors probably evolved. We can also see how the one species of man and woman would have difficulty surviving if they could not depend on each other. They could not be partners in the survival of the relationship if they did not recognize their dissimilar capabilities, and therefore assume varying responsibilities. Of course the species could not survive without the different contributions made to reproduction by men and women.

There are certain other ingredients that must be included in the recipe for success of a partnership. For some of those ingredients, it matters not who provides them, just as long as they're included; for others, they must be provided for by both partners. To be most successful, capabilities are matched with ingredients. Roles must be defined and responsibilities accepted regardless of gender.

No matter how far back you go, the differences in genders that can be stereotyped, are just basic parts of a complicated equation that makes up each one of us, and each of our relationships. They are just some more ingredients that create an environment for that ladle of soup to exist. And while most of that equation is made of individual criteria that at the very least are not gender-related, it is all those correlated parts, which allow us to function as a team.

When we generalize and lump all those men and women into nice defined categories, it provides us with a broad-brush approach to deciphering what a person is all about. We can then reach heretofore-difficult conclusions as to their motivations, expectations, behaviors and feelings. It becomes valuable if it gives us a clue that was not apparent before. The key is to use those insights to understand how to convey feelings, and to understand what is being communicated, rather then plug those insights into a ready-made equation that fits all men and women; and then treats that equation as a part of a game to be played out in a relationship.

A friend of mine had recently read a relationship self-help book and related a story that was told expressing the differences between men and women. It seems a lecturer was talking to a rather large audience at a conference focusing on the distinction of the genders. She was speaking to what she said was a typical scenario of a woman cooking dinner for a man and herself. This woman was preparing a breaded fish fillet dinner by frying it in a pan. At some point in the preparation one of the fillets had broken apart. At that point, she said that most of the women in the audience began to laugh as if knowing what else was coming. When the preparation for the dinner was complete the woman had to choose which fish fillet she was going to give the man. The lecturer then asked the audience if they knew which fish went where. She said the women in the audience screamed with laughter and applause affirming that the woman would take the broken fish, giving the man the one that was whole. She also said that most of the men sat there dumbfounded seemingly not knowing what was being discussed. Her point was that women are givers and would always subordinate their own interests to please their man. It is just this sort of comparative analysis that brings more harm to relationships than good.

I was really very offended by this story in this best-selling relationship book. To make a stereotypical point elevating the purpose of one gender over another, this author and lecturer contrived a situation that may have been typical given the position of each of the participants, but certainly not because of their gender. As someone who has cooked for all the women who have ever been in my life, I found that argument to be absurd. As a matter of thoughtfulness, courtesy and certainly to make a good impression of my cooking skills, I would always give the "better" portion to the person I was serving. As a matter of fact, I was fortunate to be cooking fish for a woman friend of mine just recently, and not only was she given the better looking of the fish, but even being the big eater that I am, I also gave her the biggest fish. After mentioning this story to her, she suggested that I should also point out that when I cook eggs over easy, I always take the eggs that don't make it over easy. But that's not just the way I am. Every woman that has ever cooked for me has always given me the "better" portion. Every man that has ever cooked for any of the women I have talked to regarding this story has also given the best to them. Now, there are men and women who take each other for granted, who don't care for each other, or who have no reason to be courteous or needing to make a good impression. Who knows, they might also be gluttons. But in a typical good relationship with typical men and women, I think it depends on who is cooking. I am sure that if I was in the audience I would have appeared dumb-founded as well. I would have thought that in a confer-ence that was dealing with relationships, it would have been much more appropriate to show the similarities of feelings so that participants could put themselves in the shoes of the other gender. To incite a crowd by attempting to solidify the oneness of a gender in opposition to the other does little good in the encouragement of attractions.

It's The Same Planet

When searching for a soul mate, you are definitely not looking for every man or every woman. You are searching for that very special person who is especially suited for you. If it means that person is a man who likes to be the pursuer, or a woman who likes to be pursued, fine; that will be indicated at the beginning of the relationship, and the pursuit will probably go according to that plan. If it means that a man enjoys giving and taking care of a woman, and a woman enjoys receiving and being taken care of by a man, fine again. If it means that a man has a sexual attraction to a woman, and that sexual attraction can be trans-lated into an intimate relationship for a woman, well, that's really fine. These are all basic instincts and expectations that flow from the societal model of typical differences between men and women, and is important information to consider when judg-ing the progress of a relationship. There are so many other fac-tors and non-typical behaviors to consider, however.

It is so much easier, for example, for two assertive people—pursuers—to meet. And clearly, for a pursuit to be successful, at least one of the parties needs to take on the role of the hunter. While men typically take on that role to provide sustenance for their family, it is not unusual for a man to wait to be pursued for the purposes of a relationship, especially nowadays if he has been faced with the rejection of being *Suddenly Single*. That's why some men end up with the first pursuer to come along, because he believes his chances of being pursued are diminished according to the stereotypical roles.

Of course, it's the same with women. If they become the hunters, they usually have no trouble meeting men. Many women, however, find that role out of character, and with those same feelings that being *Suddenly Single* has presented to them, wait to be pursued as a vindication of self-worth. That's why some women end up with the first man that pursues them. Of course, if neither of these *Suddenly Singles* is pursuing, then they will never get to meet.

Dealing with all the rejection and self-esteem problems, cause both men and women to retreat to a safe place that sometimes can only be reached by the most ardent pursuer—and many times that person is not the love of their lives, but rather just the first and only "love" to come around. It is so limiting to play the game of pursuit. After all, our goal should not be to give our love to the one who pursues us the most, but rather to the one who feels, thinks, and loves the most like we do. Unfortunately, that person is probably in the same stage of retreat that we are.

Men and women of good intention sometimes never get to meet, because they have experienced the same hurts. Their solitude is many times only visited by those who don't react the same way to those experiences, or have the same feelings. Many times we appreciate those who pursue us, because we are desperate. We become desperate for affection, companionship, and feelings of self-worth. We sometimes accept all this, and call it love. We settle, so as not to be alone anymore. Our goal becomes any port in a storm, because we've given up hope of reaching the final destination; the target of our love. It's the same for both men and women.

Male/Female stereotypes aren't fitting their descriptions anymore. Women, in general, have become more self-sufficient, and can certainly hunt for themselves. As a matter of fact, our society has encouraged women to become joint hunters with their man. And while this new attitude would indicate that they would have more of a capability to become pursuers in a relationship, many times this newfound self-sufficiency provides the opposite result. Not only do they no longer have to depend on a man to do the hunting, but they are perfectly capable of providing for themselves, therefore not feeling the pressure of having to be in a partnership. And the same goes for those men who live alone, and have added gathering to their repertoire.

Incentives for typical roles have also changed. Both men and women have realized that to survive alone they have to do it all by themselves, and when they discover that they can succeed, incentives and motivations to be in a relationship diminish. Because of past experiences, and the associated mistrusts, despairs, and regrets, partnering becomes less attractive and unnecessary. **Isolation becomes a positive solution rather than a negative consequence.** That's great for individual survival, but not so good for those soul mates who were destined for discovery, and the sharing of love. Once that dependency on coupled support is gone, it is difficult to distinguish between the benefits and capabilities of each gender.

Up to a point, some sort of planet analogy would seem appropriate, and suffice it to say, such an analysis would prove beneficial to the success and maintenance of a relationship. The complements of men and women are provided by their different capabilities, which lead

228

to their particular roles. Their gender-based motivations are evolved from their specific proficiencies and qualifications. **Men and women though are very different when it comes to what they can bring as individuals to the success of the relationship, but they can be very similar when it comes to what they can hope to receive from that same relationship.**

When I first started writing this book, I met with a couple who I hadn't seen in many years. Dave and Jane had been married about ten years and had a couple of kids. As is the case with most married couples, they appeared to everyone else to have the perfect marriage. Well, their marriage wasn't perfect, and I guess my failed relationship prompted them to ask me my thoughts on why I thought marriages fail. I felt somewhat annoyed by their question, since I really didn't know them that well, hadn't seen them in years, and thought what an insensitive thing to ask someone in my situation. Apparently though, they were desperately grasping for answers to questions they had about problems that lingered in their marriage. They were sincerely interested in solving their problems, but for the most part had gotten advice that seemed to hurt rather then help. Since they had heard of my interest and insights because of this book, they wanted my advice.

In particular, they were interested in what I thought about the differences between men and women, and how that affected marriages. The reason they were concerned with this aspect of a relationship was that they had a constant problem quarreling with each other a few years ago. They discussed this problem together, with the help of some books on relationships that Jane had read. The books were beneficial because they provided a forum for conversation, and when Dave and Jane were communicating, they weren't arguing. This suspension of tension lasted a short time and they were back at arguing again. They then got tapes, and eventually went to a counselor to deal with their problem. The books they read, the tapes they listened to, and the counselor with whom they had numerous sessions, all focused on the importance of understanding how different men and women were from each other.

Jane mentioned that, for a time they both played out the roles they were given to enhance communication. She said that whenever she had an issue, or a problem that she was discussing with Dave, that he would just sit there and listen intently and every once in awhile nod his head up and down. There was definitely no arguing, but that she felt that she was talking to a robot. It got so bad that she would sometimes exaggerate the problem and raise her voice just so he would show some expression.

After awhile, she missed the arguing, because at least that provided some interaction. Jane said, that before their newfound remedy, Dave would criticize her, but at least offer solutions. Since the books, tapes, and counselor all indicated that Jane, being a woman, saw Dave's solutions as being criticism, and that Dave's propensity, being a man, was to offer solutions; the remedy was for Dave to keep quiet and just nod his head. It was suggested that women wanted someone to just listen, and men wanted somebody to just tell something to. Maybe their characterization was oversimplified, but that's what stereotyping accomplishes.

Well, there was no arguing, and Dave had become a good listener, but what happened to the communication? That's what Jane really missed, and poor Dave said that he had all kinds of solutions bottled up inside him, waiting to burst out. Eventually it turned out to be a partially good therapy, because Jane started asking Dave why he wasn't helping out with solutions. They both realized that they had a choice of learning to communicate properly, or going back to the prescribed treatment that lumped them into a gender stereotype. Clearly, this problem was a case of Dave having the habit of not thinking before he spoke. He would always start out his solution with a phrase like, "Why did you do that," or "How could you let that happen," and then would come his explanation. It appeared to be a simple remedy that just entailed a little bit of work on Dave's part, with the help of Jane, to break a habit. But their therapy got really complicated when they started playing a game that removed them from the inclinations of their individual personalities.

They brought up a number of other examples that were given to them about how men and women needed to be treated differently because of the distinction of gender. Some were actually valid considerations that should be contemplated within the framework of individual uniqueness rather then differentiating genders. There are always some people who fit into a determined category of a general stereotype. But, chances are they are not going to fit into all of them. The mistake that is made in cases like this is that it is assumed that not only do all members of a specific gender have the same characteristics and behavior, but also that members of that gender are also included in every category of analysis.

As it turns out, Dave and Jane have very different backgrounds, and dissimilar upbringing. In many ways their parents have contributed to the way they deal with the problems that they face in their marriage. But, they certainly have the same expectations of their relationship. They just need to focus more on their similarities, because that is what is going to give them a clearer understanding of each other, so that they can deal with their differences.

Give and Get

Beyond the dependence on your partner to survive, what happens to the benefits of giving to each other? The beneficiary is not the only person rewarded. When two people love each other, giving many times becomes so much more rewarding than getting. So when we choose to be alone, **it's not so much that we lose the capability to receive love, it's just as important that we forgo the circumstances to give it.** And, it's the same for both men and women. It's not a gender thing that determines the need to give; it's the two individuals in a relationship that fuel that desire.

The ideal, of course, is for **both partners to give all that they've got, so that no one has to worry about getting.** There are so many men and women who have so much to give, and are being denied that ability because of their acceptance of stereotypes that involve givers and receivers, pursuer and the pursued, those sensitive and those logical, and all those other comparisons of the differences in the relationship. These cause an act of love—giving—to become scripted in a relationship game; a game that denies the sameness of good people who need to follow their instincts, rather than the rules of play.

A short time after my divorce I was approached by a very attractive young lady while waiting for a table at a restaurant. She just said "Hi," and we exchanged pleasantries along with some minor chitchat and we went our separate ways. A couple of weeks later we met again at the same place, this time with her asking me if I would like to join her at the bar for a drink. While I did not want to get involved with anyone yet, we did have a drink and talked for a little while, and once again went our separate ways. By the way, I paid for the drinks over her objections. The next day I received flowers and a card from her expressing what an enjoyable talk we had, and that it would be nice to do that again. A couple of days later she called and asked me to go out to dinner. I accepted but felt obligated to say that I would go only if it were my treat. It's not that I minded being pursued; it was that I felt it was my responsibility as a man to at least pay for dinner. She did allow me to pick her up. However, when I arrived at her house she had prepared a gourmet meal for us. She was also dressed in such a way that I only wanted my eyes to observe her beauty.

While I did bring her flowers when I picked her up—after all she set the standard—nothing else that I did in this situation resembled the hunter's role—the stereotypical male. And, trust me, at no point did I ever feel offended. Of course, I could have demanded that we go out to eat, but I was either too much of a gentleman, or I really liked this idea of being pursued.

My feelings amazed me, because at one point I felt I was being denied that act of giving and yet was so thankful to be getting. It made me want to give even more. And, then there was this idea about how things are supposed to be. I had flashbacks about how I was taught, through observation, how to behave with women and what my responsibilities were. There was the thought that even though I was asked out, that I still should be in control of the date, because after all, I was the man. Should I next wait, and let her open the door for me? I was confused, to say the least. There were only a few times though, that I felt uncomfortable, probably because of the anticipation more than anything. Generally though, my comfort level was at a high since I didn't have to worry about the lowered self-esteem I had recently experienced. As a matter of fact, I couldn't imagine ever being able to place myself, through my own efforts, in the position I now found myself. I decided to stop this over-analysis of my situation and go with the flow.

It wasn't so much that I thought that "times" have changed, as I thought that individuals and the way they approach dating are different. I could have challenged that experience and offered a more traditional situation, but once again, correctly went with the flow. The benefits of that night went beyond that particular dating experience. I was actually able to imagine what a stereotypical woman goes through under similar circumstances. It's not so bad being pursued.

The act of giving, of course, is involved in every aspect of a successful relationship. It is the sharing that helps a loving partnership grow and prosper. Rather than being an individual responsibility, it is a common duty, working for the betterment of each other. It reaches to the shared inner most thoughts and feelings. It embraces the pain and suffering with hugs of relief. It comforts, and changes despair to hope. It offers a belief in the equality of love. And it erases all doubt. Giving provides for two people, truly in love, to express themselves as one, with all the compassion and understanding of two souls destined to be together.

People, who love and give because of love, understand that giving of oneself is so much more important than giving, or getting "things." Whoever said, "Diamonds are forever" has never observed how quickly they disappear at the end of a relationship, when the tally of loveless possessions is all that's left because there was no love. Of course, most of my new women friends laugh when I tell them that and point out that this is just from a male perspective. They still believe that diamonds are forever because they are so easy to pack. Using that perspective, I guess for me pianos are forever. In some ways we are from different planets.

Giving of yourself involves acts of kindness and concern, shared thoughts in whispered words and written in letters and poems, promises of loyalty and commitment; relieving responsibilities and burdens; providing a happy environment; and, of course, always being there. These are the gifts that provide forever. These are gifts that should know no gender.

Giving should never be different for men and women, no matter what planet they think they come from. It's a universal act of love. It's also a way to express our own value and worth. If we truly believe that what we have to offer is so valuable, imagine how good we must feel when we are able to give it to someone we love. If we truly love ourselves for the goodness we behold, it's certainly worth the wait to bestow it on that soul mate whose goodness we will be able to receive and deserve. What a terrible waste it would be to limit that gift to a gender classification.

Battle of the Sexes

The intimacy that's allowed through the giving of ourselves, is many times merely equated with sexual interaction, especially in the formulas explaining men's versus women's needs. With all the intimacy that goes on in a healthy, successful relationship, sex is just one aspect essential to its well-being. We sometimes make the mistake of elevating sex as the essential ingredient in making love. In reality, all the intimacies we experience should give us the feeling of making love. While the holding, kissing, and touching, all provide physical sensations that are pleasurable, it is the intensity of sexual interaction that provides much more of an immediate, heightened awareness and response. But thanks in part to the media; we have come to accept sex as the **only** way to make love. That's where the confusion between men and women surfaces.

Many men are viewed as thinking of sex as the ultimate of intimacy; an intense romp in the hay that relieves tension, provides an escape from the routines and ordeals of daily life and is a reward for protecting and providing. Hence the popular notion, expressed in gender differing equations, that men respond to sex like a pressure cooker, or a blowtorch. The irony is that sex isn't any more important then all the other intimacies in that relationship. Just ask any man who has truly loved, what he longs for now that he is alone. Sex is many times a lot easier to obtain than the feelings from holding, kissing, and even just talking to someone you love, but it isn't necessarily more important to a man. Making love by just looking into someone's eyes and experiencing the feelings drawn from their heart and soul provides a satisfaction like no other. Just ask a man who has experienced that feeling that seems to span a lifetime, to compare it to even hours of great sex. Of course, most men would wonder why you couldn't do both.

Many women, on the other hand, believe that men equate sex with intimacy, and place too much emphasis on the physical, and not enough on the emotional aspects of making love, that would also lead to a much slower and intentioned arousal rate. Hence the popular notion that women respond to sex, like an oven, or a crock-pot. Just the terms alone provide different connotations. "Making love" sounds like a process; something that takes time and planning; something that involves concern and thought-fulness. Having "sex," on the other hand, sounds quick; something that's spontaneous, unrehearsed, intense, and primal. Although, when making love includes sex and sex reaches the point of arousal to an orgasm, it's amazing how quickly we forget all those differences.

We've once again allowed the experts in our differences, to de-tract from the sameness of our needs and desires. Making love and sex should not be equated with each other, and they are not as different as apples and oranges. If that overworked analogy is to be used, sex is the apples, and all the other intimacies of the relationship are the oranges and the various fruit, that make up that glorious fruit salad we call "making love." Sex is a part of making love. It's part of the process, and ideally not its conclu-sion. By comparing the two on equal terms, we open ourselves up to opting for either one or the other, and given the choice, some women choose the process of making love, and some men choose the act of sex.

By accepting this game of diversity, we've permitted each gender to proclaim the fulfillment of a separate need and make demands that while not unreasonable, certainly appear to be, given the antagonism that has been encouraged. Certainly men's, and women's needs should be fulfilled. If a man can provide for his partner, he should be assured his needs would be provided for, as well. If a woman can be accommodating for a man's needs, she should be assured that all her needs would be provided for. It really shouldn't be that much of a controversy, or even considered a give-and-take situation.

Ideally, if both people are concerned about giving in a relationship, then once again, no one has to worry about getting. And, in a healthy partnership of love, the needs of both lovers should include lots of sex, since the process of making love should be a daily event. But, the antagonisms will endure, and the separations will exist, as long as differences are stressed and the similarity of our needs goes uncommunicated.

Of course, beyond the most talked about gender differences are all the other characteristics attributed exclusively to either men or women. Do you really believe that a *Suddenly Single* male hurts or despairs less, or in a different way, than a *Suddenly Single* female? Is their isolation and desperation so dissimilar as not to offer a comparison? Is the silence of loneliness for one, unlike the absence of sound for the other? Can their grief of lost hope be so opposite of each other, as to defy the sameness of tears? Can the primal instincts of gender be the determining factor of how each one feels? How can we deny the feelings of a soul, based upon the stereotyping of a gender?

Without a doubt we are all different, but not because of some gender classification, but because of who we are as individuals. In varying degrees, we all probably encounter grief and endure the denial and its hope of return. We've felt anger, and the strength of its conviction; guilt, and its regret for blame; we've experienced disappointment, and its failure of intention; despair, and its willingness to surrender. And, of course, we've lived with the desperation. Most of us also experience faith and hope, to some degree, that enables us to endure grief, and to expect joy.

Sure, there are differences, but in the matters of the heart and soul, the capabilities of a man and woman are the same. To believe otherwise is to limit the search for a person who feels as you do. To venture into the unknown, believing that to be successful you will have to learn to understand and tolerate all the differences of genders makes the quest seem somehow a forfeiting of one's individuality. However, to understand a person based on the "letters" of their mother and father's genetic soup, and what they've learned from the lessons of life, provides insight into who they really are and what they will mean to you.

The differences are there for a reason; to provide an environment that allows the similarities to grow. In our search, we need to acknowledge distinctiveness, but celebrate the equality of feeling, with our love.

13

Commitment

With all the differences we observe in each other that can enrich and complement our relationships, and all the similarities that provide understanding, and communication of our feelings, there is a promise of tremendous potential. This potential remains just promising, however, until the assurances, obligations and security of a lasting bond are reached, providing the trust necessary to turn possibilities into realities. **Potential can only be reached with commitment to a lasting bond.**

Of all the very important demands that we place upon the ultimate recipient of our love, their commitment is, by far, the most important of all. No matter how much they say they love us, or care for us, or want to share with us; no matter how good-looking, or smart, or talented they are or how much they seem to fulfill our needs, **without their commitment to us, and us to them, everything else is temporary.**

All these other qualities that provide us with an attraction to someone, seem so important in the initial phases of a relationship. They pale in comparison however, to the extent of what is being offered by a person who understands the consequences of the monumental, compelling decision to live with someone "till death do you part," and then some. That decision says that if some, or all, of those other qualities and attractions disappear, that there is still going to be something left to hang onto, to rebuild with, to love for.

In a way, commitment is an unconditional love and respect, not as much as for the recipient as for ourselves. We put all our important qualities on the dotted line of its contract—our word, our honor. We offer a guarantee that we have an obligation to the success of even the most fragile of associations. It's a pledge of allegiance to our partner, a promise, given before and to, our God. It assumes a tremendous amount of responsibility, but its reward is the security that every relationship needs to prosper and survive. Without that total commitment, everything becomes uncertain, waiting for dissolution as a solution.

I have to admit that I never understood what commitment was, until the day my mother died. I always knew that my father loved my mother; that he was dedicated to her, and wanted to be with her as much as he could. They would always talk about how they were going to save $50,000 and retire and live happily ever after. They used to kid all the time about how they would dream, that when the kids left the house, they were going to have so much fun together. They never dreamed that they wouldn't be there for each other, always together.

I remember, right after my mother died, sitting there with my father, day after day, night after night, trying to understand what happened. And, every once in awhile, being able to talk to each other about what she meant to us. It was a time of despair, and a time of understanding, for us both.

He told me back then that, "Life might be too short, but love can last forever." And, for him, it did last forever. He was committed not only to my mother, but to the love he had for her. When she died he kept that commitment by assuring us that love would stay alive with us as a family. He never left us and was always there. It was like he had a duty and responsibility to provide for us "til death do us part."

He never married again, although both my sister and I talked to him about that possibility, since we didn't like seeing him alone. But, I came to understand that he never really was alone; that he had that love, between him and my mother, with him all the time. The reason he didn't marry, wasn't because he thought that it would be unfair to us or to our mother. He thought it would be unfair to him and his memories, and to someone else.

The valuable lessons I learned from my father makes it disheartening to see all those around me who leave one relationship after another, looking for something that seems so important. It's discouraging to see couples together, whose commitment is entrusted and directed to the things of themselves, rather than of each other. It's demoralizing to think that we could give our trust to someone, who believes that there is something more important than the commitment to love.

*What is the most powerful lesson that I could have ever learned in life? Well, after being with my father for the last 25 years of his life, without a doubt I knew. **With life too short, the most important thing is commitment to love, because it can last forever.***

Of all the qualities intertwined in a relationship, the glue that holds them all together is commitment. It is what binds two individuals together in a lasting partnership. Without that bond, the trust that needs to exist for the relationship to grow and prosper, can never flourish. The rights of the individual will always take precedence over the good of the partnership, if the limitation of time is perceived in its union. Self-protection, in such a situation, will always take priority—it's human nature. We don't share as much; we don't care as much. And then, when it gets to be too much, we don't waste any more time, because it could end at any time, without commitment.

Being physically attractive to each other certainly enhances the sexual activity of a relationship. Being financially successful would definitely enrich its standard of living. Having an intellectual compatibility would surely optimize communication. Providing friendship and companionship to each other unquestionably fills the void of loneliness. But for how long? How long does all of it have a meaning? Until the looks fade; until the money runs out; until the communication becomes strained; or until you feel alone when you're together? It all has meaning as long as you can't see the end. Once the end is probable or even possible, you're almost already there.

Without commitment, the future is like a mirage—one minute everything seems so real, and the next minute, it's nothing. Commitment ensures the future. It doesn't guarantee that all those things that you shared will always be there, but it ensures that you will. It's the one gift of love that really matters. It really does express your honor and word, and exemplifies your beliefs, values, and morality. How important is it for your soul mate to have commitment? Well, they can't be your soul mate unless they do. And unless they do, they're just people along the way. But, this is the way you'll know who the love of your life really is; the one who commits to you.

A Mirage

a mirage
so far away, existence has it not
to draw near brings it to our view
until then who knows of it
until then we cared not of its truth
when we realize its reality, it is
all of a sudden, yet gradually
the closer we get the more intense its image
then when we reach it
it disappears
it is a mirage in reality
yet in reality—nothing

14

Climbing the Ladder of Love

Now that we are more secure in understanding what we have been through and why and who we are and "who" we are looking for, it is probably a good idea to understand relationships before beginning the search for one. The complexities of joining with another in a lifelong commitment adds a new dimension to choosing a partner.

While observing what makes a successful relationship may remind you of why yours wasn't, it is a necessary step before beginning your search. Remember, you are not just looking for a person to share your love; you are also searching for someone who can survive with you in a lifelong partnership. Too many times we judge ourselves and others as individuals, rather than as one half of a joint venture. That is why it is important for someone *Suddenly Single* to understand the dynamics of relationships before seeking to change from a single to a couple. Once again, don't waste your time looking back to the "what ifs" of the past, but instead look forward with new insights as to what lies ahead. The more you know about the causes and effects of your, and others' behavior, the more successful you will be in finding and being a good partner in the future.

There are many people who look back on their previous involvements, and note that there is a tendency that even their last non-committed relationship was so much more meaningful than their first. As they got older and had more relationships, there seemed to be a growth in not only their experiences, but what they expected from these different partnerships, as well. Granted, many of these expectations and demands for more from their new partners came as a result of their understanding, that what was provided before just didn't seem to be enough. There was something missing. They wanted their relationship to continue growing, and when it seemed stifled, they became impatient. They had not yet reached the capability to give and receive true love. Without commitment, they never would.

Falling in love takes time and experience. It also takes motivation of desire. To desire means that you are perceiving what could be ahead and craving more. As you grow older in your experiences, your basic needs expand and become more complex, and your desire reaches even further, seeking higher and higher fulfillment.

Understanding who we are now, and who we are looking for in the future, completes the composite of who should enter into a relationship. Once that relationship begins however, the complexities of those individuals involved is multiplied by at least two. "At least," because another dimension is added to the coupling equation of just two people; the intermingling of needs, wants, and desires. This combination, exaggerates even more the complications of self-fulfillment. It is one thing to understand what we require for personal satisfaction, another to realize what will gratify our partner; and yet another, to comprehend the effects that each person has in a relationship.

The Hierarchy of Needs

As with Abraham Maslow's classic study of the "Hierarchy Of Needs," the fulfillment of the needs of two coupled individuals, will determine how motivated they are to move on to the next level of their union. To not understand and accept the demands of a relationship is failing to provide the complete analysis that is necessary to ensure that this commitment ladder is being climbed.

Those first needs that should be addressed and satisfied are physiological in nature. Those are air, food, shelter, and sex. Air is pretty obvious. Food and shelter are pretty basic too. If you have difficulty feeding and housing yourself, well, you are certainly going to have an obstacle to moving on to the fulfillment of other needs and desires.

That's why economic problems cause so much turmoil in relationships, not just because of the stress, and uncertainty, but because the couple doesn't have time to reach the next level of their partnership. You become stifled at the physiological level, because all your efforts are directed at providing a basic living. Sometimes, marriages of very young people fail when their desire to grow in the relationship is never fulfilled because they are so involved with just surviving and paying bills, and cannot equate just enduring with growing in love.

Of course, sex is there because it is basic to the survival of the species, and its compatibility is necessary for a man and woman to have a normal relationship. It's also one heck of a way to relieve all that stress from fighting for basic survival. But, before any hope can persist for the individuals in a relationship to grow together in love, all their physiological needs must be met.

After satisfying those physiological needs, the next level of human needs include safety, security, competence, and stability. Without the protection from harm and the security of a lasting relationship, it is sometimes difficult to provide for even more basic requirements. Being consumed with fear certainly stifles thoughts of growing together, but then again, a common need for protection may bring a couple closer. On the other hand, it presents such an underlying distraction, that it is difficult for a couple to even think about anything else. If the fear is directed to within from one partner to another, casting worry on whether or not the relationship will continue, it definitely precludes any interest in evolving the relationship any further.

Of course, after achieving protection, then you can experience competency, where you will be able to utilize your aptitudes and knowledge to provide skills and proficiencies to grow individually and jointly. These abilities will allow you to not only enhance previous basics, but will also allow you to look forward to the achievement of a better life. As you move forward, you both have confidence that all the past needs will always be met. This stability permits you to be poised, knowing that you are now firmly established and can begin to consider all those interactions that will provide growth, individually and within the relationship as a whole.

The stability that you have reached will now foster a sense of belonging that heretofore was not possible due to the unfulfilled basic needs of your past together. You have now reached a social level that includes companionship, affection, and friendship. Now that the worries of basic survival and security have been diminished, you can afford the luxury of keeping each other company. You are able to relax together and share activities, discuss daily living and share thoughts and express feelings. Your need for companionship can be so basic, and yet just being there for each other can be profoundly satisfying.

Once this sharing of time and purpose is achieved, the attachment of companionship leads to warmth of feeling. Individual tenderness evokes emotions, sensations, and compassion toward each other as a couple. This affection provides a passion and devotion from within, nurturing the relationship in such a way, that the only other way to describe it is the giving of love. It has grown from dealing with all those basic needs together, and seems to be a reward from God, for being patient. It goes beyond all the benefits of companionship, by allowing you to share your deepest thoughts and feelings. Engrossed in its meaning is the trust that sends the message of genuine concern and commitment for each other. This permits for affiliate friendships to exist without jealousy or fear of challenge to the devotion to each other. You have the confidence to encourage friendships, while realizing that only one best friend will exist from this point on.

Outside friendships provide meaningful social interaction that is necessary for you both to grow. Your friends become supporters and promoters of you as a couple. They enable diverse activity and interests, as well as expanded points of view. The intimacy that they provide does not infringe upon, but enhances the intimacy of your relationship by allowing it to become more focused. Friendships nourish the growth of all involved, by furnishing an arena for interaction and entertainment. They transform the isolation of one's self and the relationship, to a confidence of being able to share experiences beyond the confines of a coupled existence. It is a move to another level, when all the other needs essential to the maintenance of this loving union have been fulfilled.

You've now reached a point where most relationships would be deemed successful with a good outlook to the future. And, given all the caring and sharing it took to get to this level, it certainly is a credit to the partners' commitment. But as with any successful enterprise, working at maintaining your success and even building on it, requires a daily effort. There are needs of the past that still must be of concern and met. And, there are still needs in the future that must be considered.

Reaching this stage of your relationship results in a foundation to now make life better. A successful relationship however, is one that continues to grow, and at this level the rewards can be even greater. Building on the confidence of trust and commitment now enable you and your partner to reach out for yourself and to each other and seek recognition, status, self-esteem and self-respect. You've reached your ego level of needs.

To achieve success at this level requires both a concern for self, with all its independent images, as well as a regard for your partner's image of self. There must be a confidence that the person, who knows each of you best, your partner, thinks highly of you. A daily awareness and effort must exist that recognizes the worth of each of you in your relationship. It needs to reflect, not only on what you both achieved, but also on what you are capable of achieving.

Sometimes though, we neglect to glorify even the evident titles of "husband," "wife," "lover," or "friend," thinking that achievement has to be associated with some newer venture. But as with all the basic needs before, we have to first feel fulfilled at a level of predominant security. We all feel secure in a relationship when we receive daily reminders of love, respect, appreciation, and admiration. That sort of tribute paid, is recognition for not only what you achieved, but for who you are. And, recognition of the value of who you are gives you status in the relationship and pride in your accomplishment.

You both can now feel that you deserve to be where you are and who you're with. There is little need to prove oneself anymore. It presents a feeling of self-respect that was realized through the efforts of self, as well as the encouragements of a partner along the way. When finally, this satisfaction and combination of all the other needs have been completed, a level is reached where it's possible to become all that one is capable of becoming; this is called self-actualization. This is the stage where you and your partner take risks and go beyond anywhere you have been before. To seek out truths, fulfill dreams, explore feelings, and pursue knowledge. This is the phase that presents the least amount of fear of the unknown, allowing for searches into one's being and the "being" of the relationship.

At this level, a certainty exists that **all** the needs of the past are completed and secure; that each other and the partnership are genuine. There is a sense of not holding back; whatever is beneficial to one is beneficial for both. It is at this point that a culmination of all that has preceded allows that the love for oneself, and the love for each other, combine and escalate to achieve a singular "love" of absolute passion and commitment.

While I have taken certain liberties with the interpretation and premises of Maslow's hierarchy of needs, I believe his conclusion holds true. If previous, more basic needs are not fulfilled, then there is little motivation, or capability to move on to experience higher levels of needs and desires. And, there are circumstances in life and relationships that cause a retreat to a lower level starting the process of growth again from the fulfillment of more basic needs. It is the same way with couples as it is with individuals; it's just that in the dynamic of a relationship, it becomes more complicated.

Playing Catch Up

There are many relationships that start out at very basic need levels, but for the most part, those *Suddenly Single* tend to jump into new relationships at the companionship level, whether or not their partners are ready for that level of commitment. Mistaken presumptions of that sort will just probably mean being *Suddenly Single* over and over again. Companionship should only be considered the starting place of a relationship, when all the other needs of both individuals have been met. That's why "rescuers" usually have difficulty having a long-term companionship with people they rescue. Needy and desperate people, at different degrees of fulfillment, will just offer each other a short-term fix.

Another problem encountered by *Suddenly Single* people, who disregard level of entry, is the association of reward with level of fulfillment. They get so caught up in the frenzy of finding a companion to take away their loneliness that they neglect to respond to even the different motivations correctly. It's one thing to be at different phases of need attainment than your partner, it is another to exacerbate that difference with flawed encouragement. And, it is this encouragement to move from one level to the next that offers any promise at all that their partner will eventually catch up.

As a person climbs the ladder of hierarchical needs, their incentives, rewards, and motivations change as well, making it difficult for people at different levels to communicate and understand each other. In business, a pat on the back and a certificate of recognition to a minimum wage employee will not provide the same motivation as a raise in pay, allowing for the fulfillment of some basic needs. And, recognition through promotion or added responsibilities would probably provide more motivation to a high paid executive than even a raise in salary. Mistakenly, many times the same rewards are given to people at different levels of necessity.

> *I was surprised when I found out that Steve and Gina were dating, because I was acquainted with them both, but had no idea that they knew each other. They made a*

nice couple. Both were attractive, in their mid-thirties, physically fit, and seemed happy together. Just to look at them, you would think that they had a lot in common. When I mentioned to a mutual friend my surprise, he said he couldn't believe how lucky they both were to find each other. It was a chance happening that both Steve and Gina likened to fate.

Steve had gotten laid off from a local office equipment company, but was soon after hired by a major office supplier as a salesman. When he was laid off, he was just completing a lengthy divorce from his wife of four years, during which time his work habits suffered to the point where when the downsizing occurred, Steve was the first to go. Apparently during the divorce, Steve spent most of his time with his friends, either playing golf or drinking at a bar. One of the reasons for his wife divorcing him was that they never had enough money to pay their bills, creating a lot of tension. They both liked to drink and went out to eat quite a bit, which might have exaggerated their problem. They each had new cars, but lived in an apartment. You could tell, that neither one saw much of a future with the other.

One of the new accounts that Steve received at his new job, right after his divorce was finalized, was at large accounting firm where Gina worked as an office manager. Even though he didn't get to meet her right away, since she didn't do the purchasing for her company, after a few visits in a couple of months he inquired about who she was. He was definitely attracted.

He found out that Gina had two small children, and that her husband had been killed in an auto accident three years before. As far as anyone knew she had not dated since then. She had started working for the firm twelve years ago, and was office manager for the past five years. She had an MBA and was paid a very good salary. It appeared that she spent most of her time working or with her kids.

Over the next few months, Steve and Gina began by exchanging pleasantries, taking a few minutes break to talk, and then going out to lunch. They both definitely shared a mutual attraction. Steve thought Gina was sweet, thoughtful, smart, and had a great smile. It was the first time in years someone cared about what he was saying. Gina thought Steve was considerate, lovable, and funny. It was the first time she laughed in years. They started going out together; first once a month, eventually once a week. Steve even took Gina and her kids out on weekends every once and awhile to amusement parks and the zoo. They were all getting along just great. It was just what they all needed. As time passed, they began seeing each other more and more, with Steve spending most of his extra time visiting Gina and her kids at their home. That's about the time I found out they were dating.

Then disaster struck. Steve was laid off from his new job because business had slowed and he was the last one hired. He searched, but could not find other comparable employment. When his unemployment ran out he was going to have to move out of his apartment. It was then that a relative, living in a state about a thousand miles away, offered Steve a job with his company. It was similar to what Steve had done before, with the added bonus that he was promised that he would never get laid off.

When he confronted Gina with his situation, she offered him another solution. Since they both obviously enjoyed being with each other and that there was apparently a love interest involved, why doesn't he consider moving in with her and the kids. He could have his own room and could help out with the house and kids while he continued his search for employment, and maybe, even go back to school to finish getting his degree. Without hesitation Steve agreed. Neither one could imagine being separated by a thousand miles.

After Steve moved in, he conscientiously searched for work, but could not find a job. He obviously felt guilty living off of Gina, because when a friend offered him a job as a bartender, he took it. He was finally making really good money. He even went back to school part-time at nights to try and get his degree.

Then disaster struck again, in the form of Gina's family telling her, in no uncertain terms, that it really looked bad having this man living in her house. It was affecting her children, her job, and her reputation. It was then that Steve and Gina decided to get married. She first made him promise that as soon as he could, he would quit his job as a bartender and get something more suitable to raising a family. They were married.

A few months later Steve was offered better shifts, working at night, making twice what he was then. He took those shifts and had to give up school. He was now coming home in the middle of the night and sleeping all day, and he was making a lot of money. When Gina confronted him about his promise, he said that he was making much more money now than he had ever made as a salesman, and besides he was now able to pay for some of their bills.

Gina was furious, and told Steve that they could get along just fine on what she made and that he needed to get an office day job, even if it paid half of what he was making as a bartender. He told her that she was just jealous, because he was finally making good money and didn't need to depend on her anymore. She told him that the money wasn't important, but that the impression that he was making on her children, her neighbors, and her family was very important. In this conversation with him, she also mentioned that the most important thing in her life was her children. He told her that he thought he was.

The argument went on for about another month, until Steve moved out. Shortly thereafter, he was fired from his job for drinking at work. He then moved to take that job with his relative. Steve and Gina ended up getting separated, but they kept in touch with each other. First, it was a couple of times a week, then every week, then once a month, and now every once in awhile.

When Gina was telling us what happened to Steve, she mentioned how much they seemed to bring to each other's life when they first met. It seemed that they had so much in common. How, they both filled a void for one another. She said that it was too bad that he didn't realize all the responsibilities she had. She was at a time and place in her life that was looking at a different future than the one Steve was beholding. She said that it was a shame he didn't understand.

It is important to always realize, that motivation for people in a relationship is going to be dependent upon their completion of previous requirements of growth. And, both individuals in a relationship need to fulfill the satisfaction of those needs at the same time, or feelings of jealousy and insecurity will be prompted by discontent and lack of communication. It is difficult, at best, to worry about your self-esteem, or your partner's recognition, when you haven't felt comfortable expressing your aptitudes and abilities. And, wouldn't it be difficult sharing your affection, and trusting friendships, if you felt sexually repressed or feared for the security of your relationship? Both partners need to move along at the same pace. If they don't begin at the same place, one has to wait and help the other catch up, before going to the next level. Of course, that assumes that both partners agree where that next level is.

The reasons most good intentioned people enter relationships, is to provide growth to their individual natures. This growth gives meaning to a relationship, and if or when it ceases for one or both of it's partners, a stagnation is perceived. When something stops growing it appears to begin dying. That's when the individual nature surfaces to save itself, and it leaves to begin living again; growing again. It is why so many people go from one relationship to another. They feel stifled, stagnate in an association that shows no movement to the achievement of higher goals, either on an individual or coupled basis.

Of course, one of the main reasons that growth usually ceases in one of these deserted relationships is, because one or both of the partners lack the commitment necessary to encourage growth. So, we then have all these people wandering and wondering through life, searching to be satisfied and starting again at a lower level of need with someone else.

While they always assume they are growing, they are merely moving up and down and up again, on a scale of personal and coupled growth. Many of these people will never come close to reaching the heights of self-actualization, because they needed to be in a relationship long enough to provide an environment offering complementary resources of trust, dependability, understanding, and appreciation. It is only then, that they can receive the encouragement to be motivated to reach for the higher personal levels that provide for a better relationship. It takes this growth and time to have all the individual and partnered stages complete to achieve the commitment to love.

It may take a lot of understanding and communications to know what degree of needs you are each at, but without commitment, it won't matter. All the hopes and dreams of reaching self-actualization together can only be completed by being committed to helping each other fulfill each other's needs and desires. But, if you can't even insure the security of the relationship, companionship can't evolve.

So many relationships have failed that have had all the capabilities of achieving the highest level, but lacked the motivation through commitment to see it through. And in so many cases, the individuals who give up their quest for this ultimate achievement ultimately have to start all over again with someone else. This time, if you're *Suddenly Single,* be certain that the person with whom you are starting over again, is at least committed to climbing the ladder. You can never reach the top together, unless you are both committed to keep climbing.

Can't Get No Satisfaction

The motivation to keep climbing the ladder of success on a personal level, and within a relationship, is that it is our human nature to never be satisfied. Not only will relationships cease to grow if there is not movement up the levels of the ladder, but the anxiety generated by dissatisfaction of the lack of growth, causes those relationships to fail. Being stifled, being stuck at a certain level will almost always eventually lead to the perception of individual failure and then the breakdown of life together.

Since we were children, and then growing up and reaching adulthood, we always wanted, expected, and demanded more than many times, what we even assumed we deserved. And, when we became involved with a partner, that motivation continued. Our whole lives were conditioned to never being satisfied, so why should this change in a relationship? It doesn't, and it shouldn't, and that's okay. It's a good thing not to be satisfied. It's what causes us to do better; to be better. It provides us the motivation that brings us to personal success and creates relationships that achieve unbelievable fulfillment and joy.

It is only when we are not satisfied with things that can't change, that this tendency becomes destructive. Its drive produces an anxiety of unrealistic expectations and becomes a consuming desire rather then a productive motivation. It causes individuals and couples to dwell on their negative situation, draining concern and effort from positive capabilities. And of course, the one thing we should recognize that we can't change in a relationship is our partner.

Not being satisfied at a level of achievement propels us to begin achieving at a higher level. It is this dynamic, that when partnered, causes relationships to soar. Of course, there must be the trust and dependability of each companion of this venture to insure its success. It is when the dissatisfaction with achievement is directed at each other, rather then at the stage of condition, that relationships are caused to sour.

With all the balancing of concerns involved in reaching levels of success in a relationship, and with all the pressures brought to bear to realize an unquenchable satisfaction, there must be commitment in order to arrive at a better place. That commitment demands that we recognize the tendency of our human nature to be sometimes disappointed in not being satisfied with the results of joint effort, but that the goal of that effort is to achieve an actualization shared by both. **In the beginning you have to be satisfied with each other, so that at the end you can be satisfied with the accomplishments of your journey together.**

Relationships do require a lot of work and understanding. It's hard enough to figure out all the implications involved with two ladles of soup from the two different pots without putting them both together in the same bowl. It will never taste exactly like you think it should.

It's the dynamic of the relationship that determines the recipe for success. The characteristics of each individual, when combined, can equal so much more than just the sum of their parts, if they can just learn to complement and compliment each other. And, how hard can that be? Well, It does take a constant awareness of the feelings and needs of your partner. If you truly love someone, it is something that you would want to do every day. That's all it takes—every day.

15

The Limits of Choice

You should have, by now, figured out who you are and also probably have a pretty good idea as to who you would like to be with, in what you now understand can be a lasting, successful and growing relationship. Once again, you are looking for someone who feels as you do, but you also need to consider all those other traits, qualities, behaviors and needs that exist within a potential partner.

To search for and find that duplicate in feeling is wonderful, as long as that demand for duplication is not carried over in every other consideration, which if not next to impossible to find, could probably evolve to a rather dull relationship. A better match might be found with a person who is complementary to you in many ways, and would certainly increase the pool of those possibilities. There are so many more people out there who don't act, think, work or look exactly the same or aren't the same age or in the same place. This allows for so much more variety, and more possibilities of finding a match.

Sometimes we become so locked into proximity that we fail to look beyond our neighborhoods, our jobs, or our social circles to search for a recipient of our love. There are probably not very many people who can duplicate our feelings and duplicate or complement most everything else, who live within a few blocks of our homes, work in the same department or office, or who are friends of friends. When we limit ourselves to proximity, we severely decrease the number of possibilities who might be a match. Of course, the fewer the possibilities, the less hope, and the more despair, depression, and desperateness will exist, causing a revisit to past mistakes.

Such a self-confining search with hopeless limitation can only once again lead to the consequences of a previous failed match and relationship of desperation. Something as simple as just going beyond that immediate proximity can change those hopeless limitations to promising, expansive probabilities. While we can all estimate how many people exist in our immediate surroundings, and the potential match that affords, let us go beyond that number and location to imagine a broader perception. By evaluating realistic possibilities we can interpret what is probable.

We need to just simply assume realistically and reasonably, that for every 50,000 people who exist, within whatever boundary limitations we place on ourselves, there will be at least one very probable match; duplicating feelings and matching or complementing most everything else. We will then finally be able to depart from our hopeless, doomed, desperate feeling of the zero, or so, possibilities of our immediate surroundings, to the over 5,000 probabilities a plane ride away. And, that only includes most areas of the United States. It is certainly, of course, more convenient to be able to find someone around the corner, or someone with whom we work, or to be set up by a friend. But, not finding that special someone close by, and still limiting the scope of such an important decision to include just the neighborhood, could deny us the possibility of spending the rest of our lives with a soul mate who currently exists no more than a couple of hours away.

To theorize to this figure of how many people it takes to arrive at that one probable match from a number of possibilities, involves dealing with statistics. If you are not so oriented you might want to pass over this suggested statistical analysis. It is only included to demonstrate that realistically, there are many other matches out there, albeit sometimes with some effort and some distance away. Then again, sometimes closer than you think.

Statistical Match

First, let us assume, with certain statistical verification, that in the United States there are approximately 140 million males and 147 million females. Allowing for that same type of validation we can suggest that about 81 million men and 87 million women fall into the range of between 25 and 74 years of age. We can further break that statistic down, for the purpose of generally addressing those *Suddenly Single,* to 20 million men and 20 million women in the 25 to 34 years of age range; 23 million men and 24 million women in the 35 to 44 years of age range; 19 million men and 20 million women in the 45 to 54 years of age range; 11 million men and 13 million women in the 55 to 64 years of age range; and, 8 million men and 10 million women in the 65 to 74 years of age range.

Let us now postulate for the sake of argument, that only twenty percent of both the men and woman between the ages of 25 and 74 years are single and available. To some, that figure might be thought low, but when considering the duration of the range and that a higher percentage would probably apply to both the younger and older age groups, it should be reasonable for our purposes. And, we know that over twenty-five percent of the households are one person. Besides, when developing such a theory, it is better to understate than overestimate.

So now, we can also presume that there are over 33 million single men and women in the age range from 25 to 74 years old. Providing a more specific focus, involving age categories within this group of single men and women, we can generally approximately suppose that there are 12 percent of men (4 million) and 12 percent of women (4 million) in the 25-34 year old range; 14 percent of men (4.6 million) and 14 percent of women (4.8 million) in the 35-44 year old range; 11 percent of men (3.8 million) and 12 percent of women (4 million) in the 45-54 year old range; 7 percent of men (2.2 million) and 8 percent of women (2.6 million) in the 55-64 year old range; and 5 percent of men (1.6 million) and 6 percent of women (2 million) in the 65-74 year old range. This analysis should now allow an even further narrowing of focus to determine where these probable matches are located.

We can estimate, with some reliability, that over 26 million of these single men and women live in metropolitan areas. That over 5.5 million live in the Northeast; almost 7 million live in the Midwest; over 11 million live in the South; and, that almost 10 million live in the West. And, while regions and states are mostly balanced between the numbers of both genders, certain cities may have a preponderance of one gender or another. Examples of cities that have been rumored to exhibit such an imbalance are Anchorage, Alaska, with more men, and Washington, D.C., with more women. Any further analysis would therefore need to consider the peculiarities of each city.

For now however, we can certainly formulate a methodology that can provide an equation, which generally will reach the conclusion, of the number of possibilities to draw a probable match from. Using the 50,000-population number, we can figure that about 60 percent of that total falls into the age category of 25 to 74 years of age. That would present about 30,000 people in that age grouping. Of that group, it can be justified that 20 percent, or about 6000 of those people, are single. We also know that specifying further allows an approximation that 12 percent of these men (720), and 12 percent of these women (720) are in the 25-34 age bracket; a little less than 14 percent of men (820), and 14 percent of women (840), are in the

35-44 age bracket; 11 percent of men (660), and 12 percent of women (720), are in the 45-54 age bracket; 7 percent of men (420); and 8 percent of women (480), are in the 55-64 age bracket; and that 5 percent of men (300), and 6 percent of women (360), are in the 65-74 age bracket.

Visualizing a gathering of single people, inclusive of just two of the age groups, can provide anywhere from approximately 850-1500 men or women to search for that one person offering a probable match. And, unless the limitations go beyond reasonableness, there should be more than one match acceptable. Of course, it may be overly presumptuous to imagine having all those possibilities in one place, but they could be in one city. Or, they could even be attracted to something like a *Suddenly Single* seminar or conference that will be occurring in cities all across the country. The point is that we should know that these people exist and are either waiting or searching for that one person to enter their lives. The only way to find is to seek, and there are many ways to accomplish that task. However, it first takes faith in knowing that there is that perfect match out there waiting and searching, and then hope that the efforts expended to find them is rewarded.

This expanded outlook offers a hopeful scenario, and contrasts so markedly with the isolation and hopeless confinement of those typically *Suddenly Single*. Its comparison is, of one waiting at home to cross paths with a door-to-door salesperson, or waiting for a new person to get hired at work, to someone actively pursuing a personal connection in another city, or at least another neighborhood. It is changing from making a new acquaintance or two, with someone from familiar surroundings, to allowing hundreds and even thousands of possibilities to occur by searching for other people.

Applying this conservative one in 50,000 formula to metropolitan areas around the country, one can assume there will be approximately 14 matches in Albuquerque; 5 matches in Anchorage; 80 matches in Atlanta; 6 matches in Billings; 8 matches in Boise City; 4 matches in Burlington; 2 matches in Cheyenne; 180 matches in Chicago; 70 matches in Cleveland; 60 matches in Denver; 3 matches in Fargo; 18 matches in Honolulu; 120 matches in Houston; 34 matches in Indianapolis; 36 matches in Kansas City; 40 matches in Las Vegas; 5 matches in Lincoln; 12 matches in Little Rock; 340 matches in Los Angeles; 8 matches in Madison; 230 matches in Nashville; 235 matches in New Orleans; 400 matches in New York; 40 matches in Orlando;120 matches in Philadelphia; 80 matches in Phoenix; 70 matches in San Diego; 3 matches in Santa Fe; 80 matches in Seattle; 140 matches in Washington, D.C.; or 20,000 matches in India, if you are so inclined.

With all these possibilities leading to probable matches, it would be a shame to restrict our number by attaching unwarranted criteria to our pursuit. We should now realize, that in all likelihood, there is more than one match for every 50,000 people. There is more than one match in a location or gathering of over 1000 single men or women from any two age groups that you can imagine. This formula is just a guide to permit a realization that there is a reasonable calculation accessible to devise a strategy for a successful search, as well as offer a hope that there are many people waiting and available to be searched out. It is important to remember however, that equally influential to the number of people available, are the number of exclusions caused by unjustifiable qualifications.

What a different outlook, limiting the limiting of possibilities presents. For what is probably the most important ingredient of what should be the most crucial decision in anyone's life—the person with whom you spend the rest of your life—it would be foolish to add arbitrary, non-essential limitations. **The more limitations that are added, the fewer are the possibilities.**

It is critical, to carefully analyze, and eventually prioritize the qualities that attract you to others. It is equally consequential to be aware, that many limitations are dictated by preconceived notions brought on by societal influence or stereotypical grouping, which may prompt you to exclude the one who could be your perfect match. You also need to hope that the person searching for you, their soul mate, will not erase you from their list because you were in their off-limit group, or just too far away. Just being *Suddenly Single,* should not afford one the luxury of confinement in this decision-making process. The more open this process is to individual observation and analysis, the greater the numbers of possibilities exist, and the less of a chance of eliminating that one person who can provide the necessary duplication and complements.

There are so many areas of concern where an open mind, can not only expand the possibilities of the search, but can change a perceived unimportant, or unnecessary lack of duplication to the possibility of becoming a beneficial "complement". Sometimes it is better to choose certain traits in others different than your own, rather than exactly the same. There's a reason some opposites attract. Keep in mind, these choices are not commitments, they are merely choices to investigate.

Act Your Age

A person's age offers a clear example of an accepted notion that sometimes, unfairly limits choice. While we probably place too much emphasis just on the number itself, age is one of the criteria, and a somewhat reasonable gauge, to utilize in a search for a compatible partner. It is a reasonable gauge because it provides a typical measure of part of who a person is. So many measures of people, however, allow unfair judgments and exclusions.

Using age as an example, consider that each person develops their minds, bodies, and emotions at different times in their life. Due to genetics, experiences, and environments, each person progresses toward maturity at a different speed. Of course, as we learned in the experience of hierarchy of needs, in a sharing relationship it is important to grow together and to share in life's journey. Sometimes age can be an indication of that progression, but, clearly, each individual's criteria of need must be assessed before reaching a valid conclusion.

We need to be able to achieve our goals, learn, and grow old together, and help each other individually, as well. It will take a lot of communication and understanding, as well as an incredible amount of empathy. It is all a learning experience that we achieve by being together that sometimes seems so much easier to understand and accomplish if we both start out in the same place. Age is just a gauge, one of many in determining where that place is located. Using a stereotypical analysis of age, however, just limits the number of people capable of a visit.

There are so many self-help books, tapes and seminars out there which use the same type formulas for success in dating that we heard about regarding the gender factors of a relationship equation. And, as the different planet analogy provided insights into the diversity of genders that were stereotypical but not valid from an individual perspective, so to is the comparison of age.

Some of the People Some of the Time

It is really unfair to include "every man" and "every woman" in a formula that presents people as the same. We should know that it isn't true, and yet we continue to fall into the trap because it is easy. Easy, in the sense that the less work we have to do to determine who is right for us, the more prone we are to consider that particular direction. Once again, an easy or lazy approach to the most important decision you ever make will most likely bring about either no result, or the wrong result.

The best way to judge the benefit and validity of these formulas is to look within ourselves to see if we are "every man" or "every woman." We know that in many ways we are different. Wouldn't it be a shame if that someone out there who could be our match, lumped us into one of these categories that didn't fit us. And yet, here we are considering doing the same thing to our possible match.

The benefits of a quick fix formula for success is that it provides a grouping of the typical match for a typical person given typical criteria. Typically, in some categories this could be a good measure to begin a search. But not in all categories, and certainly not with all people.

We have all read stories that support the validity of these groupings, with regard to age. The younger woman who marries the older man, only to find out in ten years that he just wants to sit home and watch TV and has lost his sexual desire. Or the older woman who marries the younger man, only to find out that he would rather spend his time playing basketball with his friends, then visiting art galleries with her. Then there's the younger woman who likes to go to bars and go out dancing; the older man who doesn't like to travel anymore; the older woman who would rather read a book than make love all night; the younger man who would rather make love all night. They go on and on with these "typical" stories. But, as we read these stories, we find that we know people who could fit these descriptions at any age or gender.

What really happens is that these people get stuck at different levels of their relationships, and that's what is causing the problem; not age. There are certainly reasons for concern that need to be contemplated, such as health, goals, maturity, and things that would have significance because of a considerable age difference. But as the ages increase, the cause for worry should decrease. There might be more reason for concern if one person is 20 and the other is 40, than if one person is 40 and the other is 60. What it really comes down to is life's experiences and life's desires, and the level of need of each person.

> *Again, poor Fred. Whenever his friends think about what it was that made him really happy, it was his kids. Fred was a terrific father. His kids were small when he got divorced, and because of the problems he had with his ex-wife, he never got to experience their early adolescent and teenage years; he really misses that.*

> *When we ask Fred what his plans are for the future, he says that he would like to get married again and start a family. Well, that might sound great for someone younger, but Fred is approaching 50. All his friends have advised him to just enjoy single life, travel, and have fun. They suggest that if he really wants to get married, he should only find a companion who enjoys the same activities that he does. But, no kids. To start over at his age would be crazy.*

> *Fred wants a family more than anything, though. His problem is age. First of all, he has to find someone who is*

young enough to still want to have children. Then he needs to find someone old enough to want to have children with someone his age.

Knowing Fred with all of his capabilities and desires, he wouldn't have any problems starting over. He's in great shape and plans on enjoying a long life. His problem will be attracting someone to start over with, who is able to view him as an individual, rather than the typical 50-year old "every man" who we read about. There is nothing "typical" about Fred. Maybe someday he'll meet someone who will realize that.

Old Is As Old Does

No matter what gender you are, or what limits society places upon the judgments you utilize in your search for love, to judge another based on chronological age will certainly restrict the opportunity to find your perfect match. Age may play an important part in the communication and understanding of a relationship, and then again, it may not. People are different. They are individuals, and they grow and relate differently. Some people at 35 look and act like they are 50, and some people at 55 look and act like they are 40. There are those who at 60 years of age don't have the common sense or the maturity of someone 40 years of age. There are those who at 40 years of age will die in a short inactive 20 years, at age 60, while there are some already 60 years of age who will still actively be alive after another 30 years at age 90.

Some who are older, have many experiences in life, yet may crave to experience so many more, while some younger, whose experiences are ahead of them, may be content to watch life pass them by. There are those who have worked many years, but have accumulated little security, while others just starting careers already have great promise of financial success. Then, there are even people whose sexual interest and activity may have peaked at a younger age, while others in advancing years have yet to notice a diminishing of desire. And of course, there is now Viagra. Isn't science wonderful?

Pete has become kind of an inspiration to those of us passing through middle age. He was one of the older guys, over 60, who had reached a point in his life where his main concern was just going out drinking and dancing and dating younger women. That's how he dealt with his solitude, but that's not the reason he is an inspiration.

It seemed all of those who knew him realized that his married days were over and that he was going to live the rest of his life carefree and alone. He had a great job and was pretty well off financially. He traveled a lot and was always up for an adventure. He didn't appear to be concerned about much including his health. He already had a family that was grown and he felt that he was too old to be able to start a family again. Then he met a woman of about 35 years of age who had been divorced for about three years, from a very unhappy marriage with very little security. They dated for a while and enjoyed each other's company. After about six months of dating they got married and shortly thereafter had a baby girl. Pete's life changed.

His little daughter is ten years old now and what a wonderful sight it is to see Pete walking hand and hand with his little girl. He is a doting father whose love and joy are expressed by the constant smile on his face. It doesn't look like he has aged at all from the day his daughter was born, probably because he now takes a lot better care of himself.

Pete talks all the time about how lucky he was beginning a family again. But one has to wonder how long this luck will last and how much longer Pete will be around to be a father to his very young daughter. When I very candidly asked him, that while his situation was good for him, how did he think his age was going to affect his wife and daughter. He explained that when he first met his wife, her dream was to meet and marry someone who would love and respect her; someone who could provide her with security and maybe someday have a family with. She always wanted to be a stay at home mom, but realized that might be too much to ask.

Pete mentioned that he was almost afraid to fall in love with her because he didn't think he could help her fulfill her dreams. But fall in love he did. Not wanting to further the relationship under false pretenses, he had a very open and frank discussion with her. They both came to the understanding that while the factors of age and experience and even interests seem to divide who they are, that there was really very little difference as to what their needs and goals for the future were. And, they complemented each other in so many ways. They both wanted a family and the security and love that go along with it. Pete had enough security so that she could be a stay at home mom and they would never have to worry about finances. They could travel and really enjoy life. She also loved to take care of Pete, from the way he dressed to what he ate. She was also well educated and smart enough to communicate with him about his business. Pete loved it.

But what about Pete's age, I asked? Were there any concerns given the fact that he will not live forever? Pete said that his wife is always concerned about his health and helps him live a healthy lifestyle to insure he has as many years left as possible. It was his wife though, in that initial conversation, who told him that in life you never know what is going to happen. That if she lived with Pete twenty or thirty more years that she would be so thankful to have a marriage last that long, especially nowadays. There wouldn't be the pressures of the typical marriage involving finances and careers or transfers or even just growing up. She will be getting everything she ever dreamed about and would be so thankful to have been with Pete, no matter how long it lasted. And while their kids may not experience the longevity of a father's relationship as some might, they will certainly have a better quality life than most.

As I listened to Pete tell me his story I thought of my own that started with my mother, who was only there through my teenage years and a failed relationship that didn't last as long. Pete also mentioned to me that nothing lasts forever. The ideal isn't, after all, just to have a marriage that lasts as long as it can; it is to have an ideal marriage. If you can do that for 20 or 30 years, you've really accomplished something.

There are men and women who would make wonderful husbands, wives, and parents no matter what age they are, and there are individuals who will never be able or even want to see that measure of success. And, of course, there are people who will learn from their accomplishments and mistakes, and those who don't have that capability. Sometimes people are different because of how old they are. Most times they are different, because of "**who**" they are.

On a recent trip to Florida, I met up with a number of what some would call "elderly" men—they call themselves "seniors"—who would arise every day at 5:45 a.m. to meet at the tennis courts or golf courses to spend the morning "playing hard"—the women arrive about 9 a.m. Now, I'm a fairly good tennis player, although apparently I don't play often enough, because I was beaten in a doubles match where one of my opponents had just turned 85 years old, and it appeared like he had another ten good years of tennis in him. There was no way he looked or played like he was 85, or even 65, and there he was every day, many times beating all those "kids" of 70 years of age.

I talked to him briefly, because he was always on the move, about his motivation for playing so much and so hard. He said that tennis has helped him maintain his hand/eye coordination and his reflexes as well as keeping his mind sharp. He also said that he liked to play and have fun and how much he was enjoying life since he retired.

My uncle, who was somewhat disappointed that he had to have me as his tennis partner that day, who at probably about 70 years old—we're not sure and we don't ask—could easily pass for 60. He acts like he's 50; they call him the "kid". He really is a remarkable person. He has such an intense interest in his overall physical and mental condition. He seems aware of everything that affects his body, and, of course, because of his success, his whole family always goes to him for physical counseling.

He leads a normal single life, and doesn't go to extremes. He does exercise though, on a daily basis by playing tennis and golf, sometimes even on the same day. He has found that the best way to maintain his physique is to exercise in the morning, but if that's not possible, he will still make sure that he exercises at some point every day. He is also very cautious about what he eats, and while he doesn't diet and does eat out frequently, he always makes sure that he minimizes those foods that aren't quite healthy and balances them with healthy foods. Of course, he always takes vitamin supplements, and over the years he has noted their effect on his condition.

While retired, his job seems to be staying young, and in so many ways he has succeeded. He feels as comfortable socializing and competing with people in their forties and fifties as he does with people his own age. And, after playing tennis with him and his friends, I know he can. He thinks he has the body and capabilities of a 40-year old, but I think it's more like a typical 50-year old, and he and his friends are proof of how attitude, exercise, and diet can change what society considers the normality of the condition of one's life.

They all made a choice: their chronological age wasn't going to make a difference in how they lived their lives, and that no matter what perceptions society had about how old they were, they were going to be different because of "who" they were.

The criteria that we use in the selection of that person capable of appreciating and sharing our love, needs to include so many more important things than age or location. It needs to embrace morality, values, trust, commitment, honesty and integrity. It needs to involve everything from physical attraction to financial security, from shared interests to goals for the future, and from learning together to feeling for each other. It needs to comprehend all that is involved in a decision that could, and probably would, include sickness and health, good times and bad, and hopefully a long time till death do they part.

The More The Merrier

The only way to ensure the expansion of possibilities necessary to finding a mate is to change your matchmaking equation from firm limitations to degrees of acceptance, where reasonable. There must be a clear understanding that the more variation we are capable of accepting, the greater the number of choices we will have.

While there may be certain demands that are too important to allow variation, adjustments will allow a relationship that might not have ever existed, because of unreasonable limitations. For example, someone who has severe problems with smoking could certainly limit the possibilities of a match to someone who doesn't smoke. An alcoholic should probably not seek out someone who drinks. Limitations are justified when habits lead to bad behavior or health concerns. However, unnecessary or overzealous restrictions may just limit a probability. Maybe a person can quit smoking or drinking, or cut back to a reasonable level, if acceptable. People begin some bad habits when they are *Suddenly Single,* but given the right environment, and the incentives of a new relationship, someone with minor usage should probably not have their chances discarded. Of course it is always a bad idea to change a limitation to a degree of acceptance because of desperation rather than being reasonable.

Education is another reasonable gauge that people use to typically determine who a person is, but like age, each person is different, and each relates differently to learning opportunities. With some people, a formal education may not be as valuable to their lives and knowledge as experience. While earning an education certainly exhibits degrees of discipline, a level of intelligence, and persistence, many times a career opportunity or a different arena can allow for these same qualities to exist. While people with similar educations and intellect would have an enhanced capability to communicate, there is no hard, fast rule that states that they will make better matches.

Maybe someone with a high-powered, stressful job would be better suited to someone who can provide extraordinary care for a family and home. Or maybe a person who makes $80,000 a year and isn't having any fun in life can couple with someone who makes $20,000 a year who doesn't have much security, but knows how to have fun. With $100,000 a year they can have a lot of fun and security together. Sometimes, complements can provide so much more than duplicates. Even being opposite in certain areas can provide a satisfactory complement. Reading books, participating in sports, writing, going to school, sewing, gardening, and work-related activities, are all individual pursuits that either partner in a relationship can pursue, without threatening the security or goals of the other.

Differences in religion and politics may even be rationalized to co-exist in a relationship, although their differences may indicate deeper concerns and be a source for future conflict. Of course, if the relationship is going to lead to marriage and possibly children, then differences like these must be weighted accordingly. An Atheist becoming involved with a devout Christian or Jew might present future problems, while a Republican and Democrat might not have as significant a problem but will engage in lively debates. There are certain goals, aspirations, and beliefs which we all have, that can provide absolute limitations that should never be compromised.

To narrow the chances of crossing paths of that one in 50,000, a wish list of priorities and those absolute limitations must be established. Once again, you need to be honest with yourself. Make a list of all those "definites" of who your partner must be. Then add how you feel—your emotions and view of life—and any other qualities that you sense should be matched. Then throw in the complements that would be appropriate to enhance a fruitful and lasting relationship.

After that list is completed, begin to think beyond that general population of 50,000 to the more specific places where the probabilities of your match exist. Religious priorities would lead to theological interests; physical concerns should lead to health clubs and athletic events; an affinity for socialization would direct one to "social" clubs and outings; and intellectual attractions would point toward educational institutions or groups that discuss and analyze issues, such as political associations.

The more you try to cross paths with like-minded people who fulfill your priority list, the more probabilities you will meet. The more probabilities you meet the more you can add to your list. You know you are succeeding when you can consider your perfect match's height, hair, and eye color. Not that such minor physical attributes would mean much to a desperate *Suddenly Single,* but human nature being what it is, we won't be satisfied with someone who just feels like we do.

There is a story I have heard many times over the years. Unfortunately I am unaware of the original storyteller. It's about a soldier stationed in Florida by the name of John

Blanchard, who one day stood up from the bench on which he was sitting, straightened his wrinkled Army uniform, and glanced at the people making their way through Grand Central Station. He was looking for the girl whose heart he knew, but whose face he didn't—the girl with the rose.

His interest in her had begun over 13 months before in a Florida library. Taking a book of his interest off a shelf, he found himself intrigued, not so much with the words of the book, but rather with the notes penciled in the margin. The soft handwriting and inspiring thoughts reflected a thoughtful soul and an insightful mind. In the front of the book, he discovered the previous owner's name, Miss Hollis Maynell, and with some time and effort he located her address. She lived in New York City. He then wrote her a letter and invited her to correspond with him. A few days later he was shipped overseas for service in World War II.

During the next year and one month, the two got to know each other through the letters they sent, and each letter was like a seed falling on a fertile heart. A romance was budding and Blanchard requested her photograph, but she refused. She felt that if he really cared, it wouldn't matter what she looked like.

When the time finally arrived for him to return from Europe, they scheduled their first meeting at 7 p.m. at Grand Central Station in New York City. "You'll recognize me," she wrote, "by the red rose I'll be wearing on my lapel." Blanchard replied that he would be recognized by "the book" that he would carry. So, at 7 p.m. he was in the station looking for a girl whose heart he loved, but whose face he had never seen.

He noticed a young woman approaching him, her figure long and slim. Her blonde hair lay back in curls from her delicate ears; her eyes were blue as flowers. Her lips and chin had a gentle firmness, and in her pale green suit, she was like springtime come alive. As he started toward her, he seemed to notice everything about her, but forgot to notice that she was not wearing a red rose. As he got closer, a small, provocative smile curved her lips. He thought he heard her murmur "Going my way, soldier." Almost uncontrollably, he made one more step closer to her and then "I saw Hollis Maynell."

She was standing almost directly behind the girl in the pale green suit. She was a woman well past 50 and had graying hair tucked under a well-worn hat. She was more than plump, and in his observation noticed her thick-ankled feet thrust into low-heeled shoes. As the girl in the pale green suit was walking away quickly, "I felt as though I were split in two, so keen was my desire to follow her, and yet was so deep my longing for the woman whose spirit had truly captured me and upheld my own."

And there she stood. Her pale plump face was gentle and sensible and her gray eyes had a warm and kindly twinkle. He did not hesitate as his fingers gripped the small worn blue leather copy of the book that was to identify him to her. "This would not be love," he thought, "but it would be something precious, something perhaps even better than love; a friendship for which I had been and must ever be grateful." He squared his shoulders and saluted and held out the book to the woman even though while he spoke he felt "choked by the bitterness of my disappointment although also appreciative of this moment of meeting."

"*I am Lieutenant John Blanchard, and you must be Miss Maynell. I am so glad you could meet me; may I please take you to dinner?" The woman's face broadened into a tolerant smile. "I don't know what this is all about, son," she answered, "but the young lady in the green suit that just went by begged me to wear this rose on my coat. She said that if you were to ask me to dinner, that I should tell you that she is waiting for you in the big restaurant across the street. She said it was some kind of test."*

16

Seek and You
Shall Find

The problem most of us have is not knowing where or how to get started in this new life that has been abruptly thrust upon us. Those *Suddenly Single* typically don't have a plan, because they were committed to a relationship that was going to last forever. They weren't looking for someone else or something else to do. To those non-committed folks, starting over was part of a plan, because they recognized that their relationship might fail. When you are committed, you don't have the luxury of foresight. You must start fresh at the beginning, with a plan.

As was mentioned earlier, you can at least begin the "no brainer" parts of the plan by starting to get in shape through exercise and nutrition. Of course, to delve deep into the recesses of your mind to figure out who you are is going to take quite a bit of time, effort and soul-searching. And then, formulating a profile of who your soul mate is, within the limitations you set forth, will be an ongoing process, while all the time working through the grief of your last relationship.

It's going to be a continuing process because, as you become more secure with yourself, you will have less of a tendency to settle out of desperation. As you meet new and different people you will probably adjust your qualifications. Even some of the absolutes of your limitations may soften, if you meet that one right person who feels as you do, or in the case your absolutes are too limiting that you have difficulty meeting anyone.

The end of your journey, however, does not necessarily coincide with the end of this process of searching. What marks the ending of your ordeal, your journey, is the acceptance of change. Your journey has helped you arrive at a comfortable new beginning. You are still going to be searching, but in a more confident, relaxed and purposeful state of mind.

Just Do It

The terms *seeking, searching, finding,* all seem to indicate some sort of movement. That movement has a direct correlation to the success of your purpose. If your seeking has no more movement associated with it than sitting in front of the TV waiting for something to happen, your finding will then provide the same sort of movement. To seek someone means to actually pursue the possibilities of meeting someone. All those other people that you know, or have already met, obviously were not the "someone" you sought. So, now you have to show some movement to meet new people.

Maybe it's not easy leaving the comfort of your individual surroundings to go out into the cruel world to conduct a search. Maybe, when you get home from work, you just like to change into something comfortable, cook yourself some dinner, and relax in front of the TV, curl up with a good book, or even write a book. Besides, now you are getting used to that scenario. Maybe you have the comfort of your children or pets that deserve your attention. It would seem difficult not to spend all of your free time with them because you are probably the focus of their lives, and they need you. Maybe you are so involved with your job and the social circle it presents, that you can't imagine having any time to do or think about anything else. After all, that's what provides you your security, and has allowed you to focus on something other than the negatives in your life. Or, maybe you just like to hang out with your inner circle of friends and venture out to those same old well-worn places that you all feel safe in. These are the steady people and places that helped you through your despair, and there is a sense of comfort in familiarity.

All these situations are understandable and comforting, but they don't provide any movement to change. There is nothing wrong with relishing the security of relaxing at home, or spending time with your children or pets, or being so dedicated to your job and fellow workers, or even hanging out with your friends. But, you need to expose yourself to new people in new places. You need to broaden your activities and interests if you ever want to cross paths with that person you are seeking. All of your current associations are important and can remain so, even though you are expanding your base of comfort. Sometimes this present comfort becomes an excuse for not seeking. Maybe it's the fear of failing in the future. Or maybe you've become lazy to the prospect of having to start over.

One of my best friends had gone through a horrible divorce that, along with his recovery and healing, took a few years to complete. He was one of these really nice guys who thought he was being a good husband only to find himself alone and despairing. I used to visit him in these times of distress and found what used to be a thoughtful, decisive person, had turned into someone who couldn't think clearly and didn't know what he was going to do. When he completed going through all the processes of grief and understanding though, he was ready and committed to search for his match.

He joined clubs and attended activities. He went out on group functions and dated different women. He also traveled and took trips to exotic places by himself. And, it was on one of these exotic cruises that he got lucky. It was there he met an entertainer, a singer with a famous group.

She had never been married and had been dedicated to her profession all these years, enjoying the benefits of loving her work and traveling the world. She was at a point in her life though, where she had seen most of the world and began thinking about dating and possibly settling down with a family. While there was somewhat of a significant age difference, they both were at a place in their lives where they were searching for love, and had now found it.

My friend had been on cruises before and had traveled extensively, primarily to get out of the rut he was in: dealing with his failed relationship. He had met some interesting people and had worthwhile experiences, yet, who would have thought that he would have met his future wife on this particular cruise. He wasn't planning on it, although by taking this cruise, it was all part of his plan to eventually meet someone. After all, the greater exposure you have to more numerous and different people in dissimilar surroundings, the more likelihood there is to meet that special someone who will be part of your life forever. That was his plan, and it worked.

Now, I would never have gone on a cruise by myself, although I have gone alone to meetings around the country. To me, it took my friend a lot of courage to decide to do something like that. To him, however, it wasn't so much courage, as it was a resolve to make his life better, more enjoyable, and to welcome the possibility of change. He was always certainly looking for the woman of his dreams, but while he was doing that, he was enjoying life. There was no pressure in doing that. Whenever he ventured out on a new experience, he never regretted it if he didn't find someone, because he always enjoyed the adventure. Besides, he knew it would just take time. And, it was time well spent, rather than sitting home waiting for a miracle to happen. His miracle happened because he went looking for it.

I was best man at his wedding to his beautiful bride. I couldn't help but think how lucky they both were to be able to meet like they did. As a sidelight, they are parents to the most adorable children one could ever imagine. That's interesting because he was told during his previous marriage that he could never have children. Sometimes things happen for a reason; maybe it's not just luck.

Get A Job

Do you still feel that you shouldn't have to go through all this trouble, as you felt when you were considering getting in shape? As in our discussion about physical condition, how, while we work so hard at our jobs to provide our homes, cars, and all those other things that we need and desire and deserve, can we somehow question the value of working hard to find a recipient of our love? That is exactly what seeking is all about. It is about treating the search for your soul mate as a job, with the same intensity you have getting those other things in your life that you need. Granted, with all your other responsibilities, it may be a part-time job—but a job with a payment more valuable than any other hard work can provide.

Just imagine a job in which your goal is to find a love match as payment for all your hard work. It's like working for commission; you don't get paid unless you sell your product. I know this must sound simplistic, but once again we all need to start somewhere with a plan. Besides, now you can justify sitting around strategizing, researching, and conferring with others in a similar position, or asking the advice of friends and family. It shows your positive outlook, and your resolve to move on and in a positive direction. And every once in awhile, you need to reflect on how important this search will be in your life, so as not to lose the intensity of its purpose. It is probably a good idea to also make sure that this business plan be put in writing, so that you not only have a ready reference to your mission, but also that you really do begin treating it like a job.

Since you've already defined your product, you, it is now time to figure out who you are going to sell it to, and put it into writing. List all those absolutes and then the degrees of acceptance of all those other characteristics that exist in your equation of a match. In a sense you are painting a portrait in words that describe the person you are searching for. Eventually, you will end up with not just one picture of your soul mate, but also a morphing of pictures, where the extremes of your degree of acceptance criteria can exist in your search group, with everyone else in between.

After completing that phase of your plan, you can then begin imagining where these people exist, or where the best possibilities are to cross their paths. This does take some imagination, since obviously you have not been able to cross paths with them as of yet, in the places you have been. It also doesn't hurt to add to the equation places they would go to meet someone like you.

This is the rifle approach of marketing. In a business that was searching for a certain type of consumer, it would be likened to sending brochures to a certain demographic group or placing ads that targets a certain age or interest group. For example, if you were looking for someone who likes to keep in shape, you would go to a gym. But you would need to go to different gyms at different times to increase your exposure. A key point to remember; the reason you have this job, is that you haven't met that person yet in the routine of people and places that you currently exist. So **don't get into routines.** It will just waste more of your valuable time.

Adjust the Focus

It would be obvious to mention that if religion was an important consideration in your choice that you need to investigate religious organizations, church groups or functions. If dancing and that sort of socialization are important, take dance lessons and try different nightclubs. If politics are one of your main interests, get involved in a political party or someone's campaign. However, the rifle approach only fulfills that one area of concern or interest. A rifle only shoots one bullet at a time directed at a specific target. You might find someone at a church function who satisfies your religious interests, but doesn't meet many of your other matchmaking criteria. But it is a start, and at least you can cross paths with someone who will attract you because of one thing or another about them. Of course, the initial attraction in a case like this may not be physical, but rather shared interests.

Dating services, personal newspaper ads, vacations, seminars and clubs for singles, and of course the Internet are other ways of focusing on meeting people with similar interests. While dating services and newspaper ads can be rather costly and really only provide a limited number of possibilities, they are surely worth the investigation. You just need to put yourself in the shoes of another person sometimes and figure out what they would do or where they would go to make an attempt at finding you.

Sometimes, high-profile professionals need to go to a dating service, to participate in a service that allows for anonymous introductions, or depend on family or friends to set them up. Dating services, while usually extremely expensive, have a limited clientele. They do, however, have the advantage of attracting people who wouldn't be spending all that money unless they were serious about finding a match. There is a certain "air" of exclusivity about that sort of search. And, when you get to the point of not having the capability to meet anyone at work, through friends, or you just don't have the time and effort to conduct a search, a service of this sort, or even taking a few minutes to look through those personal ads, might work.

While newspaper ads are just a couple of sentences, there is usually a recorded voice message that offers more detail. I met two really nice people doing just that. Of course, when I mentioned to one of my dates that to some people this might seem like a pretty desperate way to meet possible matches, she reminded me that I called her, and what did that make me? Just because someone is perceived as desperate in their means of getting to meet someone, it doesn't take away from their value as a possible match. It could be that this is the only way they thought they could meet someone new. They've got to be better off than all those people with no movement in their lives. Just remember, newspapers make a lot of money selling you telephone time answering these ads, and many times that cost may be even more than other possibilities of searching for a match.

Advertise Yourself

While doing the research on newspaper classified dating, I also conferred with a friend of mine who worked at a newspaper, and a few friends who had actually placed ads. I was amazed at how well thought out the whole scheme of personal ads in the newspaper was. The newspapers had their own ready-made free resource, by allowing people to place their personal ads for free. Sometimes, they get hundreds a month that they rotate with the new ones appearing first. So there is always someone new, offering a descriptive ad as to who they are looking for and/or who they are. This encourages those who are searching for someone to regularly check the personals for that special ad that offers hope of a match.

Since the advertisers are limited in space as to the description they are offering, they are also permitted to record a message with a further explanation. In most cases, that is also free to those placing the ad. To listen to that message, however, usually costs the searching party approximately two dollars per minute. If they want to respond to an ad, it's another two dollars per minute. This part of the transaction is anonymous, and advertisers are not permitted to give their telephone numbers in the ad. So each time that an ad is answered, chances are the cost is going to be at least ten dollars, and that's if you really don't have much to say. And when someone is of the mindset to call these "personals", they probably won't limit themselves to a short response or calling just one ad.

My friends who placed ads had different experiences and actually changed their ads once they learned how the game was played. My friend Stephanie had placed what she thought was the perfect ad:

SINGLE MOM

Attractive mother of two. Late 30's brown/brown, 5'2."
Considerate, romantic, sweet. Loves gardening, cooking,
going on picnics, traveling, reading. Looking for a family
man who is trustworthy and financially secure.

It was a good ad that described a real basic description of who she was and who she was looking for. But, there wasn't much to distinguish her ad from others. She only received two responses, and decided not to go out with either one. Her friends helped write a more enticing ad that they felt was more honest and attractive than her own.

SWEETNESS

Absolutely the sweetest, nicest person you are ever going to meet. Loves to cook romantic dinners at home or traveling just for two. Family oriented, and has two fun, well-behaved kids who don't mind Mom taking off and having fun herself every once in awhile. A very attractive 5'2" who looks as good in jeans as she does in lace. Seeking equally secure and trustworthy man with similar interests to enjoy happiness together.

Stephanie received quite a few calls on this ad and within a week had decided to meet with two of the men who answered her ad. She still continues dating one of them. Her friends also helped her put together her recorded message, which was not as humble sounding as the original one. This time she was very self assured and up front on what she had to offer and what she expected.

A friend of a friend, Marti, had put together an ad in which she described herself as someone who loves to country/western dance, go to movies, travel, watch football on TV, drink beer and hang around with friends. She thought her ad would attract a lot of men because they would see her as someone who could enjoy the same things that they do. She had plenty of responses and dated three of the men she had met through the ad. Unfortunately, while each one said that they would enjoy dancing, movies and traveling, all they wanted to do during football season was sit around and watch the games on TV and drink beer with their friends. She said that in her next ad she was going to say that she hated watching football on TV, but loved to shop.

Brad had thought that he too had put together a pretty good ad. It listed all the things that he liked to do, including playing sports, hiking, biking, roller blading, going to the gym, and running 10K races. He mentioned how he likes to travel, cook, watch movies and sports at home and go to clubs dancing. He stated that he was seeking a woman to share his life with him. He didn't receive one response to his ad. I would have expected that at least one woman would have called telling him how self centered he was, but I guess with the associated charges involved, no one bothered. I told Brad that it seemed that he was advertising for a male buddy rather than seeking a love connection with a woman. While **he was looking for a woman to first play with, women were looking for someone to later love with.** It was important for him to focus his ad in such a manner. He admitted I was right, because he knew of someone who did exactly that and couldn't stop the responses from coming in.

Brad's friend Art was the one who put an ad together at about the same time. Art enjoyed all the same activities that Brad did, and thought that it would be nice if he happened to attract a woman who had some of the same interests. That wasn't his main concern though, since he was looking for a woman to complement his life by bringing her interests to him, and possibly making new interests together. His ad expressed a different tone.

SHARING

Loving, caring, sensitive man. Strong physically and emotionally. Loves to give and appreciates receiving. Passionate and compassionate and receives pleasure by giving the same. Enjoys the intimacy of conversation as much as the feelings of a touch. Thankful for the attractiveness of his

> *looks, but wants to be attractive for his loyalty, his comfort
> and his joy. Seeking a woman who shares these feelings. In-
> terests in athletics a plus, but not a must.*

The only problem with Art's ad was that it attracted too many replies. He is still sorting through the responses and occasionally has
time to go out on a date with some of the women he met through his
ad. With all his choices, he will probably meet someone who not
only has the qualities of the woman he was looking for, but will also
have many of the same interests that he enjoys.

These ads present an interesting dynamic in that they are directly competing for attention with all the other ads that appear
in that same newspaper. If you look at the ads that most men
place, they usually involve their interests and needs. That's why
Art's ad stood out so much, because he was appealing to sensitivities that a woman might find very attractive. When he read
all those other ads, he realized that, not only didn't he want to
sound like they did, but that apparently he wasn't like those other
male advertisers. Leslie, another friend of Brad's attempted to
do the same thing.

She had placed an ad about a year before, with very little response. As a matter of fact, she relates how it sounded a lot like
Art's ad. It dealt with caring and sharing and intimacy. It asked
for trust and loyalty and an understanding of feelings. She had
since given up on "personals" in the newspaper, because there
were so many women looking for the same thing. She was then
encouraged when she heard about Art's success and decided to
put herself in the place of a man looking through the ads to
figure out what might grab their attention. She picked out parts
of other ads that applied to her and that she thought would be
attractive to a man, being careful not to fall into the trap of appealing to someone looking for a TV watching, beer drinking

buddy. Brad helped her with his advice. Her ad attracted a lot of attention.

HOT

Sexy, attractive SF, 5'6", blonde/blue, 36yr. old hard body. Likes to work out and give massages. Enjoys sports, traveling, movies or just cuddling by the fire. Loves to dance either with friends at a club, or at home with someone special. Lots of fun with a great sense of humor. Adventurous and creative. Loves to start the night with a romantic candlelit dinner at home. Seeking a man who likes to be spoiled, but is also willing to share and be loyal.

Leslie got so many replies, that she had to pull her ad out of circulation after the first week. She must hold the record for number of responses and certainly made a lot of money for the newspaper that week. A few of the men responding asked if the ad was for real, thinking that it was either a prank or a ploy by the paper to make money off of their response. A few others acknowledged that if everything she said in her ad were true, why would she even worry about someone being loyal; they could never find anything better than that. Some of the answers were so long that Leslie reasoned they must have spent more money on the phone call than they would have taking her out on a date. She also realized that the words *Hot, Sexy, hard body,* and *massage* were probably the only words needed in the ad according to some of the men that called.

Leslie never went out with any of the men who responded to her ad. She didn't know if it was because there were so many, and she couldn't make up her mind, or because some of them sounded rather aggressive. When it was explained to her that her ad might have been a little too aggressive itself, she said she was just being honest. Believe it or not, she was. But she said that she is only that way with someone she is familiar with, and she got the impression that the men calling would expect to be "spoiled hot" right away.

In any dating situation that involves competition, it is important that your package is more noticeable than others. It needs to be more colorful, exciting, and enticing. It needs to attract attention and be perceived as different. It needs to exhibit quality and be well thought out. Of course, above all else it needs to be honest. There are so many different ways to describe yourself honestly, that it really shouldn't be difficult to come up with one that is clear and effective. Words that can usually be used to evoke the senses are the words that you want to visually portray and emotionally feel, who you are.

To be effective, however, requires a response. You not only have to be noticeable enough to draw attention to the product of yourself, but you have to present a package so attractive as to lure prospective responders away from similar expressions. You also need to make that attraction urgent, because of the competition and possibility of lost opportunity to require immediate action. It must somehow embrace all that will tantalize, while still being honest, clear, and to the point.

To exhibit all these qualities, if I were placing a personal ad in a newspaper, I would look to my audience and appeal to their sensitivities. My ad would simply say, "Man who loves to shop seeks woman." I am sure that all the interest generated would provide enough responses to find someone willing to match shopping with anything I wanted to do.

The Club Scene

Special interest clubs should also be considered and are certainly worth a couple of visits to meet the other members. Who knows, you might even enjoy and benefit from their activities. Clubs of this nature usually seek out and encourage new membership for the same reason you are interested in them, as well as receiving dues. The larger, long-standing activity clubs provide a steady stream of new singles who are eager to participate and meet other people. Some smaller clubs are that way for a reason. Either they don't have much in the way of interest for new members, or they intentionally maintain a degree of exclusivity.

Most of the clubs that I attended were very open and receptive. There were a couple of smaller ones however, that seemed to be exclusive to their long-term members. They were more like an extended family sharing in their isolation rather than a club open to new experiences and people. The women seemed to treat me pensively, like I was an outsider who was going to disrupt the status quo. The men treated me as an intruder who was going to steal away in the middle of the night with their women. Clearly, people like this were in a severe rut, and had accepted that their lives weren't going to change much. It appeared that while perhaps the members of their club weren't matches for them, they were satisfied enough not to accept change.

Some of the neighborhood nightclubs I visited in different cities presented the same type of a scenario except on a larger scale. People went there to feel secure, everything was familiar. The feeling of exclusivity that emanated from the small groups that clustered in these establishments did little to welcome any change an outsider might bring to their routine. You would think that the people, who frequent places that are thought of as singles hangouts, would understand that this "badge" of condition that they accept, would indicate that they are searching for other singles. Maybe they are just single people looking for more single people who want to stay single.

One night, a friend of mine called and asked if I wanted to meet him and some friends at a "singles" bar on the other side of town. I told him that I wouldn't mind going out, but that I had been to that particular bar once before and it seemed really inhospitable. He told me that was because it was kind of a neighborhood hang out and that everyone knew each other. He said that it is really different if you go with people that everyone knows. I agreed to meet him.

I arrived before he and his friends got there, and felt the same unsociable atmosphere as the last time I was there. It actually seemed from the stares I was getting, that people were wondering what I was doing there. And this wasn't a small bar. This one had an occupancy of about two hundred people and was jammed packed with apparently everyone being a regular. By the time my friend arrived, I was almost ready to leave, that's how bad the "feeling" was.

After he arrived and we walked around meeting his friends, everyone seemed really accepting and the whole atmosphere of the bar appeared to lighten up toward me. As a matter of fact, people were really very friendly, and I began to think what a great place to hang out. Though it still had that feeling of exclusivity, I was now one of the exclusive. As we were mingling I noticed that most tables included all men or all women. Even though they all knew each other, they were for the most part separated by gender. We broke that standard by sitting with three women my friend knew. They were all very good looking, very personable, and from what I could tell, very available, although I would never had been able to meet them if it hadn't been for my friend's acquaintance. I asked one of the women if she would like to shoot pool, and after receiving acceptable glances from her friends she agreed. As we were shooting pool, I told her of my previous experience at the bar about six months before, and she mentioned she thought she remembered seeing me come in then. When I asked her how she could remember that far back, she said that it's just that not many "new people" come in there. I was somewhat flattered to be remembered, but was still puzzled as to the benefit of being so exclusive.

After a while, she told me that she and her friends had been going to this same place every Friday night for the past couple of years. They always arrive at about the same time, early enough to get "their" same table. She mentioned that the benefit to them was that they get to hang out together in a really secure place, and that they wouldn't feel as safe going to other bars. They know all the guys there and everyone looks out after each other. If they went to other bars, as each had done before on occasion, they were usually "bothered" by someone they didn't want to be bothered by. She also stated that they have never dated anyone from this bar.

When I questioned that this seemed to really limit their possibilities of meeting someone to date, she expressed that they usually date men they meet at work or from other friends, and that's the trade off for feeling protected. And, when I asked her what she would have done if I had come in there alone and had asked her to play pool, she said that she probably would have declined. It may have been because I was not known, but that she and her friends had an agreement to always stick together and to not be split up on Friday nights. I guess the reason she agreed on this night was that my two companions were with her

301

girlfriends, and this was acceptable to them.

After returning to the table, we all talked some more and then danced when the band began playing. It was a very enjoyable evening and I found myself attracted to this woman. We stayed to closing and we asked them if they wanted to go out and get some breakfast. They declined, since one of the women had to get up early the next morning. They encouraged us to meet them there the next Friday night and we agreed, although I knew I wasn't going to go back. I even considered at one point asking out the woman I was with, but given a second thought, realized that she would probably decline, given their choice of not dating men they meet at this bar.

I guess I understood where they were coming from, but thought at some point they would realize that with all they had going for them, there was a reason they were all still available. It's like they were stuck in a trade off which allowed their security to be guaranteed, but that demanded that the rules of the "game" be followed. In a way, it's a shame, but at least they really enjoy each other's company.

You've Got Mail

The Internet can be a matchmaking bonanza if approached with some degree of caution. It by far provides the most exposure for your time, effort, and in some cases, money. Some matchmaking services charge a monthly or quarterly fee, while a few Internet servers and others provide some sort of matchmaking service to their subscribers without additional cost. Some of these services advertise that they have over 1,000,000 members and offer to those who don't limit their searches to the neighborhood a world-wide audience. They afford the ability to identify specific geographic locations and allow a search for requested profile specifics such as age, ethnicity, religion, income, height, weight, body shape, whether they smoke or drink, and if they have children, or want children. There are some whose primary area of concern is religious preference, while others are activity specific.

Of course when dealing with Internet dating services, you can throw the one in 50,000 probabilities of a match theory out the window. For every 50,000 members of a dating service there should be 50 probable matches, utilizing the one in 1000 criteria established for a group of single people together. And with some of these dating services you have the capability of listing your criteria for a match and they will provide you with the results. Some even do that automatically. They afford you the capability of communicating with numerous other singles who have the same interest you do—finding someone else. In most cases the odds are even better than one in 1000 since all those participating are willing and able participants.

Most services offer pictures of advertisers when available, as well as a self-describing profile, which usually includes something about who they are, their likes and dislikes, and for whom they are searching. There is, of course, the capability to communicate with each other through e-mail, or even an anonymous e-mail when provided, so until you are ready, no one will know who you are. While this feature is a double-edged sword, it is probably, for the most part, a beneficial feature from a safety standpoint, since not everything on the Internet is as it appears.

There have been cases of deception with this kind of communication, but that happens in everyday life as well. It is, after all, just like communicating with someone by phone, except with the safety that they don't have your phone number. But, just like a phone conversation, you have to assume that the person you are talking to is telling you the truth. On the phone, you can't see who you are talking to, but if they have a picture on the Internet, you just have to believe it is of them. And, it goes both ways.

Sometimes people on the Internet display pictures that are not of themselves or even a picture taken many years before, in hopes of prompting an attraction. In my particular case I didn't have a picture displayed and explained to this presumably sweet, wonderful woman that it would take me some time to get it accomplished. Apparently she had gone through this before, with some disastrous results from someone who was very nearly the opposite of his description.

After awhile she was curious and insistent enough to ask if I had ever had any pictures of myself that might have ever appeared in any publication or reporting service. I told her that I was on TV a lot and in newspapers, but that they don't usually put pictures retrievable on the Internet. But, there might be a picture of me from my work in the Legislature.

I never heard from her again, and she never answered another e-mail. I kicked myself for not getting a picture displayed sooner. Then I went into our legislative reporting service to see what they had displayed. It was the picture from hell. It was one that was taken when I was at the peak of suffering from my thyroid condition. I was 50 pounds heavier. My eyes were bulging, my hair had fallen out, and my face was swollen. It would have been nice to find someone who would have accepted me like that, because then they would have been really pleased with the way I looked now. But whether it was because of the way I looked, or because it appeared I had been deceptive by describing myself as a muscular, in shape, attractive man, she never contacted me again.

It is helpful when we can put a face to a correspondence. For some people it is the initial attraction, while for others it is to see if there is any attraction. But at the very least, in something like Internet dating, it can contribute to an honest forthcoming relationship even if it doesn't evolve past e-mail. Besides, most people don't respond to ads that don't have a picture. There was a study that indicated that for every ten people that responded to an ad with a picture, only one responded to ads without pictures. I have now become conditioned to answering only ads or e-mails that come with pictures, not just because I want to see what they look like, but I thought if I put mine out there, I would expect the same in return.

These Internet dating or match making services had a somewhat dubious reputation in the past. However, in the past couple of years, they have become more mainstream, considering how many "normal," upstanding people who now participate. Some people still feel that there is a stigma, and that only very desperate people use it.

When I first investigated the Internet's offerings, I probably had that same impression until I realized that I was using it, and was I any more desperate than those other people? Besides, how desperate do you have to be to go to a singles bar? No more desperate than using your computer. And why criticize those who recognize the value of finding a recipient for their love, and who have the insight to understand that their search may take them beyond their neighborhood or social circles. We sometimes get conditioned by society to act and perform in a way that may limit or at least discourage our abilities to interact with people who may feel as we do.

The key to being successful with your search on the Internet is the same as achieving success in more traditional dating situations; be honest about yourself. Don't make yourself out to be someone you are not. You now know who you are, and that's whom you need to portray. And don't forget that those changes that you were hoping to accomplish is not the "who" you are, it is "who" you hope to be, and that isn't you yet.

That is the problem with most relationships, especially those found in situations like the Internet. Another's expectations tend to become the person you portray. Of course, that tendency happens a lot in traditional dating, as well. People give the wrong impression. They tend to give positive impressions or even change to fit a mold of what they assume would be desirable traits or behavior. They attempt to manipulate the courting by causing the party of their interest to become attracted to qualities that are images of their creation. Then when the attraction is firmly set in place, their traits and behaviors begin to modify, reflecting more and more an accurate portrayal as to who they are.

In many cases this is a natural occurrence and not an insidious plot. We all want to give a good first impression and during courtship will present ourselves in the best possible light. The intention is one of doing no harm, but clearly the harm is done because of the establishment of the relationship under false perceptions. Yet, sometimes it is so much easier being someone you are not, especially if you have a low self-esteem that allows you to feel unworthy of another's attraction. It is always better to be honest. It is always best to accentuate the true positives of your being. That approach will always get a response from someone looking for you.

It is certainly a lot easier to create a false image on something like the Internet, where initial contacts are just conversations. In some ways, some form of exaggeration is to be expected, but it is the blatant deception that is a cause of just concern. The lies about marital status and even gender are enough to make one wary of ever getting involved in such a situation. Over time, however the truth will usually come out and the only thing wasted will be time, provided involvements are kept anonymous until reasonable accuracy is assured. I, for one, have gone to both extremes of personal portrayal; each providing little success.

After a fairly lengthy correspondence, I was asked to send a current picture of myself. At the time the only recent picture on disk that could be sent was one of me in the woods with a three-day growth of beard wearing a baseball cap on backwards. I explained that it wasn't a very good likeness, but sent it anyway. I never heard from that person again. A friend of mine viewing the picture said that I appeared to be a fugitive from justice hiding out in the woods.

I have also sent pictures of myself at a exotic beach with the perfect tan and just the right camera angle to portray me as being in a lot better shape then I was with a lot more hair on my head then I had. I heard from those women again, but always worried that I would have difficulty living up to that picture. One of those exchanges of pictures involved a woman who seemed like she had everything going for her in life except someone to share it. Her picture portrayed an extremely attractive, confident woman. Maybe it was my insensitive remarks I shared: that with her appearance and all those other qualities, it was hard to believe she wasn't in a relationship. That caused her to lash out about, "Why does everybody have to be so perfect to be attractive?"

She then accused me of being a typical male, who places so much emphasis on a woman's looks and proceeded to tell me how much less than perfect I was.

That was one of my first Internet encounters and I guess it would be fair to say that we got off on the wrong foot. We never heard from each other again. When I think back now as to what transpired, I believe one of two things occurred. Either my remarks, which I intended to be a compliment, were taken as insensitive and stupid, as I can honestly now say they could have sounded, or she was obviously offended that in order to succeed she had to be somebody she wasn't. Maybe it wasn't her picture or history. Sometimes we spend so much time wishing we could be better by somebody else's standard that we neglect to be satisfied with the blessings we already have.

Interestingly, there are a few of us senators who are accused of using our high school yearbook pictures in various campaign and government publications. Then when people meet us they can't believe how much we have aged in such a short period of time. I always tell them that it is the pressure of the job.

Our society has programmed us to be self-conscious about our looks and the way we appear to other people. We become very sensitive to the value placed on us, just because of the way we look. It is when we alter "who" we normally are to make a good impression that we eventually run into problems.

Internet Dating

My Internet experiences, for the most part though, have been positive ones, and I have even had a couple of women visit me from other states. Although one of the dating services had a feature column entitled, "You Know You Are A Dating Failure," and in it was the phrase "when you have to bring in a date from another state." I'd like to think it was because I didn't want to limit myself, and didn't think state loyalty would be a consideration when it came to dating. It was interesting though, because in both cases, we didn't know what the other looked like and had to depend on word description. While everyone appeared to be satisfied, the result of an equation that includes imagining what someone looks like and describing yourself to another is never going to be absolutely accurate. There is always the tendency to leave the impression that you are better looking than you really are. Although, as you get closer to the time you are going to meet, you tend to be a little more accurate. It is best to exchange pictures.

One nice thing about Internet dating is that you can get to communicate with someone for as long as you wish before meeting them. With the anonymous feature, they don't even have to know who you are, until you are comfortable giving them that information. Even though you think you know so much about the person you are going to meet from your extended communication, it can still be a little risky.

The young daughter of one of the women who came to visit even went so far as to call every few hours, all weekend, to make sure that her mother was all right. I thought that it was pretty neat of her daughter to do that. Her mother and I talked about it and realized that sometimes desperation, or a need for companionship, might drive you to take unwarranted risks that others might not understand. In our case, it was a good idea to give her daughter my phone number. On a future visit, I actually got to meet her daughter, and what a wonderful, sensible child she is. Sometimes when you are divorced, role reversals occur, with your children providing the sensibility. Follow-up phone calls at home and at work give even more credibility before you meet someone. There are horror stories.

One young woman from California who was going to come and visit me on weekends could have turned out to be one of those horror stories. She saw my profile on the Internet and e-mailed me, and sounded terrific. I checked out her profile, which included a picture, and she seemed a beautiful person in every way. We communicated quite a bit even though I was somewhat reluctant, because I not only knew that I wasn't ready to enter a relationship yet, but I was also in the process of writing this book. The more time I spent on my computer with her, the less time I was able to spend on my book. But she was pretty persistent, and we sounded so right for each other.

My message to her, from my first e-mail, was that while I found her very attractive, accomplished and fun, that the most important characteristic she could have was honesty. In my last e-mail to her before her visit, I told her that while we had so much in common, to get our relationship off on the right foot, no matter what we did that weekend, we were going to be honest with each other from the beginning. Two days later I received an e-mail from her apologizing for not telling me the whole truth. It seems that she was in an unhappy marriage, but was in the process of getting separated. But, she decided to tell me the truth because I was so insistent about getting our relationship off on the right foot, and wanted to know if we could get together when her separation or her divorce occurred. I e-mailed her one more time and told her to please never bother me again, and that just because she told me she was still married, it didn't make her an honest person. So sometimes, everything isn't the way it always seems on the Internet.

But now and then, its nice to have someone there to communicate with when you're lonely, and you'd be surprised how many other lonely people there are waiting for someone to e-mail them. I've met some wonderful people through my computer. I've had dates in cities I was traveling to all around the world that have made those trips so much more worthwhile. And, I've had the benefit of some thought-provoking, intellectual and emotional conversations from people I've "talked" with on my computer. Sometimes it got too time-consuming, but I always tried to answer someone who wanted to communicate. I know how it feels.

There are times when it gets a little discouraging though. When after communicating with someone for a lengthy period of time, all of a sudden the e-mails stop. What do you do? It's not like you can call them up to see what's wrong. Maybe they found someone else, or maybe it was something you said, or maybe they had an accident. I always assume it was one of the first two and never write back. I guess it's just because I get so many e-mails that I don't respond to people that don't respond to me. I may have been desperate to get a date, but I have never been desperate to get e-mails.

*One of my most frustrating experiences on the Internet was from an e-mail that I never received. I had joined a dating service for which there was a monthly charge. It was one of the largest and most well known on the Internet. They have a matching service that considers a number of different criteria and then matches you up with someone similar. Lo and behold I logged on to this dating service and there she was— their recommendation; my match at 99%. She had a picture and she was beautiful with blonde hair and a **great smile**— and that was her profile name. When I read her profile, she was everything I was looking for in a woman and according to what she said she desired, I was everything she was looking for in a man. It was amazing how complementary our lives seemed. The things she said in her profile were almost like fate had sent her to me. And, she lived in Las Vegas, a city I would be visiting in three weeks. It was perfect.*

I e-mailed her and waited. While I was waiting, I began to plan out a date with her and think of some fun things we could do to get to know each other. This was a no-brainer since we were so compatible. With other women that I had read about on the Internet or communicated, there were always doubts, but with this one I had no doubts. I waited a couple of weeks, but there was nothing. I e-mailed her again to no avail. I even tried e-mailing her when I got to Las Vegas. She never responded. Unfortunately I didn't run across her in Las Vegas either.

A friend of mine mentioned that he had heard about this happening a lot to other people. He thought that there was a possibility that some dating services might be "stacking" their profiles with good looking, complementary, available people to get others to join in hopes of a match. Or it could have even been someone who was playing games with the profile and picture. Of course, most likely she just didn't want to respond to my profile. At least that's what I'll think.

If you have access to a computer, Internet dating will afford you the ability to take your "rifle approach" on the road. You can visit web sites all around the world, and find so many people in the same boat you are. For the most part, all the people I've encountered who use the Internet, including myself, have found it to be a worthwhile experience. And for those who have difficulty meeting people in other places it can become a place to go on a pseudo date—or I guess the term would be cyber-date for those with computer lingo. For some it's nice to come home at night with messages waiting and the capability to continue a relationship with a computer as the only string attached. The only problem arises when this cyber-dating becomes a replacement for actually meeting someone face to face and beginning a real relationship. Computer "dating" is just the means to the end—which is to meet someone personally.

Numbers Game

While the Internet allows you to utilize the rifle approach as your marketing method, it can also take on the character of the shotgun approach. As opposed to the single shot, specific target rifle approach, the shotgun approach sprays multiple shots at a more generalized target. As a matter of fact, in the case of those online dating services, the fewer your limitations, the more matches you receive.

The benefit of the shotgun approach is that you become exposed to so many more people, that you are bound to eventually cross paths with your match. Typically, the prime attraction in this case is physical, since crossing paths may not have anything to do with shared interests. And, of course, to cross one's path does not mean that you will ever get to meet them or discuss common interests.

This approach though, is not as difficult to target as the more specific rifle method. In the marketing of a product, this approach would be like putting an ad in a newspaper or on a billboard that appeals to the general public. You still have to use some targeting so that you don't waste your resources; even though you know the result is going to be more widespread, you still have to point the shotgun. This method becomes a game of numbers. The more people you are exposed to, the greater your chance of success. It is certainly more time-consuming, but also more adventurous. The focus of your shotgun becomes meeting or crossing paths with people in general. That then allows you to target in on singles, then to those of mutual attraction; and then shared interests, and so on.

This broad-based approach involves everything from traveling to as many places as you can to shopping in different grocery stores. It is simply getting out more, to as many different places as is possible. It is going to conventions or industry shows—a great place to meet someone when you are alone; shopping malls, athletic events—where there is not assigned seating, fairs, outdoor concerts, receptions, and of course traveling—preferably by train or plane where you can also meet people en route.

I just returned from a trip to India that I took with two very attractive eligible single women friends. It started out, as an official visit to the country of Bhutan, which turns out is one of the most beautiful places on earth. We were only able to stay for a little while, which was regrettable because the culture is so fascinating and the people so hospitable. While our trip to Northern India didn't provide the same comfort or hospitality, it was a historical adventure nonetheless.

During our travels we came across a surprising number of Americans who were traveling either alone or in small groups. It seemed that immediate bonds were formed between us, not just because we were Americans but also because we were people who had a common interest in traveling and were all eager to share our experiences. To say that many of the women I encountered were eager for a male traveling companion would be an understatement. I was not only approached by some of these women to, among other things, redirect my travel plans to accompany them on their journey but have received correspondence from them since my return about future trips. My friends were also subject to similar offers by male travelers.

It amazed me that wherever we traveled the same phenomena occurred. I met doctors, lawyers, schoolteachers, students, and all kinds of interesting, personable women who would really be enjoyable company for traveling. It was so easy to meet with them and socialize. I had never experienced anything quite like that before in the United States. While I'm sure one reason these meetings were so willing was because of the familiarity of someone in a far off place, but there were other influences as well.

There was an excuse to start conversations; asking about where they are from or for directions and advice on where to go. There were no apparent barriers or threats to enter someone's space or time, due to worry about rejection because when people like this travel, they enjoy communicating with others of shared interests. Of course being in a strange country encourages a dependence on such communication. And, it was exciting to talk about who we were and our adventures to people who moments before were complete strangers. It was equally amazing how short a period of time it took to become friends and to know so much about someone.

We experienced an opening of our personalities to other people that we seem inhibited to present when we are in our same familiar surroundings. Maybe it's because of the perceived barriers, or the lack of excuses to meet others back home. Maybe it's because we have more confidence when we have nothing to lose because of rejection or perhaps it was because I was traveling with two good-looking companions. Or maybe, it's like that story about the soldier waiting at the train station for the woman of his dreams wearing the rose; it's the shared interest, the feelings, and the view of life that provides real attraction.

There is the theory some people espouse, that the best way to meet someone is not to look. That is a kind of destiny approach that many of us have experienced in the past, leading to our current predicament. If you don't show any interest in finding someone, in all probability you won't. On the other hand, if you become obsessive in your search, chances are you might find someone, but the rest of your life will fall apart, or you will be looked upon as too anxious and avoided at all costs. Moderation and being reasonable are the keys to success. You don't want to scare away any prospects by having them assume you are on a no prisoners march to the altar, or that you have little concern about their interests. And, of course, you don't want to appear or be desperate, or present the other extreme of being too choosy.

I recently heard of one lonely woman who had three children and hadn't been on a date in almost three years. She e-mailed a man on the Internet and told him everything about herself. It seemed they were very compatible, and she seemed to be in a real hurry to meet her match. He was in no such hurry. In her final e-mail to him though, she told him that she could tell a lot about a man by his shoes, and asked him what kind of shoes he wore. He replied that shoes didn't mean that much to him and he usually wore loafers. He never heard from her again. And he thought she was desperate?

Friends At Work

There needs to be a balance. You should never be desperate. It is good to be picky, but not too picky. Somebody should have told that shoe fetish woman, that she was lucky that she found a man who wore shoes. Most of the people we meet along the way are not going to be perfect, or perfect for us. But many of these prospects are reasonable, good intentioned people, who can become friends, and can provide help in locating the object of your search. It is a learning experience.

It really bothers me when I hear from lonely people who have had the ability to meet many others in the same predicament, only to disregard these people because they were not their perfect matches. Wouldn't it be wonderful if all these people could become just friends; to get to know each other and possibly introduce each other to others that they think would be a match. I know that with all the single people I meet in business, politics, school, and on the Internet surely there would be many matches amongst them. But, it seems that when a "match" is not perceived, the reason for involvement is dispatched—especially on the Internet. I guess no one wants to be just friends. Yet one of the most productive methods of meeting a possible soul mate is through the introduction of a friend or acquaintance who can view both subjects objectively. After all, it's a numbers game. The more people you know the greater your exposure.

One of my dearest friends Bernardo, is a high-ranking official with the Venezuelan government. Bernardo is the type of friend who not only provides the enjoyment of companionship, but the stimulation of intellectual conversation as well. We both have a lot of fun together while attempting to solve the problems of the world with the common theme of doing what is "right." As Bernardo puts it, "We are dreamers."

Bernardo is also the kind of person who truly cares for his friends and is always trying to assist them whenever he can. It is in that regard that he decided to utilize what limited matchmaking capabilities he had to search out someone he thought would be a good match for me.

One of my trips to Venezuela happened to coincide with the beginnings of a presidential election for that country. A former student of Bernardo, who was also a previous Miss Universe, happened to be running for President that year. In describing her qualifications to me, as well as expressing his admiration for her as a person, he piqued my interest in her candidacy and I offered my assistance to her campaign. Unfortunately, Benrardo was never able to make the connection, and I never got to help on her campaign. She lost that primary race for reasons apparently not due to the lack of my help.

After the election, on a subsequent trip, her name came up again at a dinner with Bernardo and his best friend Humberto. Humberto and I became fast friends because we had the same sense of humor, and he was also single, which provided a direction of common interests. We talked about her, politics, women, and business over the next few nights and all came to the same conclusions on everything, including that now the election was over, that I needed to meet her and take her out on a date. Since Humberto had the most recent contact with her, he volunteered to talk to her on my behalf and set up a meeting for my next trip. Humberto was going to give me a report on his progress when he stopped by to visit me in New Mexico, on a business trip he was taking in a couple of months. He even thought the possibility existed that she might come with him, and that while he was at his meeting I could show her around and get to know her better. Things were really looking up.

After the time had passed for his scheduled visit, I called Bernardo to ask him what had happened. He replied that he didn't know and had thought that Humberto was with me reporting how he was doing with my date, but that he would find out. All he could say was that he knew Humberto was working hard in my "interests." A few days later, Bernardo e-mailed me that, instead of coming to see me to report progress on how my date was progressing, Humberto took my future date to Greece. We both commented that we thought he was going above and beyond the call of duty in trying to get me a date with her. Well, needless to say, she and Humberto got married a few months later. I read about it in the newspaper even before Bernardo called to inform me. He did say when he called, that there were a lot of good intentions involved.

On another visit to Venezuela, I stopped by to visit Humberto and his lovely wife on the island in which they lived. She was everything that they described to me—beautiful, intelligent and so very capable of everything she attempts. And of course, with Humberto's good looks, his intelligence and charm, they make quite a couple. I guess I can honestly say that I am happy to have played a part in their getting together, in a round about sort of way.

I still believe that the best way to meet a match is to have friends set you up. Of course, in the future I think I will become more involved from the beginning.

While friends usually have the best insights as to "who" would make the best matches, they also usually have a limited pool to draw from. If you are going to use friends as a resource you need to involve as many as you can, and even though my experience didn't work as planned for me, it is beneficial to use friends of both genders. You need to go out with friends and have them introduce you to more friends and pretty soon the pool of possibilities gets bigger and you meet more people who know more people. And then, seemingly out of the blue, someone out there who you didn't even know in the past has thought of someone who would be the perfect match for you. It has to do with exposure—with numbers.

It has been proven statistically that more people met their spouses at their job than any other place of encounter. The reasons for this occurrence is obvious. The workplace offers access as well as a time for familiarity. Chances are you will not only have contact, but a capability for a more in-depth communication over time than you would in other circumstances. Of course, the drawbacks to these "office romances" are their confining nature and the ease and convenience with which they present themselves. If you are not of the mind to go out and search for your match, you might adjust your matchmaking criteria to fit that person in the next cubicle. Then you will have to ascertain whether or not this person is really the best match for you, or just someone with whom you have been able to, because of your jobs, become more familiar. If you work for a really small company, you are either going to have to credit your meeting with an extreme amount of luck, or your desire to settle for the warmest body in the closest proximity.

While working for larger companies affords the opportunity for a broader selection of potential matches, it is once again simply with exposure—with numbers, that will allow you to succeed in your search. It may be people at work with single relatives and friends, or the related business dealings with other companies or customers that offer some promise. It could also involve changing jobs or locations of work that allow for meeting new people. While there have been so many apparent successes in finding a match in the workplace, it is so very important not to be confined because of the ease of the contact.

Lori had worked for state government in Santa Fe for about ten years. She is very attractive, bright, personable and very single. She had a great job, made a very good salary and seemed to really enjoy her work. We were all surprised when she announced that she was quitting her job and moving to Washington, D.C. This was going to be an adventurous move for her since she had pets, didn't have a place to live and didn't know anyone living there. Apparently she had applied for a job working for the U.S. government in a similar position as the one she now held. The pay was comparable, and while the cost of living was probably the same, I couldn't imagine anyone leaving Santa Fe for any big city back east.

We were all surprised by her somewhat sudden departure until she explained about her priorities. While having an enjoyable job and living in Santa Fe were very important to her, she came to realize that she would probably be single as long as she stayed where she was. She had a lot of friends and co-workers, but most of them were married. The availability of single, straight men her age was diminishing with time. She had noticed some of her single friends who had hung on too long to their jobs and locations, only to find themselves with lost opportunity and few possibilities of meeting that special someone.

That's when she decided to move to D.C., of all places. I had informed her that I had heard that it was one of the worst places a single woman could be, because of the overwhelming ratio of women to men in that city. She said that didn't faze her, because while there may be more women than men, there are so many more single people than anywhere else she inquired about.

I just went to Washington, D.C. and came across Lori at a reception. She looked great and mentioned that she was having a terrific time. She gets to go to parties and receptions and museums and events. There is something of her interest going on everyday. She owns a beautiful home and loves her job. She has a lot of single friends and surprisingly a lot of them are men. She said that she has never thought about the women / men ratio because she never has trouble getting a date. Her whole outlook on life has changed. She now has hope.

What Lori accomplished was setting her priorities, and then having the courage to follow through to their achievement. She figured out that while her job was a significant part of her life, and that she loved to be with her friends, and, of course, Santa Fe was a beautiful place to live, the priority for her as a single woman was to find her match. So she gave up the comfort and security of her familiar surroundings and embarked on an adventure that will eventually provide a fulfillment that she realistically knew would take a change of exposure to conclude.

It's A Trip

While the workplace benefits of accessibility and familiarity provide an opportunity for in-depth communication from prolonged interpersonal contact, those same benefits can be achieved in a shorter span with greater exposure to a primarily single audience. This occurs with venues that are geared to the attraction of single participants, such as resorts, seminars, and trips.

Singles excursions are usually somewhat limiting due to the number of

people on a typical tour, however the fewer the number of participants, the more time can be spent meeting and conversing with the
other people on the tour. And, if you pick a trip of particular interest to you, even if you don't meet someone, you will still benefit from
the experience. Of course, matching the tours itinerary with the
perceived attraction of the type of person you are trying to meet is
certainly the best course of action. If you are searching for someone who is culturally aware, you might want to visit museums or
historical sites around the country or world. If you are looking
for someone with a sense of adventure, you might want to try a
Windjammer cruise or a safari. Just be sure there are enough
people taking part to insure some degree of companionship; that
you are experiencing something of interest to you should there
be no love connection; and that it is in fact a singles group.

Resorts and cruises that specifically cater to singles are a great
place to meet and have time to become familiar with people of
similar interest—even if that similar interest is just physical
attraction. Usually these destinations have planned activities
that encourage people to get to know each other through their
participation. Their dining facilities typically allow for mingling
of guests, which also increases exposure as well as promoting
initial conversations that "break the ice." Some have bars, shows
and dancing that provide another meeting place for guests.

The cruises that are single oriented are usually specific not only
to that group but to the dates of sailing. There is not one cruise
line or ship that just caters to single populations, which means
you have to search out those types of cruises. Resorts that cater
to singles usually do so all year, providing more comparison as
well as choice.

If you are *totally* single and want to go somewhere to meet other
singles, a singles resort is the best place to go, because they have

social directors who provide activities especially for people to meet one another. It is sometimes even easier to meet new people if you are by yourself, rather than with a group of friends, because there is always a tendency to stick with your friends. Of course, that is the way it is when you are home, so why should it be any different on a vacation. While having the comfort of your friends with you at this type of resort could certainly be beneficial. If it interferes with your capability to meet as many other people as you can in your search for someone special, you are once again wasting your time and some great opportunity.

Typically people who embark on this type of adventure do a lot better by themselves without anyone to lean on for moral support. They do better, because they are forced to learn how to meet people in a non-threatening environment, and will be able to take that knowledge back home with them. As a matter of fact, going to one of these resorts is like going to a subtle relationship school, that presents the possibilities of interaction with all different kinds of people who you have never seen before and chances are will never see again. If things don't work out, it's not like you will have to face these people at work everyday, or that your friends will be involved, or that you'll even ever cross paths with any of these people. It's just you out there by yourself, with nothing to prove to anyone but yourself.

I remember a trip down to Cancun to a singles resort. It was kind of expensive since I decided at the last minute to go and I requested a room by myself. I probably would have gotten a double room, if I had gone there with someone I knew. There were approximately 200 other singles there at the same time, and I was looking forward to a great vacation.

In the beginning it was difficult to feel comfortable since I was there by myself for the first time and there seemed to be quite a few groups who were satisfied just hanging around with each other. I managed rather quickly to become friends with a few members of the staff and began to immerse myself in the physical activities like sailing and water skiing and joined with the staff in playing tennis, basketball, and dancing. All the members of the staff were attractive and young. The young part was probably because this was not a career type employment for most of them, and the attractive part was probably to present the perception to the guests that many attractive people came to this resort. Since there were as many employees as there were guests it was difficult to ascertain who was which. If someone was very friendly, able and willing to communicate, appeared like they were singles there to meet someone, chances are they were on staff. Of course, the attractive and young part should have always been the give away.

While it sometimes appeared that the activities and shows were offered mostly for the benefit of the staff, there were a few excellent opportunities to meet other singles. There were the dining facilities that provided for seating on a first come first seated method which meant that at each meal you were probably going to be seated with different people. And there were three different sittings for each meal. With luck, I made the last servings of lunch and dinner every day. That part is good, but it involves a lot of luck if you want to sit next to a particular person. I was able to bribe the hostess with a late night drink to encourage her to sit me at tables that showed some promise of communication.

There were the dance classes that were excellent as far as learning the steps to various exotic dances and being able to meet other guests, albeit for the two minutes that were allotted for each step. Unfortunately, I found myself more interested in and involved with the dance instructors than the guests, because two minutes just wasn't enough time to even get beyond learning a person's name. It would have also been beneficial to have an actual dance afterward with the type of music you were taking lessons for. At least there would have been additional opportunity and time to meet someone. Then there was the late night dancing at the disco and bars, which provided another occasion to meet and socialize.

Of course, because of these late night activities, I never made it to breakfast except on the last day, which was when I saw HER. You could tell she was very athletic, had a great personality and smile and was very friendly toward me as we stood in the juice line. I asked her if she had just arrived and she said that she had been there all week. I mentioned that I was surprised that we didn't cross paths. She explained that she got up at the crack of dawn to go running and have the early breakfast, and then would arrange her activities so that she could get to the early servings of lunch and dinner. At night, since she didn't drink, she didn't go to the bars but rather either walked on the beach or sat by the pool and went to bed early. She was so nice, I had to ask her if she was sure she wasn't a member of the staff.

I still think that maybe she was a "plant" that hangs around on the last day to indicate to guests that perhaps they were just in the wrong place at the wrong time, and that the next time they come back, they will be able to do better. Anyway, while I guess I should have gotten up earlier at least once, I still had a great time. I met quite a few staff people, one that could have been a match had I been there a little longer, or maybe a little younger. I also had an enjoyable time with a couple of women guests who, other than being from another part of the world, would be nice to see again at a similar type of resort. And, the last couple of days I got to meet a few people who came there with a group of friends.

There was one group of three men and three women who had come from Arizona. They always seemed to be having a blast, and I just assumed they were matched up and just on a vacation. As it turns out they were all just very good friends from work who every year go on a trip together. Clearly they had a good, if not better time than most of the people there, but they had isolated themselves from the rest of the people by staying together all the time. They played sports together, danced together, and ate together. It certainly didn't appear that anyone in their group was interested in meeting someone new.

Then on the next to last day one of the men in that group, who it happened I was playing volleyball with, asked me a number of questions including where I was from and where and when I usually go to resorts and what I do and what my interests are. He genuinely seemed friendly and interested. Later that day he came up to me and said that one of the women he had come with was interested in me and why didn't I join them for drinks after dinner. I agreed and it was an enjoyable evening, even though I kind of felt like an outsider. I also had mixed impressions about what had happened. First of all, the benefits of going to a resort with friends is obvious. They had a great time. Also there is the advantage of having friends looking after you and helping to set you up with other people. I thought that was a tremendous benefit. Of course, waiting to the end of a vacation is not the ideal time to do that, which means that your group of friends has to be overtly inclusive from the very beginning.

It's a fine line from having so much fun with your friends, to the point of giving the perception that you are excluding others, which ends up causing the point to be missed as to the reason you are all going to a singles resort. And, it's not just larger groups that do this, it also happens when two women, or two men friends go to a resort. Instead of giving support and confidence to each other with the express purpose of meeting singles of the opposite sex, it appears they are like those friends in the single bar who act like they aren't there to meet anyone. While it's great to have the comfort of going away to a singles resort with friends, if you don't do it right, you'd be a lot better off going by yourself.

Singles trips, tours, resorts and cruises all present an opportunity of taking a focused shotgun approach—that exposure to numbers of single people interested enough to seek other single people. Seminars and meetings that expand upon the concept of just bringing singles together, to addressing the concerns and issues of like-minded people, bring about a further focusing of a search to the point of it being targeted like a rifle—the search for qualities and characteristics of people that "feel' like you do. These meetings can take the form of a gathering to discuss a specific topic of concern, to full-fledged seminars and conferences that not only enable participants to discuss and process the many concerns of single life, but that are attended by enough people to provide the opportunity to actually meet a compatible match.

Suddenly Single seminars have been set up to provide participants with the ultimate solutions to their predicament, offering the capability to discuss and process the many issues presented by this book, as well as being held in venues that will attract the many people who are searching for others who "feel" like they do. While the object of these seminars will be to discuss the concepts of *Suddenly Single,* the result will also provide a getting together of people who can identify with the issues presented, and thus will be able and willing to communicate their views and concerns to others of similar circumstance. After participating in the program and analysis of what it is like being *Suddenly Single* there will be a speed-dating segment that will provide those in attendance with the capability to meet with others of similar concern. It's quick, but it is exposure at its best.

These *Suddenly Single* Seminars are provided to refine the process of searching for a match. They are a hands-on approach to those who have had difficulty dealing with the steps necessary to achieving the point of being able to search for a match, and knowing who they are searching for. They provide a level of communication that is difficult to find in other single forums, because of the shared understanding of the participants who are seeking out empathy of feelings.

These seminars will provide an arena of participation that goes beyond any other form of organized searching that has been previously mentioned, because if you are *Suddenly Single,* you know of all the difficulties of meeting other people who feel like you. And if you've been *Suddenly Single* for any amount of time, you have probably been looking everywhere for that person. Or at least you've thought about looking everywhere. But where do you start? Seminars, like *Suddenly Single,* are like trips that you take hoping to find your match. While you certainly have a better chance of finding your match than doing very little about it, even if you don't succeed, you will have had a beneficial experience.

Whether you take the rifle or the shotgun approach—and of course it is best to use both—you need to experience movement. You have to trade your comfortable surroundings for new experiences.

Your plan is in place to give you an overview, and a base for your objectives. Your new encounters need to be enjoyed for adventure's sake as well as providing the possibilities of fulfilling your objectives. It's another way of benefiting from your search without the overbearing pressure of having to succeed. It's the benefit derived from traveling to new places, making new friends, and making new memories that provide so much more value to your life. So, in a way, while your search is always an underlying reason for your movement and change, and your opportunities for success are constantly improving, you are also growing, learning, and achieving enjoyment in the process.

It's a lot like fishing. Your ultimate objective might be to catch a fish, but what a wonderful way to relax and spend an afternoon with nature. Even when you don't catch a fish, sometimes the process is a reward in itself. Maybe that's what "the best way to meet someone, is not to look" is all about. Maybe if you are doing things you enjoy, it doesn't look like you are looking. Just as long as you have your line in the water, you can still catch a fish. But it does take some effort. **That's why they call it "fishing." If it were easy, they would call it "catching."**

Chance Encounters

There is a continuing process that will include so many crossed paths and chance encounters. You'll meet wonderful people who were so close to ideal, and yet because of your new security of "self," you didn't want to settle for someone who was missing something important to you. And there will be brief encounters with people who you just knew could be the "one," but you let the opportunity for further investigation slip by. Then there are the hundreds of people with whom you have crossed paths, who you noticed and "dreamed" and maybe even exchanged a smile, that for a fleeting moment were possibilities, never to be seen again.

You just know your "match" is out there, and in all likelihood if you are prone to movement, you've already let quite a few probabilities pass you by. And, if you are naturally shy or still suffer from the low self esteem of your past relationship, your chance of meeting a "crossed path match" has been greatly diminished. But it's still a game of numbers, and with constant movement, you'll eventually meet a match at a chance encounter.

When I think of all of my lost opportunities because I failed to get to know someone, I sometimes become frustrated and disappointed in myself. My encouragement comes from the fact that I have had so many opportunities. Whether I didn't look at my search as a job, or was too shy for whatever reason, it caused me to miss out. But every day I pass through new opportunities, and I think about all those people who pass me by and how many feel just as I do, with the frustration and disappointment of not meeting me. We are all in the same boat, and if we are going to take the effort to achieve access to people, we also need to take advantage of that access to not let possible matches slip though our net.

It is amazing how many opportunities can cross your path when you are not looking if you make an effort to at least get out there without becoming obsessed. It is a shame that we don't take advantage of those chances to find people who may be right for us. But, just to be exposed to new people means having the confidence to believe that there are plenty of other people out there who may be your life partner.

Since I try to travel a lot, I have already crossed paths with quite a few of those 5,000 or so possible matches who were a plane ride away. While many of the possibilities I encountered didn't turn out to be probabilities, it was certainly beneficial making their acquaintance. Even en route while traveling, I meet friendly flight attendants (don't ever call them stewardesses); a woman sitting next to me coming back from Washington, D.C. who gave me her daughter's phone number for me to call for a date; a business executive who gave me half of her airline lunch with her card, inviting me to dinner the next time I was in Chicago; and a professional beach volleyball player I met on the plane from Venezuela, who I went to see play in California. And those were just on the way. Then there was the dancer in Washington, D.C. who wants to come out and see what the Southwest is like; the blackjack dealer in Las Vegas who told me to save my money so that I could come back out and take her to dinner; the fitness champion in Texas who inspired me to get into shape; and that beautiful smile in San Antonio who became a temporary match. These were just encounters with some really nice people, but as shy as I am, if it had been up to me, I would never have been able to even get to meet them.

> *One summer a few years ago, I was given the opportunity to attend a program at a graduate school located in Dallas. It would last a couple of weeks and a few of my friends from around the world were also going to be in attendance. We were all going to be staying at the same hotel, which coincidentally was also the hotel where employees for a major airline stayed while in Dallas for training. These employees, mostly attractive, personable women, seemed to have most of their time spoken for with their training, leaving little time for socialization with us.*

While our courses were rigorous, time consuming and packed with useful information, a few of us decided that it would be in our best interests to experience the nightlife of Dallas. Usually, after dinner at one of the great restaurants located there, we would go out to local nightclubs in the area to dance or just socialize with the residents. We were having a great time, although the late nights accompanied by our "consumption" and our early morning classes began to take its toll.

After about a week of this exhausting schedule, we met a few of the airline trainees who were just finishing their courses. They explained to us that they really didn't have that much time to socialize because of their training, but were looking forward to partying for a couple of days before they had to go back to work. They suggested that we meet at the hotel hot tub that evening to relax and plan out what to do. It sounded perfect to us, especially the relaxing part.

We prepared for the evening by buying a couple of bottles of wine for relaxing in the hot tub. As the time approached for our meeting, one of my friends realized that he didn't have a bathing suit with him and that there was no business nearby where he could buy one. I offered to let him use a brand new, dark blue bathing suit with white flowers that I had bought in Hawaii a couple of months before. He reluctantly accepted, because he thought it was too wild for him. Of course, the other choice was the pair of dark blue cotton gym shorts that I was then going to have to wear.

The three of us arrived at the hot tub and met the three flight attendants clad in their bikinis. It had the makings for a very pleasant evening. The lights were low, the steam was rising and the wine was flowing. Our conversations seemed to go everywhere and we were all having a good time, as was evidenced by the laughter and the familiar way we were communicating with each other.

We must have been in the hot tub for over two hours when one of the women suggested that we all go out dancing and start spending our free time over the next couple of days getting to know each other better. Those were my sentiments exactly. I began to think about how, even with all the fun we had over the past week, it would have been so much better off had we met up with these women sooner. As they began to leave the hot tub, you could tell there was much anticipation on everybody's mind.

I thought that maybe it was the heat from my prolonged visit in the hot tub, or maybe it was the effect of the wine, but when the woman I was sitting next to stood up to step out, she seemed blue to me. As a matter of fact as I looked closer, her whole body, with the exclusion of her face and parts of her arms were pretty much a medium shade of blue. And then the other women stood up and began to leave, and sure enough, through the steam I detected that they too were blue. I looked at one of my friends who had also observed this phenomenon. Our eyes and mouths had opened to their fullest allowance as we expressed our shock and disbelief. We both then looked at the water and it had, what would appear to the untrained eye, a beautiful blue tint to it; a little darker than I had noticed in the Caribbean before, but certainly nothing that would alarm me. We each raised our elbows out of the water, since we had been resting our arms on the side of the hot tub, to reveal what looked like matching blue birthmarks on our four elbows. We then looked to our other friend who was smiling, oblivious to our observance, giving us a thumbs-up exposing his blue-stained elbow.

For all that was going through our minds, it seemed like it took those three women a half hour to reach the lights of the lobby entrance to the elevators. It was in reality only two to three minutes before we heard the first scream; then the second; then the chorus of screams and yelling. It only took about another 30 seconds before one of them came running back to the hot tub yelling, "What did you guys do to the water? This stuff will never come off." She didn't wait to hear our response.

Our previously smiling friend, who was obviously color blind, asked what it was that she so upset about. We told him to stand up and explained to him that the discoloration on his body wasn't a shadow, but was the color blue. We then asked each other if any of us had spilled wine in the hot tub. No one could remember such an accident. Our discolored friend then got out and walked over to the light as we still sat dazed from what had happened. Apparently his color blindness had been corrected as he informed us that his blue bathing suit was now light brown.

We jumped up and ran over to the light to discover that our bathing attire had also miraculously turned light brown with little tinges of blue still left in the elastic waistband. Of course, we were all blue from neck to toe with the exception of just a shading of blue on the parts of our bodies that weren't constantly in the hot tub for over two hours. I called the women up to let them know what had caused the stain to their bodies and was met with the comments,

"I can't believe you guys did this to us," and "Our bathing suits are ruined;" as well as, " This awful stuff won't come off, so now what are we going to do?"

When I told my friends what the women had said, one asked if they mentioned anything about still going out that night. The other said, "What's wrong with the bathing suits, they're just a different color." I guess there is a difference between some men and some women.

We never saw those women again, but wondered how they coped with their situation, especially since we thought that they wore short-sleeved shirts and shorts while they worked. We, of course, wore suits everyday and even when we went out at night, no matter how hot and humid it was. It took me about a week to have the shading disappear through daily baths. I'm sure there were more successful remedies, but we really didn't have the opportunity to search out a solution.

Finally, a near perfect circumstance appears that allows for personable, familiar conversation. There was not only a mutual attraction, but as luck would have it a perfect location and activity to get to know each other. And, this time I really thought I was prepared to spend some quality time getting to know someone. I guess you just have to be prepared for anything.

It gets easier each time, especially when someone is willing to start the conversation. And why are people shy about talking to strangers? Is it because as kids we were told never to do that, or is it because of that fear of rejection or fear of success thing? We always have to keep in mind that in this approach, it is again a game of numbers, and repetition. It's the expectation that normally a certain number of failures will occur before success is achieved. It is then that we can realize that rejection is a normal, temporary setback. Besides, most of the people with whom you will be making contact will not even be a probability of a match. This should diminish the intensity of your fear as relative to the importance of your success in meeting someone. But, sometimes it is still the effects of the lowered self-esteem suffered as a result of the rejection of your relationship that still lingers. While that might be one number that you will never forget, you've got to believe that none of those other numbers out there could reject you quite as bad.

When you have an encounter with someone who seems like they could just skip right over being a possibility to a probability, that's when the game of numbers goes right out the window and fear of rejection or making the wrong impression set in. Like everything else, it's a step-by-step progression. Piano, piano; little by little. The first time is always the hardest and most terrifying. It's the fear of the unknown. Most good intentioned *Suddenly Single* people, however, are thinking the same thing. They wish that someone would approach them. It does get easier, but it takes that first time and practice. That first person who talked to me may not have realized it, but what little she did for me that day, gave me hope for the future.

She was just standing on that Hawaiian beach getting her feet wet, with her golden hair glistening in the sunlight. She was a young woman, tall and tanned, with a smile that radiated every time the water tickled her toes. I was about 30 feet away, although it could have been a mile, for the chance I thought I would have of meeting her. As she started walking closer to me, I noticed a group of Japanese tourists taking pictures of her. They approached her, and asked to have their pictures taken with her. As they were taking pictures, she was getting closer to me. She then slowly turned toward me, smiled and asked, "What are these people doing?" When I answered that they probably thought she was a movie star, she laughed, came a little closer, and we talked without moving from that spot for over three hours.

After we realized we were sunburned beyond belief, she had to leave to go back home to the mainland. We talked about meeting in the winter to go skiing, but it didn't matter. I was just thankful that I got to talk to her, and that it was a start. It's supposed to get easier each time. For me it may not get that much easier, but I know there is always going to be another time. That's one thing of which I'm confident.

With all the possibilities, it's not that easy for people to actually meet with each other. All the plotting, planning, strategizing and researching, is all for naught unless you can talk with someone. And how frustrating is it to just know that you have crossed paths with someone who could have been the one? It wasn't much more than an immediate attraction, and yet there was something else that caused that person to stay in your thoughts. It was suddenly that they entered your life, and just as quickly they were gone. Maybe a lost opportunity, maybe not. In our present situation it would have certainly been worth the effort to find out.

We spend so much time and effort, or use up so much luck, karma, and destiny to cross paths and then we continue on our way, alone. We have to learn to seize the moment and take advantage of the opportunity. For some, it might be better to have dreams of what might have been, than rejections of reality. But the only way to make our dreams come true is to deal with reality. So many people I know have faced the same situations and continued on their way, alone. It recently happened to me twice.

While in Houston at an Energy Conference I seemed to be crossing paths a lot with a very attractive blond-haired woman. We both left the convention center at the same time, boarded the same convention bus to the same hotel, and I never uttered a word. With my unendingly romantic imagination, the thought crossed my mind as I changed clothes in my room that she could have been the one.

I put on some jeans and went down to the adjoining galleria for dinner, only to find her leaning over the rail watching the ice skaters. She looked up and smiled. I smiled, and continued walking, looking for a place to eat. After an hour I came back around to a nearby restaurant and went in to put my name on its waiting list for a table. As I glanced over at the waiting line, she was standing there again. I then went for a walk around the mall. When I got back she was gone.

What's wrong with that picture? Was it my fear of success or my fear of failure that kept me from talking to her? Was it my theory that if someone wants me to talk to them, they will talk to me first? Could it have been that I didn't know what to say, or didn't want to come across as being too forward? Of course, she could have been thinking the same thing. In my defense, I had another date later that night and maybe didn't want to confuse things. This might have been another one of those cases where we give up on probabilities, to spend time with possibilities.

This story must repeat itself thousands of times every day, because similar occurrences have happened to almost everybody I know. What a shame. And do we ever learn? Do we ever take a deep breath and think about how far we have come in our capacity to meet someone new, and realize how important it is to take a chance and just talk to someone? If they don't respond or they ignore the opportunity, then they are the ones missing out. I've been on both sides of that equation.

After a day of skiing with a friend in Jackson Hole, Wyoming, we were told about a local nightspot on the outskirts of town where locals and visiting celebrities went to dance. We arrived by cab and the place was packed and the dance floor filled with people swing dancing. When I saw her I couldn't take my eyes off her and her great smile. She danced every dance and was terrific—too good for me. After a while of sitting around by ourselves, it seemed like one of those places where everybody knew each other and didn't want to know us, so we called a cab to go back to the hotel. Since it takes a cab almost an hour to get there, we still had some time.

I thought it was my imagination, but it seemed she was smiling as she kept looking at me, although my friend told me that she was looking at him. I would have given anything at that time to have had the talent to dance like she could and the courage to ask her. Then the band played a slower song, and before I knew it, she came over to me and said, "I bet you can dance to this one. Let's dance." Well, we danced and it seemed like forever as we laughed, and smiled as we looked into each other's eyes. It seemed perfect. When the music stopped playing, I thanked her, and at that moment the cab driver appeared.

I still don't know why I left. When I arrived at my hotel, I did call back to see if she was still there, because I would have gone back. She had already left and opportunity had passed. Now, I don't know if I am imagining our possibilities, after all it was just one very long dance, but this was one of those classic chance encounter stories that you hear about, this time with me missing out.

After watching a movie, my friend and I decided that the woman who asked me to dance was Cameron Diaz. Of course, she may have looked exactly like her, but it couldn't have been, although even the bartender said it was. If it was, I guess I'll just add that to my list of the greatest lost opportunities of all time.

Sometimes I wonder if we really have a subconscious fear of success, or maybe such a low opinion of ourselves that we can't believe that anyone would want us, and that it must be our imagination playing tricks on us if they did. It's like the saying goes, "I wouldn't date anyone whose standards were so low that they would date someone like me." It is either that, or that we are just searching for dreams, fearful of dealing with reality or failure. But searching for dreams is not what our quest is all about.

I was recently by myself in California at a wedding of a relative of some friends of mine. It was an evening affair that began at a church that was packed to capacity. A very attractive woman, also by herself, searching for a seat, ended up sitting next to me. A quick glance and smile should have indicated that there was a probability that we would be able to talk to each other and maybe even get to visit with each other at the reception. At least, that was my thought at the time. As the Wedding Mass continued, it was evident that she and I were some of the few people who could follow and participate in the service, obviously because we attended church regularly. Once again, it seemed too good to be true.

When it came to the time in the Mass to turn to each other, we shook hands and said, "Peace be with you." Looking at her, I saw a beautiful, sweet woman with a sincere, wonderful smile. I kept thinking that she must have been there with someone. How could somebody like that be alone? She must have been there with someone in the wedding party. I decided not to talk to her just then, but rather to wait until the reception to see if she was still by herself.

After searching for my assigned seating at the reception, I realized that there was no one that I knew at my table. It was then that I saw her enter the hall, standing at the door by herself looking very alone. I decided not to sit at my assigned spot but rather wait until she sat down so that I could possibly join her. In my scheme, I thought that even if there were no seats available at her table, I would at least know where she was sitting so that I could ask her to dance. That was my plan until someone engaged me in a ten-minute conversation, at which point I lost track of where she went. I frantically searched the over 40 tables to locate her to no avail. She had left the reception. I can only assume that she left because she felt anxious as I had the many times that I found myself alone at a function where it seemed everyone was with someone.

If she just would have stayed. If I could have just talked to her sooner. It could very well be by imagination, but I think she was someone just like me, and people like us have a difficult time meeting each other. I left shortly thereafter because I realized that I really wanted to meet someone like me, and didn't want to waste anyone else's time. Someone like her probably felt the same way. It's not just that opposites are attracted to us, it's that they're not afraid of the encounter, while shy people rarely get to meet. Now all that's left are dreams of what might have been.

The negatives of these situations are pretty obvious, but the positives are that we are being attracted to other people and other people are attracted to us. The people with whom we are crossing paths are presenting some real possibilities for our future. We just need to start taking advantage of our good fortune.

I hear so many of these stories over and over again from friends and acquaintances about how they let people or relationships slip through their fingers. These are just examples of how one never gets to find out if possibilities can ever become probabilities, and if probabilities can ever become a match. Part of the problem is the lack of experience.

Be Prepared

As was observed previously, *Suddenly Single* people do not have a plan, so to many of them dating is not only a brand new experience, but something they just started thinking about. With practice, things will change. Just knowing what worked and didn't work in the past should give us a clue as to which direction to take in the future.

I know that if I cross paths numerous times with an interesting woman who smiles at me, that I will respond with a smile and a greeting and will continue escalating the conversation as would be warranted by her response. And, the next time a woman with whom I am attracted asks me to dance, I will stick around long enough to offer to buy her a drink, or attempt another dance with her. Of course, it goes without saying that I am always going to make sure the color of my attire doesn't bleed when wet. These may appear to be a simple adjustments, but they are the first steps in being prepared. Previously, I wasn't prepared; I didn't have a plan. I couldn't think on my feet, because I was out of practice. Now I have a plan, and my preparation is to imagine different scenarios and what my response should be, and to always take a deep breath before responding. Being prepared is an ingredient for confidence, and confidence is what it takes to meet new people.

> *While I was attending a business convention in Chicago, I was given the opportunity to participate in an athletic competition on the last day that was offered as a way to socialize with other attendees. It was the final day of the conference and tennis, golf, and skeet shooting were being offered to the participants. I carefully balanced the choices, and since I had the opportunity to play tennis and golf when I was home, I thought about doing something different. So, my first choice was skeet shooting.*

> *Before I actually signed up for the tournament though, I thought about my advice on increasing my exposure to meeting new single women, and how at this point in my life, that was more important than participating in a new sport. As I began to once again overanalyze my situation, I realized that very few women would be interested in skeet shooting, and that most of the men that I knew were participating in the golf tournament. Tennis was obviously going to be the place where all the single women were going to congregate. So I signed up for the tennis tournament.*

> *On the bus, on the way to the tournament site, I observed that the group was split gender-wise; half men, half women; and they were all tennis devotees. The topics of conversation ranged from tournaments and leagues that they all*

participated in, to the celebrities and tennis pros with whom they had previously played. They definitely seemed out of my league. When they began making assignments to the mixed doubles teams, I mentioned that I was an intermediate player who hadn't played in many years, so I was matched up with a very good woman player, who was also very healthy looking and attractive. She was also very married, as were all the other women playing tennis.

The good news is that we won the tournament, mostly because my partner was so good, but partly because all I had to concentrate on was tennis. I didn't have to worry about the distractions of meeting fellow single female participants, or making a good impression. I also probably had a lot more stored up frustrated energy than the other married male participants.

The bad news was that after the tournament, I did meet with a few single women as we were leaving for the airport on our way home, who informed me that quite a few of the "single" women went to play golf or skeet-shooting because that's where they thought the single men were going to be. Of course, one of the women also mentioned that there was one other event that occurred that day that wasn't as athletic as the tennis, golf, or skeet-shooting, but if my main goal was to meet single women, that this was the group that I should have been with; they went shopping.

While it may be a good idea to consider all the possibilities before the search for a mate, we must always consider that there is someone out there searching for us, considering all those same possibilities. Our purpose needs to be, not only to continue the "search," but also to make it easier for others who are searching. It is this reaching out through the realization of "who" we are, and what it means to be *Suddenly Single,* that we will have the confidence to be recognized as someone who feels just as someone else does.

Suddenly Sleepless

I am reminded of that wonderful movie, *Sleepless In Seattle,* and as I now look back, see so many of the themes related to the process of searching for a soul mate. The "feeling" that there is someone out there waiting for you, who could be looking up at the same star you are gazing at, precisely at the same moment you are. Just wishing they could find someone just like you. *Always* looking for a sign that can point them in the right direction. Understanding that the only way to ever know who is out there waiting is to keep on searching. It is this undying persistence that can never really give up until it is known for sure. It is a requirement for destiny to complete its task.

This movie also reaffirms how the time spent in other relationships, deflects from the fateful purpose of finding that one person who can make your life fulfilled. All the uncertainties exist for a reason. The doubts become a sign pointing you toward another destination. Just knowing that there is someone else out there that can present the crossed path of love at first sight, or the feeling that life can never be complete without them, is enough to be unsatisfied. The wasted time presents the dilemma of settling for the immediate security of a current association. It is the pressure from within and from others of your surroundings that dictate this settling as acceptable. But acceptable is not the love of your life, so you persist in your search.

It is finally when you give up your comfort to take a chance that someone will be waiting for you, that you are able to succeed. When you reach that success, you realize how meaningful your decision to continue searching was. You know how vital it was to the expression of your love. And you behold how crucial truly sharing your love will be to the future of your happiness. At this point, you can only imagine the consequences of not being determined and committed to seek until you do find.

Down deep inside we all know *who* can make us happy. We just have to continue our search until we find them. We will know them when we meet, because as the song in the movie goes, "We can make someone happy too."

17

Acceptance

As I continued my travels around Venezuela, the relief of my burden, the sense of freedom, and the serenity that I experienced in the jungle still remained with me. There was a time when, standing on the bow of a sailboat, in between the islands of Los Roques, that a sense of solitude occurred. It was not, however, the loneliness of previous months or years that typically accompanied being by myself. It was rather the feeling of a personal inner strength; the completion of a journey.

As I gazed into the waters of the Caribbean, I thought back to all I had been through, and all I had accomplished. All the heartache and despair that I just knew I would never **be able** to survive; all the loneliness and hopelessness, that I just knew I would never **want** to survive. And yet, here I was with a view beyond the sea; a view of security; a view of life with friendships, happiness, and of eventually again, giving of my love.

Here I was alone, feeling so strong and in so much control of my life. It had been such a long time since I had ever felt like this. What had changed? Why was this wonderful feeling of security, existing without the presence of protective barriers? Where did the need for companionship go, as I was experiencing all the joys and beauty of life? What had happened to all the anger, mistrust and despair that had always been at my side throughout this terrible ordeal? How could my vulnerability ever again allow the bad choices of the past? What had changed was that I had grown. I had matured enough to recognize that I was personally responsible for my own life. I understood that while others affected me throughout my life's journey, the reason I am where I am is because I put myself here. All those places of my yesterdays were places that I allowed myself to be.

This strength, acquired by the acceptance of personal responsibility, now enables me to look forward with a degree of confidence, leading to a sense of purpose and a faith in myself. I can now accept credit for my successes and blame for my failures, if I even choose to make such an assessment. My only dependence is on myself, unless I choose to trust depending on someone else. But it will be **my** choice and my decision that will be the basis for my future circumstance. It was always my responsibility, but I always did not accept it as such.

This acceptance of my present situation, and all that led to it, provides not so much a closure, as it does a new beginning. The terms of my current acceptance seem so much more advanced than the acceptance I had learned about years ago, as the final resolution in dealing with grief. I of course, accept my circumstance and its journey as a matter of fact, with an unchanging character, substituting belief for disbelief and understanding for mystery. And it is certainly very comforting to finally reach the stage of accepting change. Realizing that this change is now under my control because of the responsibility that I now assume, allows me a freedom unburdened by the past, and a future that will be what I choose to make of it, in a place I choose to put myself.

I have come a long way in what now appears to be a short period of time, unless of course, you have the ability of a Susana. A year and a day doesn't seem to be a very long time, looking back. Looking forward, from the beginning of such an ordeal, may seem like an eternity. To honestly and successfully deal with all that has to be dealt with, obviously takes time and effort.

Some have chosen to bury their heads in the sand with alcohol and drugs or even temporary relationships in the hope that when they pull their heads out, everything will be just fine. They think that they can continue right on course. Usually, their course never changes because they continue making the same mistakes.

Then there are those who bury their heads in their hands with self-pity, disgrace and failure, hoping that no one will see them, even though they are sure everyone is noticing. Typically, when they feel it is time to peek out through their fingers, they notice nobody else watching them in their self-absorptions. It is then that they have to begin their long-delayed healing process.

And, then there are those who hide their heads in the past with guilt, memories, and denials, seeking a resolution that will never be. They repeatedly find themselves without a plan or an idea for the future. They just wait to re-experience the ordeal they just endured.

For all those who postpone dealing with their situation, it is going to seem like an eternity reaching the comfort of self-assuredness necessary to get on with their lives. Their determination lies dormant, sleeping in the comfortable surroundings of not confronting what has to be accomplished to make their dreams come true. What they need to understand is that for any of us to ever achieve our dreams, we must first wake up.

Just like the eraser that removes items from the blackboard of our memories, we need to begin the process of going step by step through all those necessary elements of self-improvement that provide a basis for the fulfillment of our dreams. And just like the commitment we need in a successful relationship, we need to expect the same commitment of ourselves, to ourselves. We have to be totally committed to changing our circumstances or risk not allowing the dedication necessary to successfully provide its change. We have to trust and have faith in ourselves to "let go" and take the chance that we know what is best for us, and to recognize that there is no comfort in continuing despair.

Becoming better necessitates change, and positive, lasting change requires a motivation that begins with commitment. If we cannot commit to do what is necessary in a relatively short period of time, to remove ourselves from the confining circumstances in which we find ourselves, how can we ever hope to offer a lifelong commitment to anyone else? Or, expect it from anyone else?

The Grief of Growth

Sometimes the commitment to change cannot occur until levels of need and stages of grief have been satisfied. It is this intermingling of desires and emotions that complicate the healing process. It may seem difficult enough to go through the expressions of grieving, from denial, to acceptance of loss, but to have to consider going through a process of diminished need fulfillment at the same time, seems truly over-burdensome. It becomes both painful and demanding to handle all the pressures and anxieties, and emotions and feelings, at a time when it seems so difficult to just survive. But that is what survival is at the *Suddenly Single* phase of existence—movement through levels of need, while coupled with stages of grief.

Usually, when beginning at a state of denial, we are not afforded the luxury of maintaining a previously reached level of growth. When relationships fail, chances are that the self-esteem of ego also begins to fail. The security of companionship and love has disappeared. Friendships become strained. Confusion questions competency, and fear of the unknown surfaces.

Sometimes even concerns for safety arise, and of course, any relief from sex is all but gone. So here we are at the beginning stages of grief, beginning to address our basic needs all over again. It is this blending together of the complications of our lives, that exaggerate the despair. But, after we survive, these same complications and the change and commitment it took to dispense them, will only heighten the value of acceptance.

So, to reach the level of self-assuredness necessary to contemplate change and complete our journey to the acceptance of a new beginning, requires dealing with the same hierarchy of needs that was required of successful coupling. It is just that now, there is a oneness of being and a oneness of purpose. There is also probably a new starting place, and that is usually the place where the first mistake is made. Not knowing where one is beginning because of a false sense of the view of their life, causes more distress and disappointment. It is then one finds oneself stuck in the sands of denial or despair, not seeing immediate hope, because they are looking too far in the future.

They are skipping levels necessary for achieving comfort on their way to fulfilling the needs of their ego. There are those who wallow in their condition, not knowing why they can't reach the acceptance of change, not realizing that there is a step-by-step process that they must go through before reaching that level. It is certainly harder to accept change when there is no plan of resolution available or when there is little insight as to what the immediate future holds.

The plan needs to begin, once again, with taking care of one's physiological needs. This entails an assessment of physical health and condition. Stress and depression are killers of a healthy mind and body. It is important, therefore, to get that physical examination and to develop a plan with your physician's advice on how to deal with your current condition. This also will involve the nutrition your body needs to combat the pressures of your situation as well as the elimination of those things that may exacerbate your condition.

The beginning of getting in shape begins at this stage, because its efforts at this level complement nutritional changes to provide for a healthier body as well as an improved mental state. Of course, if it appears that you are having an especially difficult time emotionally coping with your current circumstance then you need to seek professional assistance to help you work through this phase. Working out to get in shape provides for a healthier body and mind by relieving the stress associated with becoming *Suddenly Single,* especially when related to sexual needs and their connected physical and mental deprivation.

While sex is a basic need, certainly at this stage of your life you should not be concerned enough about the survival of the species to deal with pregnancy or disease and the additions to grief they would bring. At this basic physiological stage, sex definitely can relieve stress. But at what cost? Worrying about pregnancy could replace current problems, or essentially make them more complicated. Then there are the possibilities of catching a disease, and how much will that complicate your future? And, how many people find themselves being relieved by sex in a temporary union, only to find themselves stuck in a bad relationship so they can keep getting sex? That's what working out is for–to quiet the urge to visit a place that you are not prepared to be.

A place of your own, a place to live, however, also must be an essential part of the plan. It is both critical and elementary to your well being and a prerequisite to even being able to think about what is going to happen next in your life, for you to have your own shelter; your home. Living temporarily with family or friends or in a month-to-month situation not only prohibits moving onto the pursuit of higher needs, but also is an indication of being stuck in the denial stage of your grief. This relationship between hierarchy of needs and the stages of grief is a constant factor in the healing process and the continuing improvement of one's condition. **Denial is a belief in the expected return to normalcy; living temporarily is waiting for normalcy to return.** Whatever the reason, having a secure place to live allows for the mind and body to function independently without the pressure or uncertainty of outside environments or influences.

Of course, basic to providing for these necessities is the capability to earn a living and pay for them. Just like the couples who are involved with surviving and paying bills at this stage of their needs, one cannot hope to move onto any other level of satisfaction until these needs are met and paid for. Many times, those of us *Suddenly Single* allow our personal lives to influence our income-producing capabilities, providing an enhanced risk of not being able to maintain even these basic necessities. This in turn causes more worry and the reduction of an atmosphere conducive to achieving basic needs or growing through the process of grief.

It is virtually impossible to grow beyond the denial and despair without the confidence that at least the most basic of individual needs have been met. Once that has been accomplished, this fulfillment provides the security necessary to experience stability. It is this freedom from fear that allows you to have the confidence to provide the basics for yourself. You are now able to go beyond worrying about how you are going to live, to addressing why you refuse to give up on your already failed relationship.

Chances are that sometime after you began to figure out that you had the responsibility to provide for all of your basic needs by yourself, you jumped from denial to anger: Anger at the partner who deserted you and anger with yourself for your contributory negligence. If this anger is not controlled it becomes regressive and prevents progression to the next level of need. And it happens right about the time when the level of need satisfaction has progressed beyond all those basic needs to a "social" level; a level, that not only allows, but craves companionship, personal interactions, affection and friendship. This level strengthens coping with your relationship's demise. You can now make friends, and you have certainly proven that you can take care of yourself. Now you are angry at, not only the pain and suffering you were caused, but for all the lost opportunities and for the lack of another chance to rectify misdeeds.

This anger changes the weakness of denial to the strength of what is perceived as acceptance. If you were never committed to your relationship, at this point, you can just go out and find someone else. Those of you committed *Suddenly Single* souls, however, find yourself incapable of jumping right into acceptance at this stage of loss, and this level of need. You now enter a new phase of dealing with your loss. It goes beyond the "what ifs" of the self-inflicted part of their anger, to a bargaining phase that allows for deals with God, Nature, Karma, or anyone or anything that might have the capacity to control the outcome of their situation.

Of course, we always think we know what the solution must be and never really leave it up to any omnipotent being to be able to ascertain what is best for us. We bargain that if things are brought back to normal, we will change anything and make any promise to bring back the status quo. There is a willingness to forego all the gains we've made and not seek any further personal development. It becomes an ultimate obligation to restoring the co-dependency of a relationship at the expense of personal growth, and appears to be a "good" thing. It is our last desperate attempt to allow our commitment to continue, even though we know in our hearts that the same scenarios will be repeated in the future if our wish is granted. It's always those of us really committed, who bargain the hardest.

When the bargaining fails as it usually does, it appears the only resolution left is acceptance. This period occurs about the same time as the ego level is approached. This is the level that is concerned with the self and conjures up images about what makes you function. You begin to have not only a clearer realization of all your qualities, but also an observation that there is no one to share this newfound understanding of self. That is when depression jumps in ahead of acceptance.

You are now depressed because you know that all that is left is acceptance. All the denial, anger and bargaining didn't work to restore the relationship or to improve your lovesick condition. All the distractions of survival and the reaching of safe, comfortable levels of existence didn't eliminate the need for final determination. So now comes the time to accept what has happened.

It is just not the finality of decision that brings on the depression. It is the giving up of commitment to a bond you never thought you could break. For those of you truly and sincerely committed, it is a recognition that your promise, your word, and in some cases your vow, is being denied its honor and it is now out of your control. It is the lack of this control of something so personal and important that pushes you to this depressing state. It is your understanding of self that drives the depression even deeper, when you realize the importance of your commitment is to not only who you were, but also to who you could become.

This deal for a lifetime has now been broken. The past's foundation for the building of the future has been crumpled. You now realize that even though commitment is such a large part of who you are, it will mean nothing in a relationship unless it is reciprocated. And you thought it was so important, so valuable, and such a powerful gift. And now, you are asking yourself to accept it as gone. That is why depression comes before acceptance. For good people, it's a normal experience.

If You Can Accept

After all the misery and uncertainty of your ordeal, you are now finally ready to accept its conclusion. You have satisfied all the needs that came before and have now reached the stage of "self" alone. All that has transpired before has prepared you with, not only the capability to accept this monumental change in your life, but has given you the ability to accept who you are. **You have now reached the other side.**

It is this knowledge of self that defines your being in a way that distinguishes it from its prior coupled existence and allows it to assume a personal nature, devoid of the influences and demands of a committed union. You are now able to determine your qualities of value, the positives and negatives of your character and the scope of your abilities, your personal needs and desires, and the direction of your pursuits.

You still know the value of love, trust and commitment, and because of your experiences, you know the results of not making the right choice in their regard. You now have the capacity to not only accept change, but to accept personal responsibility for the actions of your future. "IF" you can do that, your ordeal will have a positive effect, providing you with a personal growth and acceptance that will enable you to "be a Man, my son."

If you can keep your head when all about you
        Are losing theirs and blaming it on you;
If you can trust yourself when all men doubt you,
        But make allowance for their doubting too;

If you can wait and not be tired by waiting,
        Or, being lied about, don't deal in lies,
Or, being hated, don't give way to hating,
        And yet don't look too good, nor talk too wise;

If you can dream—and not make dreams your master;
        If you can think—and not make thoughts your aim;
If you can meet with triumph and disaster
        And treat those two impostors just the same;

If you can bear to hear the truth you've spoken
        Twisted by knaves to make a trap for fools,
Or watch the things you gave your life to broken,
        And stoop and build 'em up with wornout tools;

If you can make one heap of all your winnings
        And risk it on one turn of pitch-and-toss,
And lose, and start again at your beginnings
        And never breathe a word about your loss;

If you can force your heart and nerve and sinew
        To serve your turn long after they are gone,
And so hold on when there is nothing in you
        Except the Will which says to them: "Hold on";

If you can talk with crowds and keep your virtue,
        Or walk with kings—nor lose the common touch;
If neither foes or loving friends can hurt you;
        If all men count with you, but none too much;

If you can fill the unforgiving minute
        With sixty seconds' worth of distance run—
Yours is the Earth and everything that's in it,
        And—which is more—you'll be a Man, my son!

                        IF   — *Rudyard Kipling*

18

Epilogue

Every good-intentioned person who I talked with mentioned that they still experienced times of sadness, even years after their separation. It is difficult, especially for those who were in relationships that lasted for many years, to completely remove from memory the shared experiences that they had. And everyone agreed that it was the good memories that caused the most sadness. But that is a perfectly normal reaction for good people to have, and there are so many others like them who have the same reaction. In a way, it is good news that there are so many other good people who feel as we do.

Some other good news is that when these people meet someone who they are able to share their love with, they become focused on that new love. Their memories of the past remain as a learning process that only seems to be revisited as a measure of how fortunate they are today, in their new relationship.

For those people still alone, it is okay to remember every once in a while. It is when they continually dwell on those memories, that it indicates an inability to achieve acceptance. They need to ask themselves the question, "Would I take them back, if I could?" If their answer is "Yes, because there is no one else," then the solution is for them to find someone else. They owe it to their self-worth. They must begin to realize how important sharing their love with a partner is to them, and must actively seek out a match. **If they have time to dwell on the past, they certainly have time to contemplate the future.**

Reading *Suddenly Single* should give all those who have memories of sadness, encounters with failure, feelings of grief, the honor of commitment, and a willingness to share love, a direction toward a better place and a hope that their goodness will be rewarded. It is that hope that sometimes seems to evade us, and its elusive nature is what most of the stories of those I encountered, are all about. It's about having faith, and having expectations diminished. It's about having desires, and having anticipation dulled. It's about having goals, and having the will exhausted. It's about trust, and having wishes dashed. And ultimately, it's about having belief, and then having that faith questioned. Finally, for all those I talked with, there are only two choices that face them; to either continue to hope or continue to despair. Their only consolation was that there were a lot of other people faced with those same choices.

Even though misery loves company, it has not been a particularly pleasant experience to hear of all these stories of those *Suddenly Single*. While it is sometimes comforting to know that you are not traveling your life's path alone, and that there are people feeling the same as you do, it is still disheartening to know of their despair. But of particular sadness were those stories that ended with people giving up their search, surviving their daily routines alone. While some may be lazy, and some think that they shouldn't have to look, it's those who truly believe that there is no one else out there for them, who provide the saddest stories.

These people, have been so ravaged by their past that they have reached the point where, even if they had "faith" in themselves, they have lost faith in others. They don't want to give love another chance, because they don't believe that they will ever be able to trust again to find it. They try to become focused on everything else in their lives, so that they don't have to confront their loveless confines. It is their isolation from those who feel as they do, that causes all of us to miss the opportunity of experiencing who they are.

At the beginning of my ordeal of being *Suddenly Single,* I was going on a trip for the first time alone. A friend, whose name by the way is Angel, gave me a book called "God on A Harley," that she thought would give me comfort in my time of need. That book helped me realize that there were other people hurting just as I was, and that I had a responsibility to let them know that they were not alone. All of us who are truly *Suddenly Single* have that same responsibility. We now all need to bury our self-pity and reach out to those who need us. Besides, **you can't hold a torch to light another's path, without brightening your own.** Who knows, we might find someone who feels just as we do.

A Story Is Worth A Thousand Pictures

One of the main reasons that I wrote *Suddenly Single* was to share my insights and experiences with those who needed to know that there were other people who took a similar journey, and met with those same degrees of failure and success. It is important for those *Suddenly Single* to hear and tell these stories and to understand that they are not alone in how they feel. While this book enabled me to present my journey, which was enhanced by the experiences of those I met along the way, I would like to write another book including the adventures of people I have not met yet—maybe you.

My next book will be a compilation of real-life *stories* from different perspectives and different people. Stories that deal with all of the aspects of being *Suddenly Single* from failed relationships to chance encounters, especially including the feelings you experienced. If you have a story that you would like to share, please send it to me at:

Carraro
P. O. Box 67845
Albuquerque, NM 87193-7845

To share a story means not being *alone* anymore.

To be put on the *Suddenly Single* mailing list and to find out about *Suddenly Single* seminars, write to the above post office box, or check out the Suddenly-Single.com website.

Happy hunting!